FOOL'S GOLD

FOOL'S GOLD

The Radicals, Con Artists, and Traitors

Who Killed the California Dream

and Now Threaten Us All

Susan Crabtree and Jedd McFatter

CENTER
STREET

NEW YORK   NASHVILLE

Center Street
Hachette Book Group
1290 Avenue of the Americas, New York, NY 10104
centerstreet.com
@CenterStreet/@CenterStreetBooks

First Edition: March 2025

Center Street is a division of Hachette Book Group, Inc. The Center Street name and logo are registered trademarks of Hachette Book Group, Inc.

The publisher is not responsible for websites (or their content) that are not owned by the publisher.

Center Street books may be purchased in bulk for business, educational, or promotional use. For information, please contact your local bookseller or the Hachette Book Group Special Markets Department at special.markets@hbgusa.com.

Library of Congress Cataloging-in-Publication Data has been applied for

ISBNs: 978-1-5460-0803-3 (hardcover), 978-1-5460-0805-7 (ebook)

Printed in the United States of America

LSC-C

Printing 1, 2024

CONTENTS

O N PAPER, CALIFORNIA LOOKS like a dream house. Its cities teem with creativity, imagination, and industry. Its universities churn out brilliant minds who build inestimable wealth. Its Pacific shores are blessed with fair weather and sunshine. Its fertile fields yield the finest crops and wine to be had anywhere in the world. From afar, it does look golden indeed.

Look closer though, and the wall cracks; popped nails, termites, and dry rot cannot remain unseen. The house that was once straight from the pages of *Architectural Digest* is today ready to collapse. What self-respecting homeowner would let such a nice place fall apart like that? Don't they see it? *Don't they care?*

Americans in the other forty-nine states have been asking these questions for years as they watch the weeds proliferate in California. The leaky plumbing, popping circuit breakers, and busted windows. Brazen thieves. Squatters. Criminal gangs. And the unmistakable stench of sewage wafting through the palm leaves.

Pay no attention to those small "maintenance items," assures the realtor with the perfect hair. His dazzling smile and easy manner are well practiced. He's been selling "fixer-uppers" as though they were palaces for more than twenty years, and he's proven himself to be a pretty good "closer." But just behind him as he makes his sales pitch, we notice yet another heavily laden U-Haul truck rumbling toward the interstate, bound for somewhere—anywhere—else.

That slick salesman is named Gavin Newsom, and he is the current governor of California. Fawning press profiles describe him as the future of progressive politics, and they inevitably mention that he has "national aspi-rations." Like any salesman, what he *really* wants is a bigger territory.

The savvy real estate buyer is neither fooled nor impressed. Newsom's current "territory" looks like a shambolic money pit.

Violent crime is surging in California. Illegal drug use is off the charts, and it is subject to a daily invasion of illegal migrants crossing its southern border. Homeless addicts in once beautiful San Francisco shoot up, sleep, and defecate on its streets when they're not stealing from what shops are still open in the city. Its economy is struggling. Tent cities block the side-walks of Los Angeles as businesses leave the state's crushing regulations, extortionate taxes, and unchecked property crime. Its police force is demor-alized by negligent "Soros prosecutors" who turn repeat criminals loose. Its universities, always a source of foment and dissent, have metastasized into playthings and espionage targets for America's greatest adversary—the communist regime of China.

How did it all go so wrong? *Why* is it still getting worse?

A close look at today's national Democratic Party powerbrokers shows one common thing: California. The dangerous progressive "vision" that threat-ens America has ruled the state for two generations now. Frustrated citizens are leaving in droves, taking their dreams, money, and businesses to states that progressives don't yet run. Larger corporations are following suit.

"Voting with your feet" is a time-honored American value. The framers of our Constitution wanted each state to govern itself as much as possible. Massachusetts and Vermont were a world away from South Carolina and Florida in those days, and the Founders knew each state would do things differently. They trusted that successes in one state might be shared with the others, while failures in one state could be "firewalled" from the rest. That distance has shrunk in modern times, but still our states take pride in doing things their own way.

Here in Florida, home of the Government Accountability Institute (GAI), we are proud to welcome those "refugees" from California and

New York. Our state learned from the mistakes made by Newsom and the California authoritarians during the COVID pandemic, for example. To stop the coronavirus that originated, most likely, from a laboratory leak in Wuhan, China, Gavin Newsom locked his state and its 40 million residents down for months, while famously getting caught sneaking out to dine (unmasked) at the famous "French Laundry" restaurant in Napa Valley with lobbyists who got COVID lockdown carveouts and lucrative state contracts. On the other coast, Florida reopened its doors quickly once it was clear that the government-imposed lockdowns were hurting people more than helping them.

This is just one example of the states operating as the Founders intended, for good and bad. But if the fifty states are still America's "laboratories of democracy," California is the Wuhan Institute.

Now its left-wing politics, fermented in corruption and cronyism, threaten to breach the firewall and infect the whole nation.

Newsom is certainly not the only strain of this virus. Kamala Harris, a former San Francisco district attorney and state attorney general with few real accomplishments, was rated the most left-wing member of the US Senate before she was picked by presidential candidate Joe Biden to be his running mate in 2020. Former House Speaker Nancy Pelosi, a woman of great accomplishment and a political knife-fighter, likewise sprouted from the San Francisco Democratic machinery. Rep. Adam Schiff, from the Los Angeles area, who was censured by the House of Representatives for misusing and misrepresenting classified information he received as head of the House Intelligence Committee, was elected to the Senate seat held unto death by former San Francisco mayor Dianne Feinstein in 2023. You will learn about all of them—and many others—in these pages.

Fool's Gold peels back the layers and disentangles the incestuous web of West Coast connections that drive decision-making in Washington. Co-written by journalist Susan Crabtree, winner of the 2024 Dao Award for investigative reporting, of RealClearPolitics and GAI research director Jedd McFatter, this book is scrupulously sourced dynamite. The villains here are ambitious politicians with historic ties to international organized crime, cult leaders, and even foreign governments hostile to the United States. If you live in California, fled from it, or worry that its political pathology will infect your state, this book is necessary and overdue.

I co-founded GAI in 2012 to "follow the money" in politics. We are a small nonprofit group of investigative reporters and writers who research, fact-check, and publish books and shorter reports. Many of our books about government corruption bear my name as author, but they are the work of our marvelous team, including Jedd. With the support of our generous donors, GAI has found a niche doing the kind of enterprise journalism that reporters and editors at the major TV networks and the largest newspapers once did before they succumbed to parroting a "narrative."

We believe in the power of books to spur informed citizens to action, and I am proud to welcome Jedd McFatter as the *fourth* published author on GAI's staff, joining Eric Eggers, Seamus Bruner, and me. Jedd has been involved in every book we have done since he joined us in 2017, most recently with my latest effort, the #1 *New York Times* bestselling *Blood Money: Why the Powerful Turn a Blind Eye While China Kills Americans*.

Jedd McFatter and Susan Crabtree have each proven their mettle as fearless and tireless researchers.

Susan broke several blockbuster stories on the Secret Service's failures during and after the assassination attempt against Donald Trump, contributing to the resignation of Secret Service director Kimberly Cheatle. Her previous reporting on Secret Service lapses and corruption preceded the resignation of a previous Secret Service director, Julia Pierson. Susan is a longtime Californian and a senior national correspondent for RealClearPolitics. She has spent three decades uncovering corruption, bribery, waste, and abuse in federal and state governments, prompting several investigations by the FBI as well as House and Senate ethics committees.

This book is the first to bear the names of Jedd and Susan as authors, but it will not be the last for either of them.

I am often asked whether I am discouraged by the widespread corruption in government that we at GAI unearth and expose to the public. My

answer is an emphatic *no*. We believe in the power of the American people and of free people everywhere to resist the control schemes created by
people with more money than empathy. Our job is to arm citizens with the
facts and do battle with a cheerful, optimistic purpose.

Susan and Jedd do that here.

INTRODUCTION

A s goes California, so goes the nation," is one of Governor Gavin Newsom's favorite expressions. Considering California's free fall under Newsom's watch, it should serve as a clarion call for action.

The once vibrant California Dream is rapidly vanishing, beset by a progressive contagion that's spreading across the nation. Even after President Trump's resounding win against Kamala Harris, California Gov. Gavin Newsom swiftly declared himself the leader of the resistance and vigorously defended its leftist policies. JB Pritzker, another potential 2028 contender, joined forces with Colorado Gov. Jared Polis to launch "Governors Safeguarding Democracy," a coalition of blue-state torchbearers aiming to challenge Trump's agenda head-on with coordinated political assaults.[1] The trio of governors were doubling down on their failed far-left policies in a transparent attempt to seize the moment and fill a vacuum of Democratic Party leadership left wide open by Harris's decisive defeat. It's past time to put a stop to the madness, but to do so requires a hard look at exactly what and who have transformed this would-be paradise into an unlivable dystopia for far too many. My coauthor, Jedd McFatter, and I wrote and researched this book in constant collaboration, but as a native Californian, my experience of returning after a twenty-three-year absence to find the Golden State in serious decline fueled my desire to understand what happened to my home state and why.

Thomas Wolfe wrote a whole book, *You Can't Go Home Again*, about his tumultuous return to his hometown in North Carolina after several cultural and economic shifts that took place in the 1920s and '30s. My California homecoming in the spring of 2017 wasn't nearly as dramatic. There were many joys—time spent with my elderly parents before my father's passing, rekindling old friendships, soaking in the state's spectacular natural beauty and year-round mild climate. But I also witnessed a disturbing downward spiral that has only accelerated over the last few years. It's those lower quality-of-life issues and disturbing lack of action on them that have residents voting with their feet in a dramatic exodus, what Jedd and I view as California's reverse gold rush.

In the mid-to-late 1800s, California drew people from across the country who dreamed of striking it rich or at least harnessing the state's resources and opportunities to build a better life. Now the opposite is occurring. More than one million have beaten a path out of the state since 2019 due to California's cost of living (highest in the nation), spikes in crime, and dearth of opportunity.

The exodus from California is especially stark in San Francisco, the political home base of Governor Gavin Newsom and Vice President Kamala Harris. In 2023, the San Francisco Chronicle, the left-leaning paper of record, described the city as trapped in a "doom loop" and "on the verge of collapse."[2] San Francisco over the last five years has lost population faster than any major city in US history, more quickly than Detroit did when it went bankrupt. Between 2019 and 2021, the City by the Bay lost 6.3 percent of its population, a rate of decline larger than any two-year period in Detroit's history and a record exodus for any major US city.[3]

I spent more than twenty years in Washington, DC, as a reporter covering the White House and Congress. The first decade living and breathing politics inside the DC swamp was a thrilling tiger ride. The old-school journalism that was still alive and well in the 1990s and 2000s in DC melded perfectly with my natural prosecutorial instincts. It wasn't a job so much as a passion to expose corruption, uncover unsavory deals and self-dealing, and at times even help shape the course of political events.

Yet as a native Californian with generations of family history on the West Coast, there were days when I would feel the tug to return home, not realizing that COVID, coupled with years of absurdly bad policy, would soon drive San Francisco and many parts of the state into an abyss.

The 1980s and early '90s, when I was growing up in California, were filled with peace and optimism. I remember the mild California winters, carefree summer days, and how much more of life was lived outdoors. During our teens and early twenties, my friends and I spent our free time either on the beach or cruising along the Pacific Coast Highway, surfboards in the back of the truck, searching for the best waves. In our spare time, we would watch and rewatch *Big Wednesday*, the 1978 cult surfing classic movie about three young California surfers' coming of age. In it, a teenage girl from Chicago who is first learning about Southern California beach life exclaims, "It's really different here."

"Back home, being young was just something you'd do until you grew up. Here, it's everything," she gushes.

But for most of the last century, California wasn't just a playground for the young. In a 2019 study, Stanford and MIT researchers found that California residents are so healthy that they live on average to age seventy-nine, which beats the national average by more than two years. Only residents of Hawaii live longer. And for much of my life, California remained accessible, offering opportunities for those determined to work hard and climb the economic ladder.

Part of California's longtime appeal is the diversity of the landscapes across its 163,700 square miles. Most areas of natural beauty, including its 840-mile coastline, are public, with only a nominal fee at state and national parks. Even as a kid, I would sometimes look up in awe at the 11,500-foot snowcapped San Gorgonio Mountain in my palm-lined hometown of Redlands, a small city of seventy thousand set at the foothills of the San Bernardino Mountain range. In early 2017, when my husband and I traveled to San Diego for a work trip, we decided it was time to make our move. We signed a rental contract on a house. The price tag, at pre-COVID rates, was a no-brainer. To live a short drive from the beach, we were paying the same as our mortgage inside the Washington, DC, Beltway with more than double the living space.

The first few months of our new life in San Diego exceeded our expectations and pent-up desire for outdoor adventures. We marveled at the lack of humidity and mosquitos, the purple-flowering jacaranda trees that lined the main drag through our manicured suburban enclave, the abundance of outdoor concerts and activities, great seafood, and fresh citrus year-round. Some of Southern California's best beaches and hiking trails were just a ten-minute drive away. I picked a local gym for its view of the sparkling lagoon.

At one point during my first weeks in San Diego, I flipped the car radio to an '80s station while cruising along the Pacific Coast Highway, noticing my old haunts and surf shops, many of which still remained. I felt transported back in time. Yet just a few months into our new life, we started noticing cracks in California's golden façade.

While taking our daughter, who was then less than two years old at the time, to a pier in downtown San Diego for a sandcastle-building exhibit, we were confronted with an eerie sight. Horton Plaza, once a vibrant, state-of-the-art five-level outdoor mall occupying six and half city blocks in the city's historic Gaslamp Quarter, was now boarded up and covered in graffiti. Nordstrom, its anchor store, had closed in 2016. While making our way down to the sandcastle exhibit on the pier, we encountered a stench so putrid that we quickly covered our faces. An incoherent man covered in human excrement and barely clothed was walking toward us in the middle of the road. He didn't threaten us, but the sight of someone in such a desperate condition shook me to the core.

Later that month, San Diego County officials acknowledged that the city was in the midst of the deadliest hepatitis A outbreak in the United States in decades. Officials identified 592 cases, twenty of which resulted in deaths. Seventy percent of those afflicted were homeless, living on the streets without access to twenty-four-hour public restrooms.

There were other troubling signs. In 2017, our first year in California, the state was struck by a wave of deadly wildfires, three of which were the most destructive in state history. Hot, gusty Santa Ana winds in the south and Diablo winds in the north fanned the infernos, which killed forty people and burned over a million acres, destroying more than ten thousand structures and causing $1 billion in losses in that year alone. The deadly blazes continued unabated every late summer and fall through the pandemic and into 2022.

Some of the first things visitors to Southern California beach towns notice is the ban on plastic straws, along with the number of Teslas sharing the streets with gas-guzzling Range Rovers, a $100,000 to $160,000 status symbol for the upper-middle class. Straws become litter and eventually find their way to rivers and oceans, endangering marine life. It's all part of California residents' greater focus on environmental impacts—at least superficially. But in 2017 alone, wildfires released millions of metric tons of carbon dioxide, black carbon, brown carbon, ozone precursors, and toxic compounds into the atmosphere, impacting both the regional and global climate, polluting water and soil, and endangering public health. After several back-to-back record fire seasons, Stanford University researchers in 2022 found that wildfire smoke had reversed decades of air quality gains, and instead had exposed millions of Americans to extreme pollution levels.[4]

The wildfires kept coming fall after fall. And I, like every other resident of the state, began to brace for them as an inexplicable part of modern California life. One autumn day, when several wildfires were raging more than fifty miles away, orange haze filled the air, and the sun looked like a blazing apocalyptic sphere. Even after the courts found Pacific Gas and Electric (PG&E), the gas and electric utility serving sixteen million residents in Northern and Central California, guilty of manslaughter in some of the most destructive blazes, it seemed like the utility—and others across California—were acting with impunity.

No matter how many fires, gas leaks, and explosions California's utilities caused, whenever PG&E and other companies like Southern California Edison, Southern California Gas, and San Diego Gas & Electric ask for rate increases, California regulators sign off on them. By 2024, the wildfire fallout included insurance companies either hiking premiums for homeowners or dropping policies altogether.

Coming from Northern Virginia, which ranks tenth in the nation for the most expensive utility bills, I didn't expect the sticker shock when I saw some of my first gas and electric bills. I soon found that San Diego has the best weather in the nation but absurdly also the most expensive electricity. And despite paying the highest utility costs in the nation, California customers somehow have the most unreliable service. We, like millions of others, experienced rolling blackouts with no air-conditioning in the hottest summer months at the height of the COVID pandemic in 2020.

The electric grid failures weren't as bad as in the early 2000s when then-Governor Gray Davis was successfully recalled over his inability to keep the lights on. But the blackouts highlighted the state's overreliance on renewable energy sources, which can't keep the electricity flowing after sundown, when solar panels stop producing. The summer blackouts and brownouts were the least of our concerns during the pandemic. California's restrictive COVID lockdowns and laws took a grim toll on the state's economy. When they were finally lifted, the state's recovery lagged behind, with one of the highest unemployment rates in the nation.

Unlike other states, California's unemployment system was woefully unprepared to handle the onslaught of layoffs plagued with problems.

People in service-industry jobs were hit the hardest. My hairdresser was forced out of work for more than seven months, threatened with hefty fines if she continued to serve her clientele. She never could navigate the fraud-plagued unemployment system to receive the tens of thousands of dollars in compensation she was owed.

Then came the skyrocketing home prices. During the pandemic, housing prices surged in California, as they did across the country, but it was especially steep in coastal Southern California areas where homes were expensive by national standards but still affordable compared to San Francisco and New York prices. The new, looser remote work policies at many Silicon Valley firms made relocating to sunnier, laid-back San Diego County a no-brainer.

In 2021, San Diego real estate prices increased at their fastest pace in seven years and were rising quicker than in any other area in the nation save Phoenix, surging a whopping 17.4 percent in a year. Home prices in some coastal suburbs skyrocketed an unheard-of $1 million in one year. A home costing $1.5 million before COVID was now $2.5 million. The end result: most Californians are now forced to rent, with prices growing out of reach for the vast majority of residents.

The summer of 2020, race riots and looting protesting the death of George Floyd broke out in big cities across the West Coast, as they did across the country. But once the unrest died down, brazen criminal acts started occurring in affluent and urban areas and urban inner-cities. The first smash-and-grab crimes, in which flash mobs of masked thieves brazenly ransack department stores, began in 2021 and are continuing to plague high-end and convenience stores alike. An undeniable contributing factor: Proposition 47, which California voters passed in 2014 as part of a far-left criminal justice reform push, eliminated the felony penalty for theft for goods worth $950 or less.

Soon, there was a new, unnerving element of life in California. The state's sanctuary state laws that protect illegal immigrants accused of crimes from federal deportation began attracting "burglary tourists." These marauding gangs from Chile, Ecuador, Colombia, and Peru ransack homes then flee back to South America with the stolen goods. The professional burglars enter the country illegally or exploit a visa waiver program intended to spur tourism from dozens of trusted countries.

San Francisco's dramatic downturn over the last decade is the most alarming in the state. In late 2023, workers in the Nancy Pelosi Federal building, in the heart of the city's Tenderloin District, were ordered to stay home as crime, open-air drug markets, and drug-addled homeless threatened their safety. The cost of living has always been high in California. But since 2021, we've also had some of the highest gas prices, most expensive housing markets, and highest home insurance rates. With all the costs of living spiking at once, coupled with lower levels of personal security and opportunity, hundreds of thousands of residents each year find the costs impossible to continue to bear.

The sad reality is it doesn't have to be this way. While the pandemic accelerated some of California's problems, most can be traced back to failed progressive polices or public corruption—or both. When you strip away these self-inflicted wounds, the state is one of the most richly blessed places on earth and worthy of saving.

California's dramatic landscapes and amazingly livable weather have for centuries drawn settlers from around the world. It's served as the embodiment of the rugged American West, home to the glamourous golden age of Hollywood, and more recently, Silicon Valley's tech revolution. The internet and iPhones were born in California; the state also produced two Republican presidents, Richard Nixon and Ronald Reagan (albeit with disparate legacies).

Despite having more going for it than just about anywhere on the globe, statistics and new research back my experiences over the last seven years: California's golden patina of optimism is dimming. According to *U.S. News and World Report*'s 2023 rankings of US states, California ranks dead last in the category of opportunity.[5] What this means is that when experts analyzed various metrics and data related to equality, affordability, and economic opportunity, they found that every single state is doing a better overall job than California.[6]

Newsom and Harris have touted California as a model for the nation. In reality, the opposite is true. The not-so Golden State leads the nation in a litany of dishonorable distinctions: no state taxes personal income and gas more than California, and only two states have a worse tax climate for business. It has more poverty than any state, and at the time of this book's writing, its unemployment rate is the highest in the nation. In 2023, 28 percent of all the homeless people in America called California home, despite the state including only 12 percent of the national population, and drug addiction and violent crime are on the rise amid a statewide mental health crisis that worsens by the day.

If your state has the fourth-best health care quality in the nation but ranks thirty-fourth in health care access, this means many of your poorest and most vulnerable never receive the top-notch health care that's right at their fingertips. And if your higher education system ranks third but your K–12 Education ranks thirty-eighth, then it's clear your priority is catering to the exclusive class of financial elites, while throwing scraps to the middle- and lower-class Californians reliant on public schooling. The state also has the biggest budget and the largest budget deficit in the nation. California's deficit was an estimated $68 billion in 2024, while many other states were running surpluses.

The beloved historian of California, Kevin Starr, once wrote: "From the beginning, American California was caught in a paradox of reverent awe and exploitative use...there has always been something slightly bipolar about California. It was either utopia or dystopia, a dream or a nightmare, a hope or a broken promise—and too infrequently anything in between."[7]

Wild banking scandals and investment fraud now plague the state, but consider this: during the Great Depression, when banks across the country were crashing, not a single California bank went bankrupt. Fast-forward to 2023 and we see two California banks collapse in the same year: Silicon Valley Bank in Santa Clara and First Republic Bank in San Francisco.

In short, the Golden State is now a shadow of its former self. Like fool's gold, California life retains a glittery allure but has lost much of its true luster. For too many residents, pursuing the California Dream has now become a fool's errand.

It would be tragic enough if this devastation were contained, but what's happening in California is not staying in California—and, shockingly, that's by design. Take a look at the power brokers of the Democratic Party and you'll quickly notice that nearly all are from California. What you are about to read reveals a darker side of the Golden State:

- We meet powerful politicians and family dynasties with close ties to mob bosses and cult leaders.
- We show how world-class con artists defraud, plunder, and literally poison the people and institutions of California, including illegal immigrant drug dealers getting rich and avoiding prison and deportation while poisoning Americans with fentanyl and other illicit drugs.

- We chronicle the myriad schemes in which officials line their own pockets and sell out the state to foreign interests, including the Chinese government and its nefarious transnational Triad organized crime syndicates.

Many of the narratives that follow have been downplayed or left undiscovered by mainstream media because collectively they expose the failure and futility of California's progressive agenda and governance. Ultimately, these narratives will reveal who is influencing California's influencers, and how they stand to benefit from the economic, social, and cultural—and even physical devastation of America from coast to coast.

—Susan Crabtree and Jedd McFatter

CHAPTER ONE

The Failed Progressive Vision

ONE CRISP AUTUMN DAY IN 2023, residents of San Francisco awoke to find their city transformed.[1] Almost overnight, the city by the bay had become virtually unrecognizable. Street corners and plazas previously crowded with homeless encampments and open-air drug markets were clear, and the trash heaps, piles of feces, tainted needles, soiled mattresses, and ragged tents were gone. Storefront windows that had long been boarded shut now shone. All the crude graffiti, scummy debris, and filth were replaced with painted murals, brand new flower boxes, and colorful new crosswalk markings. Freshly pressure-washed sidewalks—the forgotten pathways through the city—now gleamed.[2]

After decades of failure and $24 billion squandered in the previous five years on statewide strategies aimed at ending homelessness, San Franciscans witnessed a bona fide miracle: their city (or at least the downtown) was golden once again.[3] Perhaps most shocking of all, the homeless population had vanished, and no one seemed to know where they went. How could a problem that plagued authorities for decades be solved overnight?

The closer that residents looked, the more unsettling the answer became: large concrete barricades and steel fences had been erected downtown, and the formidable police presence could best be described as a "shock and awe" campaign. Stranger still were the cheering crowds waving giant Chinese flags on long poles while acrobats and Chinese dance troupes performed on the sidewalks. Hundreds of blood-red lanterns were strung above the streets.[4]

And it was certainly ironic that the leader who unabashedly touted the cleanup of San Francisco that day, Governor Gavin Newsom, was the very same career politician who had failed the city for so long.[5] Chinese President Xi Jinping was there for the Asian-Pacific Economic Cooperation (APEC) summit held at the St. Regis Hotel on November 10, 2023. And Newsom was locked in, ready to prove he was a serious player on the global stage. His lucrative and long-standing business relationships with Chinese apparatchiks gave him an affinity for China that most politicians do not possess.

The transformation of San Francisco was so striking, not because of how sudden it was, but because of who Gavin Newsom is. For more than twenty years, Newsom claimed that he was trying to fix the problems of crime, drugs, and homelessness in San Francisco and across the state. And on his watch, those problems only got worse. Why? Because, under ordinary circumstances, Newsom cannot fix those problems. His ideology prevents him from doing what is necessary.

At his core, Newsom embodies the sinister progressive vision that has seeped outward from California and now threatens every American, whether they live in the cities, suburbs, or even remote rural locations. The progressive vision for America maintains that crime should be made legal; jails should be emptied; dangerous drugs should be freely available; borders should be opened; illegal aliens should be given amnesty and free health care and interest-free loans. San Francisco became one of America's first "sanctuary cities" when it passed its "City of Refuge" resolution in 1985, and in 2021, after Black Lives Matter demanded that cities "defund the police," San Francisco was among the first to do exactly that, slashing $120 million from the city law enforcement budget.[6] Accordingly, Newsom's progressive vision enforces "racial justice," "social justice," "restorative justice," "economic justice," and "climate justice"—everything but *actual* justice.[7]

More than any current politician, Newsom has executed the progressive vision across his city and state with swiftness and precision. Every problem he encounters, Newsom addresses in typical performative progressive fashion:

convene a commission, appoint a czar, hold a press conference, and ultimately, just throw more money at it. The result of his decades-long reign in California has been abject failure. Compounding Newsom's ruthless drive to enact the failed progressive vision is his boundless and selfish ambition. Despite his policy failures, he has amassed personal success, thus incentivizing his current course. For an unimaginative political creature who sprang from the loins of California's corrupt Democratic establishment, Newsom's first response to a problem has always been to trot out the progressive platitudes and boring bromides of the Left Coast elite. It's pure reflex.

Newsom has learned that actually solving problems is not necessary for personal success in a one-party progressive state like California, where an endless geyser of bad policy spews forth schemes of extreme permissiveness and dysfunction. For Newsom's political opponents desperate to tackle the perennial problems of crime, drugs, and homelessness, Newsom's enforced leniencies are not just policy failures; they are existential crises as criminals inevitably gravitate toward his sanctuaries of lawlessness. For nonprogressives, ending these policies seem to be common sense.[8] Newsom appears capable of tapping into common sense when convenient, as demonstrated with the instant cleanup for Xi's visit or, earlier, when he ran for governor. Speaking to the *Chronicle* in 2018, Newsom admitted that San Francisco had become "too permissive" and tolerant toward "bad behavior on the city's streets."[9]

The aspiring governor addressed one particularly heinous spectacle that had become an everyday occurrence in his state: "People shooting up [drugs] on the streets and sidewalks, where kids are in strollers, is not acceptable—it's just not."[10] But once elected, Newsom's fickle aversion to junkies overdosing in front of toddlers never translated into policy. Newsom's soft-on-crime strategy also aims to decriminalize prostitution, public intoxication, and retail theft, as well as so-called "quality of life" crimes such as loitering, sleeping, and panhandling in public spaces. The progressive alternative to punishment for crime, "incarceration diversion programs," have released many dangerous or drug-addicted criminals back onto the streets. The results have been devastating.

*   *   *

North Highlands resident John Oliveira experienced Newsom's dangerous policies firsthand. In the summer of 2022, Oliveira noticed a foul odor coming from his neighbor's house, and he immediately knew something was very wrong. Oliveira had first met seventy-seven-year-old Pamela May a few days before the overwhelming stench began to waft from her property. When the police arrived to investigate, they found May's decomposing body, which had been "dismembered beyond recognition."[11]

The man eventually arrested for the "heinous psychopathic murder" of May was Darnell Erby, a repeat offender who had been released in April 2021 after serving less than half of a twelve-year sentence for first-degree burglary and fraud. Erby's life of crime began in 1999. In the interim, he racked up a rap sheet that included twenty arrests, eight felonies, and sentences totaling twenty-four years.[12] Such cases had become numbingly familiar in California.

Several months later, David Fidel Mora-Rojas killed his three daughters, ages nine, ten, and thirteen, and another man inside a church in Sacramento before turning the gun on himself. Mora-Rojas was in the country illegally but wasn't handed over to US Immigration and Customs Enforcement (ICE) after being arrested for drunk driving, assaulting an officer, and attacking a medical professional shortly before the killing spree. When Mora-Rojas went on the deadly shooting rampage, he had been free for only five days.[13]

Later that year, a young police officer, Gonzalo Carrasco Jr., was shot and killed while on routine patrol in the small town of Selma. He left behind a pregnant girlfriend, his parents, and siblings, all of whom lived in the same Central Valley farm community. It was the first loss of an officer in the line of duty since Selma's 1893 founding.[14]

Authorities say Officer Carrasco was slain by a convicted felon named Nathaniel Dixon, who had been released on probation in July 2020. Dixon has pleaded not guilty on first-degree murder and other charges. In 2019, Dixon was convicted of second-degree felony robbery and was in jail until July 2020, then released on probation. Sheriff's Office officials say that a month after his release, the felon was arrested again for carrying a loaded gun and possessing drugs. He was arrested yet again (a third time) shortly afterward on five felony charges, including possession of meth and having a firearm, the latter of which is prohibited for felons, according to court documents.[15]

Dixon stayed in jail until September 2022, when he was released on probation for time served and in accordance with a new state law that allowed the release of lower-level felons to provide relief for prison overcrowding.[16] Dixon was then back in jail again (a fourth time) one month later after he ditched a meeting with his probation officer. He was released again just two and a half months before murdering Carrasco.[17]

"When I see someone who was sentenced to prison...who was later released and commits a crime, and they have served a fraction of the sentence they received, I get angry," the district attorney said after Darnell Erby was arrested and charged with dismembering Pamela May. "I think our community gets angry. And the next question is, how did this happen?"[18]

None of these crimes should have happened. Each of the perpetrators should have been in jail but were set free thanks to Newsom's failed progressive vision.

These three cases paint a grim picture of California's soft-on-crime system, but the state's crime epidemic is only growing worse. And there are countless tragic and preventable stories just like these. Under Newsom's watch, violent crime in California has skyrocketed. Homicides jumped by 33.9 percent and aggravated assaults by 25.3 percent in 2022, with gun-related homicides and aggravated assaults soaring by 37.7 percent and 61.1 percent, respectively.[19] The actual rates are likely much higher. Crime data only captures incidents reported to police, and many crimes go unreported.

The rapidly rising crime rates didn't just occur in a vacuum. They directly correspond with Newsom's decade-plus-long progressive experiment with criminal justice reform, which has resulted in far lighter sentences and the premature release of violent criminals from jail. After Newsom released tens of thousands of prisoners during COVID, ostensibly to prevent the virus from spreading among California's incarcerated criminals, the state prison population dropped from 160,000 in 2011 to around 91,556 by mid-2024. As we discuss in Chapter 4, Newsom has been accused of releasing these prisoners under a false premise. COVID death rates in the state corrections system have been markedly lower than in the outside population. Even as crime surges, Newsom's administration estimates the prison population will drop to roughly 86,000 by 2028.[20]

Newsom is not only emptying prisons; he is also shutting them down. His administration has closed or is closing four state prisons, and has plans to "reimagine and transform" San Quentin, the state's oldest and most notorious prison (and previous home to the largest "death row" in the United States), into a rehabilitation center.

"We are literally tearing down walls to reimagine our prison system, incentivize true rehabilitation, and end cycles of violence and crime," Newsom said in a 2024 press release.[21] "Brick by brick, we're building a new future that will make all of us safer."

But Newsom cited no evidence that the state is growing safer because there is none. As we will explain in Chapter 5 the state's corrections agency won't disclose rehabilitation results for the years Newsom has served in office. Again, Newsom and the progressives' failed COVID policies exacerbated the problem. During the pandemic, when millions were out of work and the state had the highest unemployment in the nation, flash mobs of masked robbers stormed through the doors of Nordstrom and other high-end retailers in San Francisco and Greater Los Angeles, stealing thousands of dollars of purses, clothes, and jewelry. This type of organized retail theft has become such a massive problem that many retailers are closing their doors for good. By mid-2024, Nordstrom, Macy's, Whole Foods, Anthropologie, Old Navy, Office Depot, 7-Eleven, and Denny's all announced plans to close stores in downtown San Francisco or nearby Oakland. Starbucks and Target have also closed locations.[22]

Newsom attributes business closures in downtown San Francisco to "macroeconomic" shifts, not rampant theft, drug use, and violent crime.[23] In August 2023, downtown San Francisco was such a hotbed of crime, homelessness, and drugs that the US Department of Health and Human Services advised employees at the Nancy Pelosi Federal Building in the

Tenderloin District to work remotely "for the foreseeable future." Showing up for work at the building had become just too dangerous.[24]

In January 2024, California's homegrown, beloved burger joint, In-N-Out Burger, announced that it would close a store for the first time in its seventy-five-year history, citing crime. The franchise no longer considered the store near Oakland International Airport safe for operation. "We feel the frequency and severity of the crimes being encountered by our customers and associates leave us no alternative," the company said. "Despite taking repeated steps to create safer conditions, our customers and associates are regularly victimized by car break-ins, property damage, theft, and armed robberies."[25]

Southern California isn't faring much better. More and more businesses in Santa Monica and Los Angeles, even on once tony and vibrant Wilshire Avenue, have boarded up due to vandalism, crime, and homelessness scaring customers away.

"Mayor, we need your help. We need your help in this area," Sean James, an independent contractor who runs a business in Santa Monica pleaded in an interview with a local Fox News affiliate.

The surge in violent murders, rapes, organized retail thefts, and other crimes that shock the conscience are directly the result of Newsom's failed progressive vision and can be laid squarely at his feet. Back in 2014, when Newsom was lieutenant governor, he was the highest-ranking official pushing the specific progressive ballot measure responsible for the chaos: Proposition 47. This was the George Soros–backed policy that decriminalized drug, property crimes, and even certain sex crimes. Prop. 47 turned theft of items valued under $950, and some drug offenses, from felonies to misdemeanors. Newsom vocally supported the progressive activists and organizations pushing Prop. 47, while his boss, then-Governor Jerry Brown, remained quiet. The measure passed by a wide margin.[26]

Despite the bedlam that has ensued, Newsom now seems in denial over the disastrous effects of Prop. 47. In early 2024, he revealed that he witnessed a shoplifter steal from Target without workers intervening to stop. When he confronted an employee about it, the woman blamed the

California governor for passing laws that emboldened criminals—before realizing he was in fact the governor. "Why didn't you stop him?" Newsom recalls asking the Target employee. "The governor lowered the threshold… there's no accountability," the employee said. Newsom's description of the encounter was widely ridiculed for his failure to recognize the obvious truth in the Target employee's accusation.

Prop. 47 was coauthored by a George Soros–backed prosecutor named George Gascon. (Soros is famously a key architect of the failed progressive vision.) Newsom, who is very close to the Soros family, and Kamala Harris, endorsed Gascon for district attorney of Los Angeles despite his record of failure as San Francisco district attorney. In fact, Newsom set Gascon on his political glidepath by appointing him chief of police, then turned to him again in 2011 to be district attorney when Harris left the post after her election to attorney general.[27]

Gascon's lenient prosecutorial record led to a sharp increase in crime in both cities and two failed efforts to recall him from office during his Los Angeles tenure before voters ousted him in 2024. In addition to freeing criminals and unleashing lawlessness, Gascon's office has waged a secret war on police. In December 2021, Gascon's chief of staff, Joseph Iniguez, and his partner, Dale Radford, were arrested for suspicion of public intoxication and for driving under the influence, respectively, when they were stopped on their way home from a wedding.[28] No charges were filed and Iniguez later sued the local police department for allegedly violating his civil rights. He eventually received a $10,000 settlement which critics described as a "nuisance" payment.

According to the arresting officer, Gascon's chief of staff allegedly threatened to put his name on the "Brady list"—a database that indicates an officer must not be trusted to testify—effectively ending his career, although this alleged threat does not appear in the videotape Iniguez made of the incident.[29] However, during an investigation of the charge, the California Department of Justice discovered that another Gascon aide, Diana Teran, had been inappropriately accessing and using confidential police files for years. In April 2024, Teran was arrested and charged with eleven felonies relating to "unauthorized use of data from confidential, statutorily-protected peace officer files." According to an unsealed affidavit in the case, Teran "accessed computer data including numerous confidential peace officer files in 2018, while working as a Constitutional Policing Advisor at the Los Angeles County Sheriff's Department (LASD), and, after joining the LADA in January 2021, impermissibly used that data at the LADA."[30]

The corruption in the district attorney's office has hardly deterred Newsom from continuing to defend Gascon's Prop. 47 agenda. If anything, Newsom has doubled down in the most unethical ways. Since Prop. 47 was implemented, there have been numerous efforts to reform the measure, staunch the bleeding, and end the carnage, as even some of California's most liberal mayors are opposed to it. The latest effort—the Homelessness, Drug Addiction, and Theft Reduction Act—was sponsored by a non-partisan group of former district attorneys, public safety and crime victim advocates, and big box retailers, including WalMart, Home Depot and Target.[31] Newsom and the progressives smeared the bill as a "Republican-led initiative," and fought against it tooth and nail. Leaked emails revealed that Newsom's administration refused to negotiate any crime bills unless the district attorneys pulled Proposition 36, a separate 2024 ballot initiative designed to gut Prop. 47. Progressive lawmakers allied with Newsom put a poison pill into the crime reduction act that would automatically repeal it should any Prop. 47 reform ballot measures pass.[32]

In a bizarre twist, Newsom and Democratic lawmakers then backed away from plans to put a competing crime measure on the November ballot in 2024 that would have largely overturned Prop. 47.[33] Reality had dawned on them: they simply didn't have the votes, even in their Democratic super-majorities in the state legislature, to pass it. By the end of the summer of 2024, Newsom had signed ten carefully crafted bills focused on cracking down on retail theft and increasing prison time for offenders, while still preserving Prop. 47's core tenets.[34]

On Nov. 5, California voters sent an indisputable message: Proposition 36, which eviscerates its soft-on-crime predecessor, won in a landslide, and Gascon suffered a resounding loss to Nathan Hochman, a Republican turned Independent former federal prosecutor. California voters abruptly ended the progressives' decade-long soft-on-crime experiment in their state. But the early architects of the disastrous era should not be allowed to skirt responsibility.[35]

Newsom and Harris—while she was serving as attorney general—were two of the biggest proponents of Prop 47. In California, attorneys general are responsible for writing the titles of ballot initiatives, which are often manipulated to deceive the public into backing or opposing the proposed new laws. Harris was notorious for this practice during her attorney general tenure and seemed all too eager to mislead voters that Prop 47 was tough on crime. Backers promoted the ballot measure as the "Safe Neighborhoods and Schools Act," and Harris gave it the innocuous title: "Criminal Sentences. Misdemeanor Penalties. Initiative Statute."[36]

State Democrats were aggressively reversing tough-on-crime laws in response to a Supreme Court order to reduce its overcrowded prison population.

This extreme approach to prison reform earned an embarrassing public smackdown in mid-2024, when a transgender-identifying California convict with a long record of criminal violence had to be transferred out of a women's correctional facility and back to a men's prison after being indicted for rape.[37]

Illegal drug use has skyrocketed during Newsom's tenure, and his policies are partially if not directly to blame for creating a culture of drug permissiveness, starting with cannabis. His support for legalization of widespread pot smoking has been unequivocal: "For me, you can't be neutral here. This is a social justice issue. It's an economic justice issue. It's a racial justice issue."[38] After Newsom came under heavy fire for his efforts to legalize cannabis in California, he began bucking his party's efforts to likewise legalize harder drugs in his state. To his credit, Newsom vetoed the progressives' bills to legalize hallucinogenic drugs and create drug injection sites. Newsom may have simply learned from Oregon's mistakes. California's neighbor to the north recriminalized hard drugs in mid-2024 after a deluge of overdose deaths and chaos in the streets of Portland led to a surge in homelessness and an exodus of downtown businesses and record homicides. The three-year experiment with addicts' lives that focused on treatment over punishment as a model for the nation had failed miserably.[39]

It's worth noting that Harris, in filling out a 2019 American Civil Liberties Union presidential questionnaire, supported decriminalizing federal drug possession for personal use, including hard drugs like crack and fentanyl, along with defunding ICE and using federal funds for sex-reassignment surgeries for illegal immigrants. In an interview at the National Center for Transgender Equity Action Fund conference in 2019, Harris bragged that she worked "behind the scenes" when she was California attorney general to change the state's law to support taxpayer-funded gender transition surgeries for prisoners.[40]

Many observers noted an obvious reason for Newsom's calculation: "It's not hard to see why Newsom was unwilling to touch the issue," *Politico* reported. "Every move he makes is now being scrutinized nationally. He's quickly become a Democratic contender for president, without ever saying he has any interest in the job. His veto has become the latest evidence of his national ambitions as he shows a wariness of swinging too far left and a willingness to anger the progressive wing of a party that helps keep him in office."[41] But cannabis and hallucinogenic drugs like LSD are not California's biggest drug problem.

Much like the rest of the United States, California is in the throes of a fentanyl overdose epidemic that grows worse every day. The deadly synthetic opioid is now ubiquitous in the open-air drug markets in San Francisco's Tenderloin and South of Market neighborhoods. A video released by Hochman, during his campaign for Los Angeles district attorney, shows how the Hollywood Walk of Fame, with its famous pink stars bearing the names of the industry's most glamourous and notable actors and actresses, has been transformed into a Walk of Shame. Its once glimmering sidewalks are now home to drug-addled residents in various stages of stupor and filth.

Fentanyl is assembled by Mexican cartels using chemicals manufactured in China, then smuggled up the West Coast and distributed throughout the interior of America.

Local sheriffs and law enforcement officials have blamed Kamala Harris, while serving as California attorney general, for undercutting their efforts to stop criminals and Mexican cartels from flooding the state with guns and drugs from across the border. Harris, they argue, repeatedly defunded and disbanded antidrug task forces across the state just as fentanyl trafficking was on the rise.

Deadly fentanyl is now a booming industry for California's illegal immigrants. A disproportionate number of the street dealers are Hondurans who are in the United States illegally, a recent *San Francisco Chronicle* investigation revealed.[42] Los Hondos, as they are called, send so many remittances to their hometowns in Siria Valley, Honduras, that a boomtown of attractive new homes—mansions by local standards—have sprung up there. And there's often a distinctive theme: a connection to San Francisco so strong that the homes and gates are often embellished with the Golden Gate Bridge, San Francisco 49ers, or Golden State Warrior logos. The Golden Gate Bridge has also become a popular neck tattoo for dealers, as San Francisco's sanctuary city status carries a lower risk of deportation in addition to more lenient prosecution and sentencing.[43]

Even if Los Hondos are arrested and convicted, the state's sanctuary policies mean they are rarely deported; and drug-dealing profits are so high that even if these pushers are imprisoned they are quickly replaced by more Honduran immigrants. "They're poisoning people," one local business owner told the newspaper. "They're this cancer, this aggressive, metastasizing cancer on the Tenderloin—the dealers and the addicts."[44]

The irony of Newsom clearing out the homeless in San Francisco to welcome an authoritarian kleptocrat like China's Xi Jinping was particularly stunning, given that—as the *Washington Examiner* put it—"no one has done more to put more homeless people on San Francisco's streets than Xi and his fentanyl-exporting minions."[45] In his 2023 best seller *Blood Money*, Peter Schweizer provides ample evidence that China is the source and purveyor of all the precursor chemicals used to create the fentanyl that's killing Californians in record numbers.[46] And Xi has tacitly blessed this twenty-first-century Opium War. Recent stats on the fentanyl devastation wrought in California are frightening. In 2022 and 2023, the number of drug overdoses in America topped two hundred thousand, with fentanyl comprising the vast majority. Deaths from fentanyl in 2024 were just as bad.[47] Governor Newsom's office released statistics in February 2024 showing that the California National Guard seized a record 62,224 pounds of fentanyl in the previous year—an increase of more than 1,000 percent since 2021. According to Newsom, that amount of fentanyl "is enough to potentially kill the global population nearly twice over."[48]

The fentanyl wave has undoubtedly pushed many desperate Californians off the cliff into homelessness. But it's those who are already unhoused who suffer the most. In Los Angeles alone, deaths among the homeless surged 300 percent over the past ten years, with fentanyl accounting for a third of these deaths in 2023.[49] Tragically, most of the homeless who die of fentanyl overdoses are not seeking out fentanyl. They're actually using meth and crack and other stimulants to help them stay awake during the night so they don't get attacked or robbed, unaware that some of these drugs have been laced with fentanyl.[50]

Newsom's failed progressive vision that facilitated California's crime waves and drug epidemic has fueled another crisis every bit as tragic: homelessness. Newsom's history of supporting "Housing First" programs is based on the misguided notion that issues such as crime, unemployment, drug addiction, or mental illness should only be dealt with *after* the homeless have received housing. This approach poses special problems when you consider that housing construction, labor, and land cost significantly more in California than in other states, and local fees imposed on developers for city infrastructure improvements currently add tens of thousands in costs per affordable housing unit built.[51] Over the past five years, the state's homeless population has grown more than 40 percent to its current level of 181,000 unhoused individuals, nearly twice the number of its closest rival, New York. In 2023, 28 percent of all people experiencing homelessness were in California, even though only 12 percent of the US population resides there.[52] In 2023, the number of homeless *women* in California spiked to sixty thousand, which is nearly as many as Florida, Texas, and New York combined.[53]

Unfortunately, 68 percent of California's homeless are defined as "unsheltered," which means they experience their homeless plight outdoors.[54] On any given night in 2023, 50 percent of unsheltered individuals nationwide were sleeping on the streets of California, including half of America's unaccompanied homeless youth.[55] Unsurprisingly, 60 percent of all unsheltered individuals in the US suffering from *chronic* homelessness can be found in California.[56] In 2019, Gavin Newsom broke his promise to appoint an official "homelessness czar" for the state, which would have been a cabinet-level secretary working full time out of Newsom's office to solve the state's homeless crisis. Newsom's promise was silly because it's clear that appointing an individual figurehead does nothing to resolve serious social problems.

A year into his governorship, when reporters were peppering him with questions about making good on his promise, an irritated Newsom pounded on a podium at a budget news conference and snarled, "You want to know who's the czar? I'm the homeless czar in the state of California."[57]

Thankfully, Newsom changed course. Instead, he decided to trust the homelessness task force he'd previously created to do the job. "That committee is profoundly important and I'm looking forward to big things coming from their work," Newsom said.[58] The name of the committee is the Homeless and Supportive Housing Advisory Task Force, and it's cochaired by two Newsom appointees: Los Angeles County Supervisor Mark Ridley-Thomas and Sacramento Mayor Darrell Steinberg. Newsom appears to have been a big fan of Ridley-Thomas: in 2020, the governor created a thirty-second ad endorsing Ridley-Thomas during his election campaign for Los Angeles City Council. Here's what he had to say about his future task-force cochair:

I'm urging you to support Mark Ridley-Thomas for City Council. I've had the privilege of getting to know local elected officials all across this state. A lot of folks hold hands, talk about the way the world should be. Other people get things done. Not only does Mark Ridley-Thomas get it, but he knows how to deliver. And so, I could not encourage you more to take this opportunity, take this moment, and make sure that we have a doer in the City Council of Los Angeles, Mark Ridley-Thomas.[59]

When he was appointed to the task force, Ridley-Thomas took a serious tone in his response, stating that he looked forward "to partnering with California Governor Gavin Newsom, Sacramento Mayor Darrell Steinberg, and other members of this Task Force to ensure that the State of California steps up its efforts in confronting the defining civic and moral crises of our time."[60]

Indeed, Ridley-Thomas's framing of California's homelessness as a "moral crisis" was fitting and accurate. But Gavin's favorite LA councilman was also dealing with his own personal "moral crisis," which would soon be splashed all over the front page. In August 2023, the US Attorney's Office issued a press release announcing that Ridley-Thomas had been sentenced "to 42 months in federal prison for a bribery and fraud scheme in which the longtime politician demanded benefits for his son from a university dean in exchange for Ridley-Thomas's political support for a lucrative Los Angeles County business." He was also ordered to pay a $30,000 fine. In Ridley-Thomas's sentencing memo, the prosecutors put it bluntly:

This was a shakedown. Not the kind in movies with bags of cash or threats of force. But the kind that is polite and pervasive. The kind that happens too often by sophisticated, powerful people. The kind to which society, sadly, has become so accustomed that it often goes unreported and rarely yields consequences for the offender but strikes a devastating blow to the integrity of our democratic system…One's public service cannot be a bargaining chip for personal, private gain.[61]

Here again we see Newsom's lack of discernment, to say the least, in choosing his allies, but more importantly, it undermines citizens' faith in their governor's ability to develop creative solutions to the homelessness crisis.

As the homeless numbers continued to rise, Newsom shifted to blaming local governments' failures in reducing California's homeless numbers and threatened to withhold state funds for city needs and even to marshal the state Department of Justice's powers to take legal action against localities.[62] But at least on paper, the state already had a mechanism for coordinating and overseeing homelessness. It's dubbed the California Interagency Council on Homelessness, and the governor is the one who appoints its members. (The state auditor in 2024 would issue a sharply critical report on the Interagency Council on Homelessness, finding that it had not tracked the funds the state deployed, nor had it collected any outcomes from the programs.)

When that didn't work, Newsom blamed a federal appeals court that ruled against Grants Pass, a city in Oregon that ticketed people for sleeping outside, arguing that it violated the Constitution's ban on "cruel and unusual punishment," and ruling that cities cannot clear encampments unless they can provide alternative housing for all the people in them. Newsom seized on the ruling, arguing that it tied his and local officials' hands when it came to sweeping encampments off city property.

All the while, Newsom continued his housing-first policies. But there was little success, and there were plenty of abject failures.

The federal government paid an undisclosed sum during COVID to convert the Mayfair Hotel, a 294-room boutique hotel in Los Angeles's Westlake neighborhood, into apartments to use as part of the Project Roomkey program (Newsom's initiative to convert hotels into low-cost homeless residences) to provide temporary shelter for the homeless during the pandemic. But the hotel shut its doors in 2022 after a disturbing and turbulent period.

There were reports of rats, mounting trash piles, defecation in the hallways, chaotic assaults, and rampant drug use. Windows were smashed, bathrooms had been spray-painted, and objects had been hurled from windows. A staff of nurses, security guards, and hotel managers complained about all kinds of criminal activity in rooms, stairwells, the parking garage, and nearby streets.

After just two years, the city paid $11.5 million to cover the damage, and residents of the neighborhood are now fiercely opposing Mayor Karen Bass's efforts to purchase the Mayfair and spend $83 million converting it into homeless housing again.

Nobody likes to ask the question, but it needs to be raised: who benefits from California's chronic homelessness?

The obvious big winners are all the nonprofits, foundations, and NGOs that receive a nonstop stream of public and private funding to operate the state's "homelessness industrial complex" with little oversight or accountability.

Los Angeles–based developer Shangri-La Industries won a $121 million state contract to turn motels across the state into housing for the homeless. The massive funds were awarded under Project Homekey. Despite numerous ribbon-cuttings featuring Project Homekey's top officials and a golden spade emblazoned with its logo, much of the work on the motels came to a grinding halt or never began at all in early 2024. According to the lawsuit that followed, that's when the company discovered that its twenty-something CFO, Cody Holmes, had spent millions of the funds on Beverly Hills real estate, a Ferrari, a Bentley, and other expensive cars, private jet travel, and VIP passes to the Coachella music festival. He'd also spent millions of dollars on jewelry and handbags, including a $111,000 Birkin bag, for his girlfriend. Many of the properties went into deep debt, then slipped into foreclosure and were taken over by lenders.

How was the housing contractor with such a heavenly name chosen in the first place?

Shangri-La Industries had a politically connected partner in Step Up on Second Street, which helped Newsom come up with his housing-first HomeKey grant program, then turned around and raked in big contracts from the program. Step Up aspired to take its model for solving homelessness to the national stage, but the nonprofit is now mired in controversy.

Attorney General Rob Bonta filed suit against Shangri-La and Step Up in January 2024.[63]

Lobbyists for Shangri-La Industries include Panorea Avdis, a partner at Sacramento Advocates, a public affairs and lobbying firm.[64] Before becoming a lobbyist, Avdis was the chief of staff to Newsom's deputy, Lieutenant Governor Eleni Kounalakis, and served as the director to Newsom's Office of Business and Economic Development.[65] Through Avdis, there was also a direct link to the agency providing the homelessness contracts. Avdis previously served a stint as the director of external affairs at California's Department of Housing and Community Development.

Because there's no consensus among California progressives of what programs work best, the *Santa Monica Daily Press* has argued that "officialdom has taken a scattergun approach, providing money to a bewildering array of often overlapping programs and services."[66] In San Francisco alone, there's a maze of 232 service providers that have received billions from nine city agencies.[67] Such a long track record of failure has forced some to conclude that California's harnessing of the nonprofit sector to combat homelessness has only intensified the problems it sought to remedy. From 2018 to 2021, California spent around $10 billion fighting homelessness, but the number of folks without a roof over their head only increased during that time.[68] In 2022, the state spent $42,000 per homeless person, a mindboggling sum when you consider that a family of four earning $42,000 would place them well beyond California's official poverty line of $39,900.

The hidden beneficiaries of California's homeless explosion were the wealthy elite (including Chinese billionaires) who had enough cash to snap up devalued urban properties that depreciated significantly from all the unresolved chaos in the streets.[69]

In what became a viral video, a sneering Newsom, standing outside a 2019 presidential debate, bristled when we asked him about his failures to curb homelessness during his first year in office. He then blamed Trump for holding back hundreds of millions of dollars in federal housing voucher money he said he needed to help jump-start their failing housing-first remedies.[70] When we pressed Newsom on whether he would address the mental health and drug addiction crisis afflicting many homeless people, he simply put the blame on Republicans for shuttering insane asylums in the 1970s and '80s, including former Governor Ronald Reagan.

Local cities cited other reasons for the lack of progress. They countered Newsom's periodic complaints that cities still weren't bringing down homeless numbers by pointing out that they couldn't help homeless people get housing and complicated treatment for mental illness and drug addiction if the state was only sending a lump sum for those efforts once a year.

Newsom continued to harp on the locals, even while Step Up and Shangri-La's corruption was exposed, and the motel conversions came to a halt across California.

In 2023, as Newsom worried that his homelessness failures could foil his presidential ambitions, he rolled out Proposition 1, a ballot measure providing $6.4 billion to build more treatment beds and permanent housing for people with existing mental health issues who were chronically homeless. It narrowly passed in March of 2024 without the support of conservatives and far-left disability advocates who argued it would fund coerced mental health treatment.[71]

Newsom called the ballot measure's passage a "victory for doing things radically different" and once again placed the onus for its success and failure on localities, lest he be blamed for its failures in the future when he runs for president, as expected in 2028. "Now counties and local officials must match the ambition of California voters," he declared. "This historic reform will only succeed if we all kick into action immediately."[72]

In the summer of 2024, the Supreme Court shredded Newsom's main excuse for his failures to address homelessness, ruling in favor of the Grants Pass law ticketing homeless people who set up tents on city property. The decision gave cities more power to arrest, cite, and fine people living outside in public spaces.

By the time this ruling was in place, the Democratic Party had already kicked Joe Biden off the ticket and installed Harris, ending speculation that Newsom could leapfrog her and cinch the presidential nomination for himself.

Newsom had finally run out of excuses for the squalor and the blight. He began ordering state agencies to remove homeless encampments throughout California, even though many had nowhere to go.

"This executive order directs state agencies to move urgently to address dangerous encampments while supporting and assisting the individuals living in them—and provides guidance for cities and counties to do the same," Newsom said in a news release. "The state has been hard at work to address this crisis on our streets. There are simply no more excuses. It's time for everyone to do their part."[73]

Newsom's sudden demand for instant action on the homelessness problem was an obvious attempt to paper over the past and erase his role in causing the scourge. Decades of "housing first" policies by him and other far-left politicians incentivized homelessness in California, enabling the problem to worsen while failing to address its root causes. In response to Newsom's pressure for swift solutions, skeptics wonder if the unsheltered will merely migrate to the most liberal areas of the state where residents and authorities are more lenient.

California's homelessness crisis is ultimately caused by a failure of leadership, and no leader has had more chances to solve it than Gavin Newsom. The problem is that Newsom's only options are ipso facto failed approaches, because his entire political career is just a reflection of the failed progressive vision he's locked into. That's why Newsom will never have the courage or creative thinking that's needed to solve the homelessness problem. Just imagine if Newsom had dared to step out of the progressive ghetto years ago and push a different set of innovative policies that genuinely reduced the number of unsheltered Californians. Such a huge win would have undoubtedly garnered widespread political support for Newsom and likely made him a leading contender for president. But Newsom has always been more puppet than pioneer, and in a state that seems to value propaganda over tangible results, he'll continue to use sly rhetoric and even outright lies to gloss over his failure to address the full-blown humanitarian crisis unfolding in the urban wastelands of California.

* * *

As Chinese Premier Xi Jinping's rocket-proof armored vehicle made its way through the freshly cleaned streets of San Francisco to the St. Regis Hotel, throngs of pro-Beijing activists heralded his arrival.[74] As it happened, the activists were United Front operatives on the payroll of the Chinese Communist Party (CCP) and had been bused in from their stations embedded across the United States. In Newsom's California, the paid CCP foot soldiers assaulted American human rights activists protesting Xi's arrival with impunity.[75]

"The world has entered a new period of turbulence and change," Xi declared during his APEC speech and stressed the need to continue the cooperation that had characterized the relationship between the East and West over the past thirty years. The summit was attended by more than twenty thousand foreign leaders and dignitaries who were there to discuss open trade and investment between nations in the Asia-Pacific region. American titans of business, including Apple's Tim Cook, Blackstone's Steve Schwarzman, BlackRock's Larry Fink, Boeing's Stanley Deal, and Pfizer's Albert Bourla paid $40,000 a table to fête Xi as a guest of honor at a banquet at the Hyatt Regency drawing nearly four hundred attendees, including Commerce Secretary Gina Raimondo. After Xi's remarks, attendees gave him a standing ovation while just outside the dinner CCP goons in surgical masks and wielding long metal pipes attacked human rights activists who were promoting democracy in Hong Kong, autonomy for Tibet, and freedom for the estimated one million Uyghurs imprisoned in forced labor camps under Xi's rule.

In addition to persecuting millions of his own people, Xi's laudable record apparently includes waging a silent war on the West, intentionally exporting the coronavirus, and killing roughly one hundred thousand Americans per year with fentanyl.[76]

The theme of the summit was ambitious, albeit vague: "Creating a Resilient and Sustainable Future for All." Such platitudinal rhetoric comes straight from the failed progressive playbook: always announce progress toward some grand utopian goal, especially when the results are intangible, elusive, or potentially disastrous. One needs to look no further than the issues of crime, drugs, and homelessness in California under Newsom's tenure. Newsom has consistently asserted that progress has been made on all these fronts. But because he is so wedded to the failed progressive vision, he cannot fix these issues—not in any meaningful way.

Critics mocked Newsom's preparation for Xi, calling it a "convenient scurryfunge," and likened it to frenzied teens rushing to clean up after a house party before the parents returned.[77] Newsom admitted as much. "I know folks say, 'Oh, they're just cleaning up this place because all those fancy leaders are coming into town,' that's true," he said, "because it's true."[78]

So the streets were sanitized, but where did all the criminals, drug addicts, illegal migrants, and homeless people go? Did the cleanup also magically lift them from their predicaments? Of course not. It turned out that, on Newsom's orders, most of them were merely rounded up by police and herded, like cattle in a rotational grazing loop, to other parts of the city. Many of the homeless ended up in the Sunset District, some congregated on Willow Street, others huddled in alleyways and camped under freeways. The Marina was crammed with as many as possible. The problems were pushed out of sight so that Newsom could impress the elite guests and benefactors who will fund his political ambitions.

As soon as APEC ended and all the dignitaries jetted home, reporters began to ask the question on everyone's mind: will all the unhoused chaos return to the streets? The answer came fast and hard. Just hours after the summit concluded, the homeless returned to their encampments and open drug use was once again ubiquitous. Within a week, the shiny streets that only a fool would believe could remain golden were scummy once again.[79] Vagrants were back in the Tenderloin urinating in public, and "pretty quickly the mentally disturbed folks, the fent zombies, started making their way back into the neighborhood." Shop owners and other leaders in the Tenderloin were shocked at how quickly all the problems returned and now claim the homeless crisis has grown worse than ever: "the post-APECalypse."[80] Referring to city leaders, San Francisco Deli Board owner Adam Mesnick said, "They are very good at creating an illusion and they are very good at performance art…it's a Band-Aid and indicative of a poor administration."[81]

Progressives identify innumerable "root causes" for crime and homelessness, including some combination of economic factors, racism, predatory capitalism, mental illness, drug addiction, broken families, illegal immigration, climate change, or even all the above. Newsom's solutions have nothing to do with the problems. In fact, progressive policies tend to mask the problems, at best, and more often make them worse. Newsom and his Left Coast mentors did not only spawn the failed progressive vision for America. They also abetted the infiltration of America by the CCP, which is now waging unrestricted warfare against US citizens via fentanyl, TikTok, intellectual property theft, massive hacking enterprises, subversion in academia, social unrest, and other methods of what our adversaries in Beijing call "disintegration warfare."[82]

CHAPTER TWO

Growing Up Getty

G AVIN NEWSOM WAS NOT BORN RICH, but he was born connected. Newsom's connections to the progressive elite in California paved the way for him to ruin San Francisco as mayor, then the state as governor, and soon, if he has his way, Newsom's billionaire-backed quest for power may ruin the entire country. Like most ambitious politicians climbing the ladder of success, Newsom has carefully constructed a narrative about his life and how he rose above his station. Newsom's story is that he pulled himself up by his bootstraps—it was his hard work, business savvy, and political acumen that led to his financial success and rapid, steady rise to become governor of the most populous state in America. But that narrative is a fiction, and the truth is far simpler: he had Getty Oil money and deep family connections turbocharging his accession. Perhaps no greater story illustrates who Gavin Newsom is at his core than the mystery of the bronze bust.

One fine day in 2016, San Francisco's City Hall got a gleaming upgrade to its facilities: a larger-than-life sculpture of a well-coiffed head (and chiseled torso) appeared atop a black granite pedestal in the rotunda to greet every local Bay Area bureaucrat, resident, and visitor. The finest sculptor in town had been chosen to immortalize Newsom, the former mayor, in bronze. The legendary Bay Area sculptor Bruce Wolfe was busy working on a Clint Eastwood statue and had to split his time between that project and crafting Newsom's likeness. "They're both handsome guys, they really are," Wolfe said. The artist noted that Newsom's defining physical trait is his hair: "It looks great on him. And I want to make sure that it translates to the bronze as well." Newsom "likes the open-collar look," said Wolfe, who took great care to accentuate the neck bones, square jaw, and stern and focused visage. "I think that's a breath of fresh air."[1]

When asked about his mayoral bust, then-Lieutenant Governor Newsom said that the idea had been "floating around" for a few years, but he insisted that he didn't know who was supporting or fundraising for the project. "I don't want to call it embarrassing," he said, "but it's a strange thing."[2] Newsom assured the public that the bronze bust's $91,000 price tag would be paid for with private funds, not taxpayer monies. And a private group called ArtCare, which partners with the city's art commission, wrote a letter to the city of San Francisco reiterating that Newsom's bust was "fully funded through private donations" to the organization.[3] The precise source of the funds that paid for Newsom's bust had remained a mystery, until now: Newsom paid for his own statue to be eternally housed in the city's pantheon among his mayoral mentors, Dianne Feinstein and Willie Brown. And he took great care to ensure no one knew it.

An analysis of Newsom's "behested payments" reveals that in 2016 three private organizations each donated $30,000 to a nonprofit called Community Initiatives, which then funneled the $90,000 to ArtCare for a portion of the sculpture's cost. As it turns out, two of these payments came from companies owned by Newsom—Balboa Cafe Partners and PlumpJack Management Group (as it happened, Newsom built these companies with help from his lifelong benefactors, the Gettys).[4] When the bronze bust was finished, it was placed in the City Hall rotunda with a quote from the former mayor inscribed on its pedestal that reads: "If you distill the essence of everything, what life is about, every single one of us is given a short moment in time on this planet, and we all have one universal need and desire, and that is to be loved and to love."[5]

Creating a larger-than-life statue in one's own flattering likeness for subjects to admire is something that strongman dictators achieve as an effortless by-product of their egoistic rule. And they are proud of it.[6] For

Newsom, funding his own bronze sculpture and placing it prominently in the city's headquarters took effort, and he tried to conceal his role out of what little sense of shame he possessed.

But the bronze bust story reveals a side of Newsom that is much deeper than his pure unbridled egoism. It exhibits the "dark triad" personality traits that ought to disqualify a person from achieving power of any kind: narcissism, psychopathy, and Machiavellianism. However, rather than disqualifying Newsom, his dark triad tendencies only propelled him higher up the ladder of political power. And the secret money behind the bronze bust reveals the other force propelling him toward an eventual White House bid: the billionaire Getty family.

California's fortieth governor was five years old when his parents divorced in 1971. He and his younger sister were mostly raised by their mother, Tessa, in a home where money was tight for several years despite his grandfather's success in real estate and politics. His father, William A. "Bill" Newsom III, was a Stanford-educated lawyer who ran an unsuccessful race for state senate in 1968 before serving as corporate counsel for the highflying Trans-International Computer Investment Corporation (TCI). TCI, a groundbreaking computer leasing and investment firm, helped develop navigation systems for oil tankers and founded several high-tech companies in and around the San Francisco Bay Area, a precursor to Silicon Valley.[7]

There, the elder Newsom worked alongside several of the state's most powerful business figures. But the once wildly successful firm went into a tailspin when the state government launched a wide-ranging stock fraud investigation, eventually forcing it into bankruptcy in 1971. Newsom III wasn't implicated in the financial scandal involving illegal syndication of the firm's stock, but it had a devastating impact on the Newsom family all the same.[8] Some accounts have blamed Bill and Jesse Newsom's divorce on the stresses of the elder Newsom's ailed state senate campaign, but the company's implosion wreaked the most havoc on the couple's marriage and home life. Gavin Newsom recalled that some of his earliest memories are about his parents fighting about money—and it had a lasting impact.[9]

"One night," he said he heard, "my mother yelling and screaming at my dad because he wasn't able to help us financially, because he was very close to bankruptcy. He didn't care about money, but I *never* wanted to be in that position."[10]

It was back in junior high that Newsom began using hair gel and wearing blazers and business suits, a look he has said was inspired by *Remington Steele*, a TV show that starred Pierce Brosnan as a con artist who assumed the identify of a glamorous private detective.[11] "The suit was literally a mask," he recalled. "I am still that anxious kid with the bowl-cut hair, the dyslexic kid—the rest is a façade. The only thing that saved me was sports."[12] But it wasn't all tough times and penny-pinching. Through the happenstance of his father's and grandfather's business and family connections, young Gavin fell into an elite circle.[13]

His grandfather, William A. Newsom, the son of an Irish immigrant, was the family's original political animal. Newsom's grandfather cut his teeth in the bare-knuckle political world of San Francisco's midcentury machine politics, controlled by party boss William M. Malone, the most powerful Democratic leader in the state.[14] Thanks to his friendship with President Harry Truman, Malone controlled most federal patronage appointments across the state in the postwar period. Newsom thrived in this world, running eventual Governor Edmund Gerald "Pat" Brown's 1942 campaign for San Francisco district attorney. Later, Newsom's grandfather helped steer Brown's successful 1958 campaign for governor.

Originally a Republican, Brown became disillusioned with the probusiness party during the Great Depression and became a New Dealer and an active Democratic Party member.[15] Pat Brown's son Jerry followed in his legal and political footsteps, becoming the state's thirty-fourth and thirty-ninth governor and serving as attorney general, as well as serving as the chairman of the California Democratic Party. The liberal father-and-son tag team occupied the governor's mansion in Sacramento and dominated state politics for over thirty years.[16] One of Pat Brown's many legacies was developing Squaw Valley for the 1960 Winter Olympics. After the resort, which changed its name to Palisades Tahoe in 2021, was built, Brown awarded a contract to operate it to Bill Newsom II and his partner, John Pelosi, the patriarch of what would soon be another ruling California family.[17]

John's son, Paul Pelosi, married Nancy, daughter of Congressman and Baltimore Mayor Thomas D'Alesandro Jr. In 1969, the pair moved to San Francisco, where Paul Pelosi's brother, Ronald Pelosi, was a member of the city and county of San Francisco's Board of Supervisors, a position Gavin Newsom would eventually win more than two decades years later.[18] Ronald Pelosi had made his fortune in the securities industry and was married to Newsom's daughter and Gavin Newsom's aunt, Belinda Barbara Newsom, from 1956 to 1977. Like so many of these intertwined Bay Area clans, a private San Francisco school had served as the conduit. The pair had known each other since they met in grammar school.[19]

Paul Pelosi also followed his father's path and grew wealthy through real estate and venture capital investments. The Pelosi family money catapulted Nancy into campaign success in San Francisco politics and ultimately enabled her to become the first woman speaker of the US House of Representatives.[20] Like his Squaw Valley partner Ron Pelosi, Newsom wanted his children to reap the benefits of his hard work and connections. He sent his son Bill to St. Ignatius, a Jesuit prep school popular with the city's old-money upper crust. Jerry Brown also graduated from the same school a year ahead of Newsom. Their social circles were so close that Bill once dated Jerry's sister.[21]

In the intervening years, Newsom managed to successfully navigate San Francisco's intense political turf wars. After Senator Estes Kefauver, a Democrat from Tennessee, led investigations into organized crime, Malone's machine-style approach was no longer in vogue and the investigations imploded. In the late 1950s, Malone was outflanked by brothers Phillip and John Burton, a formidable tag team ushering in a new era of socially progressive bourgeois liberalism that quickly spread from San Francisco to Los Angeles and continues to dominate the state's major cities today.[22] While Gavin Newson's grandfather was trying to carefully transition from the rough-and-tumble era of party fat cats to the new culturally progressive period, his son was making the most of his prep school connections.

At St. Ignatius, Bill met Gordon Getty, son of oil magnate J. Paul Getty, and the two became best friends. While J. Paul Getty was a shrewd businessman, his personal life was a disaster. He was an absentee father, spending most of his time traveling Europe. By his death in 1976, he had had five wives and countless lovers, leaving behind five sons. (Two others had died.) After their 1936 divorce, Ann Rork, Getty's fourth wife, moved sons Gordon and John Paul Jr. to Clay Street in San Francisco, near the Newsoms' residence.[23]

The timing of the move couldn't have been more fortuitous for young Newsom.[24]

The Gettys were the richest family in the world for a time—true American oligarchs. Their sprawling oil dynasty captivated the public imagination and enthralled the national media, which reported on every detail of its members' cartoonishly extravagant lives, as well as their mischief and misdeeds—drug addictions, overdoses, court battles, and divorces.[25] The family owned a mansion and hotel in Manhattan where it entertained the rich and famous. Its real estate empire included the luxurious 2,500-acre Wormsley Park outside of London, where the Gettys hosted cricket matches attended by British Prime Minister John Major and Queen Elizabeth and soirees with Rolling Stones frontman Mick Jagger and his then-wife, Bianca. The Getty family also owned vast properties in Italy, Morocco, and other exotic locales.[26]

Gavin Newsom's father and Gordon Getty were such close childhood chums they were nearly like brothers, with Gordon Getty spending most of his free time at the Newsom home. The pair spent the next six decades intertwining their families and businesses, using their connections and Getty wealth to fuel Newsom's financial success and launch his political career.[27] After Getty and the elder Newsom graduated from high school in 1951, four years ahead of Pat Brown's son, Jerry, Bill Newsom went on to Stanford Law School and afterward worked for the Getty family and Getty Oil, becoming one of the family's closest confidantes and legal advisers. The elder Newsom served as the family's tax attorney and even as its bagman after young John Paul Getty III, grandson of John Paul Getty, was kidnapped at age sixteen. When the notoriously tightfisted Gettys balked at paying the $3 million in ransom money his Italian mobster-captors had demanded—suspecting it was a prank to pry money from them—the kidnappers cut off part of John Paul's ear and mailed it to a newspaper. The Gettys quickly sent Bill to deliver the cash and retrieve John Paul.[28]

It was the Getty connections and the city's well-worn paths of patronage that led to Bill Newsom's role at TCI in the late 1960s. Gordon's brother, J. Paul Getty Jr., who served on the board, offered Bill a position on the board.[29] The job gave Bill entrée into the highest levels of California's burgeoning high-tech business world. Newsom's colleagues included the company's eventual president, Otto von Bolschwing. Bolschwing had been a Nazi SS officer, eventually becoming a member of Austria's intelligence corps and a CIA spy before shifting to international business. (Years later, the Justice Department ultimately caught up with Bolschwing and accused him of assisting in Hitler's Holocaust and associating with Adolf Eichmann, the architect of Germany's mass killing program.)[30] Bill Newsom spent good portions of 1969 and 1970 traveling throughout Europe with Bolschwing, relying on his connections and network of banking contacts to find new business opportunities.[31]

He has since claimed that he believed the story Bolschwing told him: that he had worked for US security agencies during World War II. "He was suave and plausible," Newsom told the *San Jose Mercury News* in 1981. "He seemed to have all the credentials...He looked kind of world-weary. He had a long cigarette holder—his hair was slicked back."[32]

Newsom also counted Thomas Fransioli, a top Boston banker, and Albert Driscoll, the former New Jersey governor who served as a top executive to Warner-Lambert Pharmaceutical, as TCI colleagues. The company received classified contract work from the Department of Defense, and the entire team of executives and top employees had to attain security clearances.[33] But TCI never lived up to its grandiose dreams. In the early 1970s, the firm ran into trouble with the state Department of Corporations. Several major stockholders were syndicating its stock and selling it to small investors in Sacramento. The trading was deemed illegal under a 1968 law requiring security sales to be registered. The San Francisco district attorney prosecuted several stockholders, calling it "possibly the biggest stock fraud in California history."[34]

After TCI's demise and the divorce, money in the Newsom household became tight. Newsom grew up mainly with his mother in San Francisco, while his politically connected father lived in Placer County, home to Lake Tahoe's tony ski resorts. Newsom earned extra cash by holding down a paper route, then later worked stints as a busboy and in construction.[35] For several years, his mother, Tessa, took in foster children and rented a bedroom to boarders to help pay the bills. Newsom's sister, Hilary, has recalled sharing the family home with a "creepy guitar-playing guy" and a single mom with her son.[36] After a long stint of inconsistent work, it was clear that Bill Newsom needed a steady income. This time, it was the Brown family who came to the rescue. Almost immediately after being sworn in as governor, Jerry Brown appointed Newsom to a judgeship in Placer County in January 1975 and later to the California Court of Appeal in San Francisco.[37] A year later, J. Paul Getty passed away, leaving control of his massive $2 billion family trust to Gordon, a classical music composer who quickly handed management off to his friend Bill Newsom so he could spend more time pursuing his dream of making it as an opera singer.[38]

Through all the financial ups and downs, Bill Newsom's father's extraordinarily close ties to the Gettys granted him access to the jet-setting life of power and privilege. Gavin Newsom vacationed with the Gettys in places like Africa and Hudson Bay, where he experienced a rarefied world of luxury.[39] Gavin Newsom's time with his father included many trips to North Beach Restaurant, an iconic Italian eatery in the heart of San Francisco. The restaurant was a popular watering hole and gathering place for politicos, artists, and executives for half a century.[40] The young Newsom rubbed shoulders with Jerry Brown, Ron Pelosi (Nancy Pelosi's then-brother-in-law), state Senator and retired Judge Quentin Kopp, and San Francisco Mayors George Moscone and Willie Brown.

He also got to know John and Phillip Burton, brothers who helped shape the modern California Democratic Party and who each represented different parts of the Bay Area in Congress and spent several years serving in Congress together.[41] Philip Burton represented San Francisco in Congress from 1964 to his untimely death at age fifty-six in 1983. Burton's legacy includes passing legislation to create the Redwood National Park along the Northern California coast and the Golden Gate Recreational District, stretching along both sides of the entrance to San Francisco Bay. After his death, his wife, Sala Burton, took over his seat. It's the same San Francisco House seat held by Nancy Pelosi, who won a special election when Sala Burton passed away in 1987.[42] In the 1980s, Philip Burton was so close to Gavin's father that he attended some of Gavin Newsom's high school basketball and baseball games at Redwood High, a public school on the San Francisco Peninsula, just a twenty-five-minute drive south of the city. He also employed Newsom's sister, Hilary, in his district office.[43]

While each San Francisco pol played a role in Newsom's political education, the Gettys provided young Gavin instant entrée into San Francisco's "first families." The exclusive high society included the Pelosis, as well as the Pritzkers and the Fishers, moneyed dynasties who made their fortunes in hotels and fashion and "whose names grace the city's art galleries, charity ball invitations, and hospital wards."[44] By his midtwenties, Newsom was no longer a normal middle-class kid; he was a Getty-funded millionaire and a rising star in the leftist oligarchy of his Bay Area billionaire patrons. Gordon and his late socialite wife, Ann, viewed Newsom as a son, especially after two of their four sons died from drug overdoses relatively young (one related to methamphetamine use and the other to a fentanyl overdose). The extended Getty family readily helped Newsom amass a personal fortune and fueled his political rise.[45]

In a story the governor likes to tell, his boundless political destiny began on a humble baseball diamond several hours' drive to the north, in a pleasant suburb south of San Francisco.

"It shaped me. I love sports. I don't just like sports—I love sports. It's the reason we're having this conversation. It's the reason I'm governor of California," Newsom told *The Lead*, a popular sports podcast in 2019.[46]

Friends in high places always come in handy, but for an eighteen-year-old Newsom, with his tall frame, square jaw, and swagger beyond his years, the cliché was an understatement. After a dyslexia diagnosis early in his childhood, Newsom suffered through elementary and high school in the early 1980s with middling-to-poor grades and even worse college entrance exam scores. "You don't even want to know what I got on my SATs," Newsom once remarked to a reporter about his college admissions prospects.[47]

Newsom fully admits just how uncertain he was about his future as a senior in college, recalling at different times throughout his political career that, as a struggling student, the best he could hope for was a stint at a junior college with a chance of transferring to a four-year school after two years if he could manage to get by with a B or better average.[48] But Newsom, as he tells it, had athletics on his side. He's even boasted of being scouted by the Texas Rangers while still in high school. There's a big difference between being scouted and being recruited, and there were far more professional baseball scouts crisscrossing the country and showing up at local high schools at the time than there are today.

Newsom's claim that he was scouted by the Major League franchise owner George W. Bush would go on to own has been repeated so often it's morphed into an urban legend in San Francisco. In a 2004 home opener, the San Francisco Giants invited Newsom, then the city's newly minted mayor, to throw out the first pitch. As he took the mound, the announcer stated that Newsom had "played first base for the University of Santa Clara and was drafted by the Texas Rangers."[49]

But beyond the difference between merely being scouted versus being fully recruited—or even drafted—Newsom's entire narrative about pulling himself up by his cleat laces is a myth.

Over the last three decades, Newsom has claimed to be a baseball high school standout who managed to win a partial athletic scholarship to Santa Clara University, a well-regarded small Jesuit liberal arts school in the heart of what is now Silicon Valley.

A left-handed pitcher, Newsom often recalls that he played that key position on his college baseball team until the beginning of his sophomore year when an ulnar nerve injury forced him to quit, and he never pitched again.

But the story isn't so simple. Most of the Newsom accounts fail to mention that a personal recommendation from Jerry Brown, who had finished serving his first tenure as governor two years prior, accompanied his 1985 application to school.

In every version, Newsom also leaves out the key detail that he is not included on an official Santa Clara baseball roster from his years there because he only played on the junior varsity team, where scholarships were exceedingly rare or completely nonexistent. Many varsity baseball players, even all-stars with much better stats and grades, never received an athletic scholarship, according to several fellow Santa Clara varsity athletes who attended the college during Newsom's time there and spoke on condition of anonymity.

As it turns out, William Connolly, who played for the Santa Clara baseball team in the early 1960s and went on to become a wealthy San Francisco investment banker with ties to Newsom's father, pressed his alma mater's coaches to take a look at Newsom, according to Mike Cummins, Newsom's assistant coach at Santa Clara who currently serves as the head coach at California State University, East Bay. (Brown also attended Santa Clara University his first year of undergraduate before leaving for a Jesuit novitiate with plans to become a priest that he later set aside.[50])

Newsom was offered a scholarship of $500 in the fall of his freshman year, according to his spokesman Nathan Click, who provided a photograph of a section of the paperwork to *CalMatters*. It was a fraction of the $10,251 annual cost to attend Santa Clara University at the time, the website reported. Click suggested Newsom could have received more scholarship funds but was unable to locate the original scholarship document.[51] That scholarship, whether earned or manufactured by powerful alumni, likely provided him entrée to the school, considering even Newsom admits he would never have been admitted based on grades and SAT scores alone.

After Newsom's injury, the details of which Cummins couldn't recall, the coach said Newsom "chose not to play" anymore.[52] In some interviews about his short-lived college baseball career, Newsom, the consummate performative politician, implies that it was more than the injury that led him to quit. It was really hard work.

"College sports took my love of baseball away," he said. "It was work. The requirement to do all the voluntary classes and then the workouts, and then the weekends and the summer league and winter—it became a job almost."[53]

The fact that Brown stepped in to recommend Newsom is undisputed and hardly surprising. On at least one occasion, Newsom has publicly acknowledged Brown's letter on his behalf, once joking that it was "just a blanket letter of recommendation that someone probably wrote for you."[54]

While the story is far more complicated than Newsom has ever admitted, one thing is clear: his college admission was courtesy of his family's political connections, specifically former Governor Jerry Brown, not his outstanding athletic prowess.[55]

In reality, Newsom only spent a season on Santa Clara's junior varsity baseball team and likely received only a miniscule scholarship. So why does he continue to highlight it time and time again at events around the state and repeatedly credit his early baseball skills as the secret behind his ultimate success? Given the truth—that he was born connected to the most powerful political families in the state—perhaps the question answers itself.

After college, Newsom briefly served as an assistant real estate salesman before he and one of Gordon Getty's sons, Billy Getty, went into business together, opening a wine shop in 1992. Billy Getty and Gavin Newsom had developed a taste for good wine from their fathers, both wine connoisseurs and best friends.[56] Gordon Getty dubbed the business PlumpJack Wine & Spirits, after one of Shakespeare's most memorable characters, Sir John "plump Jack" Falstaff. A fun-loving and irreverent muse, Falstaff appears in three plays, including *Henry IV, Part 1*, when he bonds with Prince Hal (Henry) over several goblets of wine at a local tavern.[57]

The wine enterprise was, of course, underwritten by Getty largesse.[58]

Gavin Newsom and Billy Getty would go on to open more than twenty businesses—wineries, restaurants, and resort hotels, including the popular Balboa Cafe in San Francisco's Marina District, a winery in Napa, and the Squaw Valley Inn. For the Newsoms, the PlumpJack Management Group helped boost the bottom lines of the entire family. Gavin's mother, Tessa, kept the books, and his sister, Hilary, served as an early president and has helped lead the PlumpJack Foundation, a charity the business eventually spawned.[59] Gordon Getty was the lead investor in at least ten of the business ventures involving his son and Gavin Newsom—even after Newsom and Billy had a bitter falling-out in 2000. The dispute involved Newsom moving into a Pacific Heights house that he and the young Getty were remodeling as a business investment because he was struggling to pay the mortgage on his home in the Marina District and was busy running for reelection to his county supervisor post. Billy wanted Newsom to renovate and sell in what was quickly becoming a hot housing market. Gavin and Billy ended up off-loading the home for a tidy profit—upward of $4 million.[60] Even though he was Billy's father, Gordon Getty publicly backed Newsom, telling a local paper that caught wind of the dispute, "I believe 100 percent in Gavin, and when he is accused of wrongdoing, I'm on his side."[61]

While Getty money fueled Newsom's wealth and campaigns, it was then–San Francisco Mayor Willie Brown, the former long-serving speaker of the California State Assembly and one of the most powerful politicians in the state, who gave him his first political job. Brown is now perhaps best known for having a very public affair with Kamala Harris and serving as her political benefactor, but he also was instrumental in Newsom's political rise. At Newsom's father's urging, Willie appointed Gavin as chairman of the city's Parking and Traffic Commission.[62] In 1995, the elder Newsom had reached out to Brown through John Burton to suggest that Gavin hold a fundraiser for him at one of his restaurants.[63] Brown, a former civil rights activist turned expert legislative dealmaker, was still serving as speaker at the time. He chose to run for mayor of San Francisco after being forced out of the California State Legislature by newly passed term limits.[64] After serving three decades in the assembly and a record-long stint as its speaker, Brown knew the value of Newsom's connections to the insular world of San Francisco's deep-pocketed elite.

Brown also appointed Newsom to the San Francisco Board of Supervisors, the equivalent of a city council, when a vacancy arose in 1997. Newsom was then elected to the board the next year.[65] Brown was term-limited as mayor, and tapping him for supervisor position set up Newsom for a run to succeed him. In November 2003, Newsom easily won the first round of mayoral balloting, garnering 42 percent of the vote. In a December runoff, he edged out Green Party–backed Board President Matt Gonzalez by just 5 percent despite outspending him roughly ten to one.[66]

Newsom met Kimberly Guilfoyle several years earlier at a John Burton fundraiser. A registered Republican, Guilfoyle worked for San Francisco's district attorney when they married in 2001. Gordon Getty and his wife reportedly covered the $233,000 bill for the lavish wedding reception at their home after the ceremony at St. Ignatius Church at the University of San Francisco.[67] The *San Francisco Chronicle* deemed the nuptials the "social event of the year," hailing the pair as the "next liberal power couple." Among the five hundred celebrities, artists, politicians, and luminaries gathered for the wedding was Ed Asner, who flew in from Rome with his wife, Cindy, Gavin's aunt.[68]

The September 2004 issue of *Harper's Bazaar* ran a splashy photo spread of the couple, dubbing them "the New Kennedys."[69] Guilfoyle, then thirty-two, soon became known for her own career triumphs. She tried a case involving a dog-mauling incident that left a woman dead in her Pacific Heights apartment. She gained national fame for prosecuting the case and quickly shifted to a television career.[70] Guilfoyle soon decamped to New York for a job with Court TV, also regularly appearing as a legal commentator on *Anderson Cooper 360°*. It was tough timing for a bicoastal relationship—Newsom had just been elected mayor.[71] With Newsom and Guilfoyle pursuing their demanding careers on opposite ends of the country, the marriage quickly grew strained and fell apart. The couple announced their plans to divorce in 2005, and less than a year later, Guilfoyle married furniture heir Eric Villency in a ceremony in Barbados, giving birth to son Ronan Anthony five months later. That relationship also was short-lived, ending in divorce three years later.[72]

Newsom seemed intent to show he, too, was moving on, and his active romantic life was on constant public display. Dubbed "Mayor McHottie" by the news media, Newsom briefly dated a model and restaurant hostess half his age and a collegiate lacrosse player who wasn't old enough to drink but was photographed with Newsom drinking a glass of wine at a gala the couple attended.[73] He also dated several television actors, including Italian actress Sofia Milos, at one point attending a Scientology-backed fundraiser with her.[74] Newsom's series of love interests attracted attention and intrigue, but it was his early political decision to lean into the burgeoning culture wars that helped win him accolades from the Left and big approval numbers from San Francisco's influential gay and lesbian community.

Upon taking office, Newsom rejected the predominant view of most mainstream Democrats, including that of President Bill Clinton, who followed the state Supreme Court rulings making gay marriage illegal.[75] Soon after becoming mayor, he started issuing marriage licenses to same-sex couples in defiance of state law, cementing his brand as an unabashed liberal who embraced the gay community and was willing to fight for them. His image was often featured in campaign advertising opposing Proposition 8, the initiative backed by Governor Pete Wilson that banned same-sex marriage in California.[76]

While Newsom's popularity as mayor was soaring, his personal life was spinning out of control. During the same year of his divorce, he was drinking heavily and began an affair with Ruby Rippey-Tourk, the wife of Alex Tourk, his close friend and campaign manager. Rippey-Tourk was also his subordinate, serving as his appointing secretary in the mayor's office. The two kept the affair a secret for nearly two years until February 2007, when it was leaked to the *San Francisco Chronicle*.[77] Alex Tourk immediately resigned from Newsom's reelection campaign, and he and Ruby Rippey-Tourk divorced. The fling made national news, with the *New York Times* leading its story by describing the affair as a "fast-unfolding scandal with all the sex and betrayal of a tawdry novel."[78]

Amid the #MeToo movement, when Newsom was running for governor in 2018, Rippey Gibney (using her remarried name) came forward to defend Newsom against charges that he was guilty of having an affair with a subordinate like other prominent politicians, producers, and celebrities under fire for sexual harassment in the workplace.[79]

Although the affair destroyed Rippey Gibney's home life, she argued that it shouldn't be part of the discussion about sexual misconduct surrounding the #MeToo movement. In a Facebook post, she described herself as a "free-thinking, 33-year-old adult married woman & mother" at the time of the affair. She also admitted having an "unfortunate inclination towards drinking-to-excess & self-destruction."[80]

There was a reason Rippey Gibney came forward so publicly to defend Gavin. At the time of her defense of him, the state capitol in Sacramento was in the middle of a #MeToo meltdown. Several California Democratic lawmakers resigned, another had been suspended, and documents had just been released the day before detailing multiple sexual harassment allegations against lawmakers and staff members since 2006.[81] It was just one year after several well-known actresses came forward with decades of sexual misconduct allegations against Harvey Weinstein, a former film producer who cofounded Miramax, an entertainment powerhouse, with his brother, Bob Weinstein. With Weinstein's dramatic fall, the #MeToo movement went viral across California and the country, taking down powerful men in Hollywood and the media like falling dominoes.[82]

Back when the Rippey Gibney affair first leaked in 2007, the revelations shook the San Francisco political scene and cast Newsom's personal reputation in a far more negative light. He suffered another blow when reports surfaced that he had allegedly arrived drunk at a San Francisco hospital on a Friday night to comfort the family of a murdered police officer.[83] Though he never admitted to being an alcoholic, Newsom sought counsel from a life coach rather than going to an official rehab facility. He quickly emerged from the experience in a new relationship with actress and producer Jennifer Siebel, a solid member of San Francisco's upper crust. The couple married in 2008 and now have three children.[84] The California press corps didn't spend too much time on the affair and betrayal story once Siebel was in the picture. They were too busy covering—often even lauding—every aspect of Newsom's same-sex marriage battles, which became a model for his time as mayor and were making national and international news.

Newsom's willingness to take on social conservatives in his party and across the state won him plaudits from California's liberal hegemony, who encouraged him to continue tacking left. He racked up a laundry list of symbolic liberal wins: his municipal government declared San Francisco a sanctuary city for illegal immigrants, he committed to paying for universal health care for the city's poorest citizens, and he joined the Kyoto Protocol, an international treaty extending the 1992 United Nations Framework Convention on Climate Change.[85] Even as Newsom was awash in positive headlines, serious city problems were brewing. San Francisco's crime and homelessness were on the rise, the city's budget was overloaded thanks to Proposition 13, which keeps property taxes low, and deficit spending spiked.[86] Luckily for Newsom, but tragically for San Francisco residents, most of the state's left-leaning media never pressed the young mayor on the two developing issues—crime and homelessness—that would go on to plague the state and tarnish Newsom's legacy as its leader.

As far back as when he was serving as mayor, predictions surfaced that Newsom would eventually run for president.[87] That raw ambition has placed him in Jerry Brown's crosshairs several times over the years. As a brash, young San Francisco mayor, Newsom decided to challenge Brown in his 2010 comeback run for governor but dropped out early in the face of poor poll numbers. It was the right choice. Newsom wisely chose to take a back seat to Brown and jumped into the 2010 race for lieutenant governor, which he handily won. Newsom sat in Governor Jerry Brown's long shadow as the state's No. 2 for eight years before he could run to succeed him. When Brown was term-limited out of the job, Newsom ran for governor in 2018 and sailed to victory, capturing 61.9 percent of the vote to GOP business-man John Cox's 38.1 percent.[88] Getty money fueled all of Newsom's polit-ical campaigns, and his first gubernatorial campaign was no different. Numerous Getty family members donated a combined $500,000 to the successful effort.[89]

In Newsom's second year as governor, his handling of the COVID pan-demic lifted the curtain on an imperious attitude and personal double standards. He imposed the strictest lockdown policies in the nation and then violated them several times. The country witnessed one of these mis-steps when he was caught in November 2020 dining without a face cover-ing at an exclusive French restaurant in Napa called the French Laundry. Two months later, Newsom and several other prominent Democrats were photographed sans masks at an NFL playoff game in Los Angeles while he continued to force children to wear masks in public schools. He was caught on camera at the football game just weeks after a state agency permanently shut down a Christian preschool for not consistently keeping masks on two- and three-year-olds.[90]

The backlash over his "rules for thee, but not for me" hypocrisy jeopar-dized his hold on the governorship, and his opponents launched a successful recall petition. Newsom then raised a mountain of cash—$80 million—eventually beating the recall attempt to oust him by a slightly higher mar-gin than he had held during his first gubernatorial win. Sixty-four percent voted against removing him from office, while just 36.1 percent favored ousting him.[91] True to form, the California media quickly depicted the win as a crushing blow to Newsom's opponents, with several editorials arguing such a strong victory had bolstered his presidential chances.[92]

Newsom was emboldened by those positive press reviews even though his record as the state's chief executive has been anything but stellar. In fact, Newsom has managed to accelerate California's downward spiral in nearly every key category. During his time as governor, the state's population has declined; homelessness has increased; violent crime and drug-related deaths have skyrocketed; taxes and utility costs have become the highest in the nation; and housing affordability has sunk to its lowest level in fifteen years.

The pandemic posed more challenges for Newsom as he imposed strict lockdowns that wreaked havoc on small businesses, churches, and other nonprofits while carving out loopholes for Hollywood and other allies and allowing teachers' unions to keep schools shuttered longer than in any other state.[93] Newsom also presided over the biggest financial scandal in state history. After Newsom's COVID lockdown policies forced millions of Californians out of work, more than a 5 million unemployed workers had their unemployement payments delayed while 1 million had payments improperly denied. Years later, hundreds of thousands of workers were still fighting with the state's unemployment agency to get their promised unemployment payments.[94]

Despite these failings, Democratic and Republican political prognosticators alike continued to spur talk of Newsom as an attractive 2024 Democratic candidate. In 2023, seemingly overnight, the California governor transformed from a conservative punchline about the state's crime, chaos, and broader decline to a political force. His near-instant rise struck a mixture of disbelief and uneasy fear into the hearts of Republican presidential candidates and all Americans who blame far-left policies they see playing out in California. A smooth talker with an imperious air, the fit and handsome and brazenly liberal Newsom has no qualms about attributing spiraling homelessness rates, record fentanyl deaths, and the exodus of more than half a million residents under his watch to anything or anyone other than himself —the pandemic, shifting economics, his predecessors, the federal government, or his frenemy foil, Donald Trump.[95]

After challenging Florida and GOP presidential candidate Governor Ron DeSantis to a debate, he poked fun at the Florida governor for accepting, then whined afterward that DeSantis and Fox News had cheated when his reviews were less than stellar.[96] Newsom had no response when DeSantis blamed his policies for the mass exodus from California. When pressed by *Fox News* host Sean Hannity to explain why so many people were leaving, Newsom sidestepped the issue and never explained it.[97] The fiery ninety-minute faceoff, moderated by Hannity, was branded as "The Great Red vs. Blue State Debate." DeSantis, however, "sought to nationalize the debate at every step," warning that California's failed far-left experiment would spread to the rest of the nation if Biden or Harris were reelected or if Newsom took their place.[98]

"He's very good at spinning these tales," DeSantis said. "He's good at being slick and slippery. He'll tell a blizzard of lies to be able to try to mask the failures. But the reality is they have failed because of his leftist ideology. Driving the point home, DeSantis wielded a "poop map" of San Francisco tracking all the instances where people have confronted human feces on city streets.[99]

Minutes before the debate was set to end, both Newsom and DeSantis agreed, at Hannity's urging, to extend the debate past the allotted ninety minutes. But during the commercial break, Jennifer Siebel Newsom came on stage and put an end to it.

"We're done," she said, pulling her husband off.[100] At least one Newsom knew when to exit the political stage.

CHAPTER THREE

Feeding the Dragon

ONE BRISK JANUARY DAY IN 2004, the youngest San Francisco mayor in over a century strutted into America's oldest Chinese enclave.[1] Gavin Newsom had chosen the one place he wanted to celebrate his narrow victory: Chinatown. Bay Area elites with impressive pedigrees had filled his election coffers, but the Newsom campaign conceded he had probably lost the white vote.[2] Instead, Chinese voters had catapulted "baby Gavin" into office. And he was ready to show his gratitude.[3]

Twirling parasols and crashing cymbals heralded Newsom's win as he paraded down the streets and narrow alleyways, reveling in one "lion dance" after another. Stopping at several historic Chinese venues, Newsom showered gratitude on his supporters and made clear that Chinatown's interests would be a priority for his administration. Standing in one of Chinatown's oldest banquet halls before an audience of six hundred, Mayor-Elect Newsom spoke of their shared victory. "There is one reason I won a very close election, and that is the support of the Asian community, and the Chinese community in particular," he told his new constituents. "I could not have done it without you." He declared to a gathering of young Chinese community leaders a few blocks away: "It can't be understated. I think what we're seeing is the future of San Francisco."[4]

During another Chinatown excursion a year later, Newsom promised a group of neighborhood leaders that his first trip as mayor would be to Shanghai, and "that he would emphasize his pro-business credentials in the new year and would do more to make it easier for new enterprises to set up shop in San Francisco."[5] One might infer that these new enterprises would be Chinese companies that Newsom would recruit to the Bay Area from across the Pacific. At one point, Newsom "wowed the crowd by wishing them good health in Cantonese," and he made sure to purchase some fortune cookies and energy-boosting ginseng while making the celebratory rounds.[6]

One of Chinatown's biggest Newsom supporters was the longtime fundraiser and grassroots activist Julie Lee. Prior to her 2018 conviction for mail fraud and attempted witness tampering that was part of a scheme to funnel state grant money into Kevin Shelley's Secretary of State Campaign, Lee had championed Willie Brown in Chinatown during his reelection campaign. After winning, Brown appointed her to the city's Housing Commission. So when Brown's newest protégé entered the mayor's race, Lee immediately began setting up precinct walks and phone banks and using her radio show to advocate, and Newsom appointed her to his mayoral transition team. Lee also held a preinauguration celebration for Newsom after he won the Chinese vote by a significant margin.[7]

From then on, Newsom was ready to go full steam ahead with Chinatown's interests. As the *Fog City Journal* put it in 2005, "Gavin may be many things, but he knows who brought him to the prom."[8]

A year later during Thanksgiving weekend, when most Americans were enjoying a holiday of family and football, Gavin Newsom and fifty of his colleagues boarded a plane bound for Communist China. Once there, Newsom was escorted to the most exclusive precincts in Shanghai to meet some of China's top leaders, including a rare visit with former President Jiang Zemin. The official reason for the trip was to celebrate the twenty-fifth anniversary of the Shanghai-San Francisco Sister City Alliance, which originated in 1980 when Senator Dianne Feinstein was mayor of San Francisco and Jiang was mayor of Shanghai. This led some observers to frame the meeting as a "passing of the torch" from Feinstein to Newsom, who was more than willing to continue Feinstein's dangerous alliances with the Chinese government and businesses. A month earlier, when Governor Schwarzenegger visited China on an unrelated trade mission, he wasn't given access to Jiang.[9]

During the trip, Newsom organized and signed memorandums of understanding between the countries that covered various activities, including biomedical joint ventures, artistic collaborations, real estate deals, and short-term exchanges involving police officers, attorneys, and judges.[10] Newsom also met with Shanghai business leaders to promote San Francisco as the best US city in which to set up shop and invest, using the opportunity to forge relationships with future Chinese government and party leaders.[11] But the trip had the trappings of something far more consequential than a business and civic exchange visit. The evidence of that is Newsom's meeting with Shanghai billionaire Vincent Lo, who was, in his own way, more important than President Jiang Zemin.[12]

At that time, few in San Francisco had heard of Vincent H. S. Lo. Still, in China, he was well known as the king of *guanxi*, a Chinese word indicating social connectedness that is often used to describe someone highly skilled at "parlaying social connections into business opportunities." In 2004, the *Economist* claimed that Vincent Lo's *guanxi* was unmatched because "his avowed desire [was] to contribute to China's success and not just his own profits," which "earned him the trust of many of China's elite."[13] As chairman of Shui On Group, one of China's largest developers, Lo had personal ties to many high-level Chinese Communist Party (CCP) leaders who had supported and prioritized Shui On's real estate projects for more than three decades.[14] Lo's foray into commercial property began in 1985 when he partnered with the financially struggling Communist Youth League to build the first joint venture hotel in Shanghai. Years later, when these communist youth became the leaders running China, they didn't forget what the *guanxi* king had done for them.[15]

Lo hosted Newsom in downtown Shanghai at his vintage "clubhouse" mansion known for its "fretted wooden balustrades" and soaring "carved stone balconies" overlooking landscaped gardens. Lo had received exclusive rights from the Chinese government to develop the historic property in Xintiandi (translated as "New Heaven and Earth"), which was a new commercial and entertainment district surrounding the original site where Chairman Mao held the first Communist Party Congress. A year before Newsom's visit, Vladimir Putin had taken over the entire clubhouse lobby for a grand dinner.[16]

It was during this meeting that Newsom and Lo hatched a long-term plan to turn San Francisco into the premiere gateway through which Chinese companies could invest and expand their businesses in the United States. Upon his return from China, starry-eyed Gavin told his staff that he was going to set aside a couple of million dollars to set up a public-private partnership called ChinaSF that would open the floodgates to Chinese money and business like never before.[17] It turns out the young mayor wasn't just blowing smoke: three years later, Newsom and Lo joined forces in Shanghai to co-launch ChinaSF.[18]

One could argue that ChinaSF impacted the Bay Area more than any other program Newsom created as mayor. For the years 2008 to 2018, ChinaSF claims they hauled in nearly $5.5 billion of economic impact to San Francisco and directly recruited 108 Chinese companies to establish official operations in the city. This new wave of Chinese infiltration included more than one thousand Chinese companies that ChinaSF helped move to locations across North America. Mayor Newsom once proclaimed that "as the gateway to the Pacific, ChinaSF builds [on] San Francisco's history of shared cultural and economic ties with China and strengthens mutual economic prosperity through enhanced relationships between San Francisco and Chinese businesses."[19]

Over the years, media and government officials have described this "gateway" known as ChinaSF in countless ways. Sometimes, it's referred to as a unique "public-private partnership between the Mayor's Office and the San Francisco Center for Economic Development."[20] Others have called it a "quasi-government agency," an "international business program," or an "economic development organization."[21] It's also been labeled as merely an "initiative," a "collaboration," a "project," or a "platform."[22] Some

Chinese business documents refer to ChinaSF as "the China Office of the City and County of San Francisco"—which is probably the most accurate description.[23]

At one point in time, ChinaSF described itself as a nonprofit. On its now defunct website—www.chinasf.org—every webpage stated at the bottom, "ChinaSF is a 501(c)(3) Non-Profit Organization."[24] The website also provided links where nonprofit donations could be made to ChinaSF. In 2016, when speaking to a group of business investors, ChinaSF Director Darlene Chiu Bryant clearly announced: "We are a non-profit, we appreciate donations, that's how we survive and that's how we're able to operate."[25]

However, according to the state of California, between 2009 and 2014, ChinaSF actually was a limited liability corporation (LLC), a private company whose only member was the San Francisco Chamber of Commerce, which is a 501(c)(6) entity.[26] The LLC has been listed as "inactive" since 2014. In other words, for a period of time, ChinaSF was a private entity embedded in a local chamber of commerce. Technically, however, "because of requirements of the Chinese partners, the effort is housed at the San Francisco Center for Economic Development", which is the "economic development arm of the chamber that is functionally integrated with but financially independent of the chamber."[27]

Claims like this one from the2018 *San Francisco Business Times* article are even more puzzling: "ChinaSF is a nonprofit organization that works in partnership with the San Francisco Center for Economic Development [SFCED], also a nonprofit, to promote economic growth in both San Francisco and China."[28] SFCED (which is now defunct) also had never been registered in the United States as a nonprofit—or even as a private US company.[29] However, from 2009 to 2014, a company registered in Hong Kong had the exact name: San Francisco Center for Economic Development.[30] It's hardly a coincidence. Was this Hong Kong entity the one that was "housing" ChinaSF?

If so, it wouldn't be surprising, given that ChinaSF has opened offices in four different Chinese cities—Shanghai, Beijing, Shenzhen, and Guangzhou.[31] Before the state of California had reestablished an official trade office in China after a ten-year hiatus, it appears the city of San Francisco may have already had three.[32] No other US city, or even state, had as many "China offices" as San Francisco.[33] ChinaSF has been operating as a de facto satellite of the mayor's office in Shanghai since at least 2011, when the international law firm Nixon Peabody donated a portion of its Shanghai office to ChinaSF operations.[34] A few years later in 2014, Nixon Peabody described itself as a "founding sponsor" of ChinaSF, so one can assume Nixon Peabody supported Newsom's vision of bridging business between the Bay Area and China. While it's unclear whether Nixon Peabody still provides office space to ChinaSF in Shanghai or whether it benefited in any way from its support of the organization, between 2010 and 2022 Nixon Peabody donated more than $94,000 to Newsom's campaigns, far more than any other law firm.[35]

ChinaSF's website states that it serves "as a facilitator, advocate and case manager for Chinese businesses navigating City, State and Federal governmental issues."[36] Yet despite being an extension of the mayor's office, in 2008 "supporters of the ChinaSF idea said they wanted to solicit private funding instead of relying on taxpayer money to avoid having the office's funding caught up in political fights that sometimes erupt on the San Francisco Board of Supervisors."[37] In effect, this private funding mechanism prioritized streamlined services for Chinese companies while shielding them from the oversight and accountability that local companies face when taking part in a government program. Furthermore, ChinaSF was structured to operate as some kind of hybrid international joint venture between the mayor's office and the San Francisco Chamber of Commerce—some would argue not for the sake of transparency, so Bay Area citizens could be made privy to the massive influx of Chinese cash streaming in, but so Newsom and subsequent mayors could personally involve themselves in every deal without having to answer for any conflicts of interest.

Whether deliberate or not, ChinaSF was structured in a manner that helped several corrupt Chinese corporations come to America. For example, let's look at one of the first Chinese companies that Mayor Newsom lured to San Francisco through ChinaSF: Suntech Power Holdings.[38]

Based in Wuxi, China, Suntech was one of the fastest-growing solar companies in the world in 2005 when it became the first private Chinese company to ever list on the New York Stock Exchange and the first to invest in "green tech" manufacturing in the United States.[39] In 2007, Suntech's CEO and chairman, Dr. Zhengrong Shi, made the *Forbes* World's Billionaires List, and *Time* magazine dubbed him an environmental hero.[40] CNN, the *New York Times, Fortune,* and many other media outlets heaped praise on Dr. Shi.[41] The *Guardian* honored him as one of the "50 people who could save the planet."[42] Thomas Friedman even lauded Suntech's green technology model as the "Sputnik of our day."[43] Mayor Newsom was known for his public admiration of China's green technology, so it was no surprise when he aggressively pushed for Suntech's move to San Francisco. After all, Newsom had dubbed San Francisco "the pace car for municipal solar projects," and it had yet to rev its engine.[44]

"The self-evident fact is that China will clean our clocks in terms of addressing the green economy if we don't wake up to the opportunity and do the same," Newsom told a journalist during a 2010 press conference. "China gets it, the United States needs to wake up."[45] In a 2010 interview with *Forbes* in Shanghai, Newsom explained how he had recruited Suntech: "It was a big deal to get Dr. Shi [Zhengrong] in first. We sent my team back here to encourage him. I [also] tracked him down in the Mission District in San Francisco. He was having a casual lunch, and I surprised him, saying, 'We really want you here.' It's what it takes."[46] Newsom also sent his top economic advisor, Jesse Blout, to visit the company in China and "underscore how important this was" to the mayor.[47] When Suntech finally agreed to set up shop in San Francisco, the *Chronicle* claimed it was "a coup for Newsom," because other US cities had also been pursuing the solar giant.[48]

Why did Suntech choose San Francisco over rival cities?

"It doesn't hurt that the space that Suntech subleased from law firm McNutt and Litteneker LLP at 188 Embarcadero falls in a new state enterprise zone that encompasses much of the financial district," the *Chronicle* reported.[49] Newsom explained it another way in his Shanghai *Forbes* interview:

First, we did tax incentives, so we had something to offer these companies the minute they came into San Francisco. We changed our zoning to support these green tech companies. So, we said: "We have the right zoning. We have public-private transaction teams, so that you have one person to meet, and you will never have to deal with the bureaucracy. We will carry your permits through the entire bureaucracy. We've got workforce incentives, payroll tax exemptions, and other enterprise support incentives from the state of California, and we'll pull all of them together for you."[50]

No other mayor rolled out the red carpet for Suntech like Newsom did. Dr. Shi was even appointed to the Shanghai Advisory Board of ChinaSF.[51] The *Atlantic* represented most left-leaning observers of the Suntech deal when it proclaimed, "San Francisco has got it right...We need China, and China needs us, now, more than ever."[52]

When asked by *Forbes* if US citizens should be nervous about the possible security threat of large Chinese tech companies setting up shop in their backyard, Newsom offered a vague, dismissive answer:

Obviously, that generates a lot of headlines and concern. We always need to be considerate of those things...But that doesn't mean that because you've had some bad experiences or there's a general climate of concern that you just give up and walk away. Those that do will pay the price in the future. We've got to keep at it...China gets it in a very pragmatic way. There is just no other choice.[53]

It was clear that if ChinaSF was going to tout San Francisco as the premiere economic gateway to the United States from China, it had to haul in their biggest green tech company, security be damned.

Shortly after Newsom signed the agreement, CNN reported that it was local communist leaders in Wuxi who had bankrolled Suntech since its inception in 2001 and that they "quickly got [their] money back, with plenty of interest, when Suntech (STP) went public in late 2005, raising

$400 million on the New York Stock Exchange."[54] Then, in March 2011, Dr. Shi welcomed Wuxi's Communist Party secretary, Yang Weize, to the company's headquarters for an event. Yang was the Chinese Communist Party (CCP) leader who originally helped Suntech secure loans from Chinese state-owned banks. During a speech that day, Shi publicly acknowledged that "Suntech is a seed sown by the Communist Party of the Wuxi government."[55]

California utility Pacific Gas and Electric (PG&E) ignored the possible security threats entailed by partnering with a CCP-linked business when, a month later, it kicked off a massive power plant construction project utilizing 150,000 solar panels purchased from Suntech. Later that summer, the US Department of Energy (DOE) offered a $359 million loan to a solar-power project in Arizona that was using Suntech equipment for its operation, clearly unconcerned that the loan would directly benefit a Chinese company that openly admitted it was a spawn of the CCP.[56]

Suntech continued to rapidly expand over the next year, until news broke in the summer of 2012 that Suntech was on the hook for nearly $700 million in nonexistent German government bonds.[57] According to AP reports, "A business partner faked $680 million in collateral for a loan Suntech had guaranteed."[58] Almost immediately, Dr. Shi was forced to resign, but nothing could stop the downfall that was coming. Soon it was revealed that some of Suntech's European managers had previously worked with an individual associated with the Sicilian Mafia. One of these managers was accused of orchestrating the fraudulent financing scheme. Lawsuits against the company began to pile up.[59] By March 2013, Suntech had officially filed for bankruptcy and was delisted from the New York Stock Exchange.[60] And Dr. Shi, the solar savior handpicked by Newsom to lead the Bay Area's green tech revolution, lost close to $4 billion in net worth, nearly wiping him out.[61] In the end, however, US investors were left holding the bag. When Suntech's massive bankruptcy was filed, its dissolved assets were used to repay Chinese creditors, leaving US lenders with zilch.[62]

While most of us have heard of the colossal collapse of US solar giant Solyndra, there's been very little reporting on the $1.5 billion lawsuit that

Solyndra filed against Suntech and two other Chinese solar companies, Trina Solar and Yingli Green Energy Holding. In their legal complaint, Solyndra accused the companies of operating as "an illegal cartel of Chinese solar panel manufacturers" who conspired in tandem "to flood the United States solar market with solar panels at below-cost prices."[63] The US Department of Commerce also found all three companies guilty of dumping their solar panels in the United States "to eliminate legitimate competition and to gain monopoly power over the market" and to "materially injure United States manufacturers like Solyndra." These "cartel" companies could sell their solar panels dirt cheap because they had received a combined $17 billion in "below-market" interest rate loans from the Chinese government to prop them up while they forced US solar companies out of business.[64]

What else do these disgraced Chinese companies have in common with Suntech? Each was recruited into the United States by ChinaSF and unabashedly praised by Mayor Newsom. In a 2008 press release, he said: "In the race to become the premier US gateway for Chinese companies expanding into the North American market, San Francisco has scored another important win with Trina Solar."[65] Several months later, Newsom announced: "We are proud to welcome Yingli Americas to San Francisco. Their choice to locate in San Francisco is yet another affirmation of our ChinaSF initiative strategy."[66]

ReneSola is another problematic Chinese solar company recruited by ChinaSF. In 2021, the analyst group Grizzly Research published a blistering report titled *We Believe ReneSola Is a Fraudulent Company; Most Projects Never Existed.*[67] The report alleges that for years ReneSola had been "misrepresenting its project development pipeline" in legal filings by claiming that many of its solar projects around the world were in the "late-stage" phase and construction was near finalization when in reality many of these projects were "either non-existent or delayed for years." Grizzly argued that ReneSola fabricated these "ghost projects" to "give the appearance of a stronger business trajectory" to investors. Renesola has denied all of the claims made in the Grizzly report, but the former chairman of ReneSola currently faces at least nine court judgments in China for failing to pay back debt and other issues and owes multiple parties more than $200 million.[68]

It wasn't just green-energy companies that streamed through the ChinaSF gateway. Most recruits were real estate companies—a fact that presents troubling issues.[69] Many of these Chinese businesses engaged in corrupt practices to gain a foothold in the Bay Area. One such company was Z&L Properties, led by Chinese billionaire developer Zhang Li. Z&L, which ChinaSF recruited to San Francisco to work on a large development venture known as the 555 Fulton Street project, is privately funded by Zhang Li's parent company, Guangzhou R&F Properties. In May 2014, ChinaSF posted photos on its Facebook page celebrating R&F's groundbreaking ceremony for the project. In one photo, ChinaSF's director, Darlene Chiu Bryant, stands next to Zhang while both hold shovels adorned with red ribbons to memorialize the first work performed on the property.[70] Shortly after this, Z&L Properties became owners of at least twelve more development projects throughout California.[71] In 2017, Gavin Newsom joined ChinaSF at Z&L's San Francisco office for a celebratory photo in front of the logo of the company he had recruited to San Francisco.[72] On that same day, Z&L donated $23,705.12 to Newsom's gubernatorial campaign.[73]

Looking back, the recruitment of Z&L to San Francisco was another ChinaSF boondoggle. Within a few years, the 555 Fulton Street project faltered after a series of mysterious delays and a growing stack of lawsuits kept the project in prolonged limbo.[74] Then, in 2023, Z&L pleaded guilty to bribing former San Francisco Public Works Director Mohammed Nuru and was forced to pay a $1 million fine.[75] The company admitted it seduced Nuru with expensive food, drinks, luxury lodgings, and trips to China "so that he would provide favorable treatment on decisions and city approvals needed during the construction and development of a mixed-use property at 555 Fulton Street."[76] US Attorney Stephanie M. Hinds said that Mohammed Nuru confessed to "a staggering amount of public corruption in his plea agreement…For years, Nuru held a powerful and well-paid public leadership position at San Francisco City Hall, but instead of serving the public, Nuru served himself. He took continuous bribes from the contractors, developers, and entities he regulated."[77] During Nuru's sentencing hearing, Judge William Orrick told him: "You made the city's competitive bidding, permit processing and decision-making a farce...During my time on the bench, I've had to sentence people for horrible things—gang murders, drug dealing, really deadly stuff. In many ways, what you've done is at least as reprehensible, in my opinion."[78]

But Nuru didn't act alone. As state assembly member Matt Haney told the *San Francisco Chronicle*, "The entire apparatus of city government was polluted with [Nuru's] corrupt behavior."[79] A close examination of the scandal reveals that several individuals involved had close ties to Gavin Newsom, including Mohammed Nuru, whom the *San Francisco Chronicle* described as "one of Newsom's inside circle."[80]

During Newsom's first run for mayor, Nuru was San Francisco's deputy director of Public Works while also serving as a Newsom election campaign volunteer. Newsom won the race, but in January 2004 nine street cleaners working for the San Francisco League of Urban Gardeners (SLUG) filed a complaint with the San Francisco Human Rights Commission, claiming that Nuru had pressured them into voting for Newsom. Because SLUG operated solely under a city contract with San Francisco Public Works, Nuru was the one holding the purse strings, and according to the complaint he lorded it over the street cleaners by threatening that if they didn't vote for Newsom, they would lose their jobs. Nuru allegedly even pulled workers from their jobs during the election and assigned them "to walk precincts, knock on doors and distribute campaign literature." Some were ordered to carry Newsom posters while walking "up and down the streets," perhaps sidestepping the trash and debris they were being paid to clean up.[81]

One of the street cleaners told City Attorney Dennis Hererra, "I felt like I was in another country, like it was some kind of dictatorship taking place." Some SLUG employees also claimed they had to provide voting receipts showing they voted for Newsom: "It was put to us like, nobody's going to get paid if we don't get these stubs." In the end, Newsom received around twenty-six thousand more absentee ballot votes than his challenger, whom he narrowly beat in a runoff election. Nine street cleaners have alleged that they were coerced to fill out absentee ballots for Newsom in the days leading up to the runoff.[82]

So how did the city of San Francisco respond to an ethics investigation of Nuru? In an extraordinary move, the Board of Supervisors organized an expensive fundraising dinner at the Four Seas restaurant in Chinatown to help Nuru raise legal funds to hire a top criminal defense lawyer.[83] A San Francisco State University political science professor, Rich DeLeon, observed that it was "unprecedented to have members of the city's legislative body raising money to aid the legal defense of a city official under investigation by the city attorney...I haven't heard of anything like that happening in my 20-odd years of observing local politics."[84]

Eventually, in 2004, the city attorney proved that SLUG used city funds inappropriately to benefit Newsom in the election and that Nuru had coerced employees to engage in unlawful election activities. In response, the city controller barred SLUG from ever receiving another city contract. But the director of Public Works at that time, Ed Lee, decided not to discipline Nuru, and the matter dissipated.[85]

Over the years, several other well-documented complaints about Nuru were ignored by Newsom and other officials until eventually he was convicted and sentenced to seven years for accepting bribes from Z&L and other financial crimes.[86] A similar fate awaited another former high-ranking city leader, Harlan Kelly, who got snared during the Nuru investigation. In July 2023, Kelly—who for years served as the general manager of the San Francisco Public Utilities Commission (SFPUC)—was convicted by a jury of six felonies that were part of two fraud schemes in which he accepted bribes and gifts and used his public position in various ways to benefit himself and his wife.[87] The city could have been spared Kelly's corruption if Newsom hadn't overlooked a major red flag from Kelly's past.

When outgoing Mayor Willie Brown appointed him as deputy director of the SFPUC in 2004, Kelly spent $4,000 of city funds to pay for a new paint job and other extras on his city-owned SUV, which Kelly was allowed to use as his personal vehicle. As the new mayor, in response to the scandal

Newsom was obligated to order Kelly to pay back the money, but he didn't fire him.[88] Instead, two weeks after the scandal, Newsom gave a speech to a group of SFPUC employees with Kelly standing next to him at the podium. Newsom encouraged city workers to "unleash your imagination" and be "willing to take risks," and he promised to support them if they "ma[d]e mistakes" in that endeavor. The *San Francisco Chronicle* notes that at this point in the speech, "Newsom, not missing a beat, smiled when he turned to Kelly and said, 'We've learned from that mistake and we're not going to repeat it.'"[89] Yet, as we've seen many times with Newsom's overly optimistic forecasts on ending homelessness or constructing bullet trains to nowhere, this prediction was comically inaccurate in light of how things unfolded. Harlan's wife, Naomi Kelly, who had been appointed city administrator by Newsom, resigned soon after her husband was indicted, and just like that, a longtime "City Hall power couple" was down for the count.[90]

Real estate maven Victor Makras was another Newsom appointee (and substantial campaign donor) convicted and fined in 2022 for bank and mortgage fraud springing from the Nuru investigation.[91] In the past, Makras—who's been described as "the man in every room for every mayor" and "tied into the inner sanctums of San Francisco politics"—was twice appointed to city positions by Newsom.[92] He was first assigned to the Fire Commission in 2005. Then in 2015, Newsom moved him to the Retirement Board because, according to the *San Francisco Chronicle*, "Newsom felt Makras would be better used helping to oversee the city's multibillion-dollar pension fund."[93]

Former Newsom appointee and political backer Rodrigo Santos was also convicted in the Nuru fallout. In 2023, Santos pleaded guilty to bank fraud, lying to the FBI, and evading taxes while working as a permit expediter for city contractors. But back in 2004, Newsom thought highly enough of Santos to promote him to president of the San Francisco Building Inspection Commission.[94]

Florence Kong owns Kwan Wo Ironworks, and over the years has donated thousands to Newsom's campaigns.[95] In 2010, Newsom appointed her to the City Hall Preservation Advisory Commission.[96] In 2021, Kong was charged and sentenced for bribing Mohammed Nuru with a $36,000 Rolex watch in exchange for city contracts and then lying about it to federal agents. Kong and her companies now face a $750,000 fine, the majority of which is to pay back money received for tainted city contracts, including $109,000 for "one of the largest ethics fines in San Francisco history."[97]

Are you starting to see a pattern here? During his political career, Gavin Newsom has directly hired or appointed more than least twenty individuals to official administrative positions who were later found guilty for financial crimes or ethics violations.[98]

Ask yourself: Why does Newsom keep stuffing foxes in the henhouse? Does he have poor judgment when it comes to choosing his appointees? Or were these cronies exactly the people Newsom needed to build the ladder for his political ascendency?

Newsom also had long-standing connections to Walter Wong, a well-known "permit expediter" in San Francisco who, in addition to pleading guilty to bribing Nuru and conspiring with a building inspector on Z&L Properties projects, was charged with fraud, money laundering, and cheating the city to obtain nearly $1.5 million in contracts.[99] In 2003, Newsom's company PlumpJack Development Fund was an investor in a partnership called Ecker-Folsom that hired Walter Wong, although Newsom claims he was unaware of the hire and that he has always refused to pay politically connected consultants to push through permits. Newsom told the *San Francisco Chronicle*:

> I never used an expediter in any of my projects where I was proactively engaged in the project. I didn't think it was right or fair that I'm filling out the exact same forms as anyone else [to] actually pay extra as a taxpayer to have someone else give the forms to the same clerk that I can hand the clerk the forms to. And then miraculously they're way ahead of the line and the rest of us standing holding a ticket.[100]

Gavin's ethical stance against hiring consultants to expedite permits unfairly is purely performative, given his express desire to encode the practice into ChinaSF operations. Remember Newsom's words, quoted earlier in this chapter: "We have public-private transaction teams, so that you have one person to meet, and you will never have to deal with the bureaucracy. We will carry your permits through the entire bureaucracy."[101]

In other words, Newsom wanted ChinaSF to perform the role of permit expediter for Chinese companies coming to San Francisco, operating directly out of the mayor's office. So while Bay Area developers had to pay corrupt consultants to hack through the bureaucratic jungle on their behalf, Newsom cleared a wide path for Chinese companies so that they could leap administrative hurdles and bypass all the grafting middlemen.

As mayor, Newsom also used ChinaSF as a tool to build San Francisco into a global hub for biotechnology and pharmaceutical science. Dozens of Chinese biotech companies were drawn to the Bay Area with huge tax breaks and other incentives, but it appears that there was very little vetting. One of ChinaSF's most concerning recruits is the biotech company JOINN Laboratories, which has close ties to China's military.[102] The company's cofounders are husband and wife Zhou Zhiwen and Feng Yuxia. In 2021, Forbes listed Feng in an article titled "Meet the 40 New Billionaires Who Got Rich Fighting COVID-19." With a net worth of $1.1 billion, Feng made most of her money conducting "clinical studies of potential COVID-19 treatments in the disease's early epicenter of Wuhan, China."[103]

Feng and Zhou both graduated with degrees in pharmacology from the Academy of Military Medical Sciences (AMMS), one of the Chinese military's highest-level research institutes, and Feng worked there during the 1990s. JOINN Laboratories General Manager Zuo Conglin was a researcher for the Chinese Air Force during the 1990s after also graduating from AMMS.[104] The company's chief of pathology and toxicology, Hemei Wang, is another product of AMMS,[105] and the director of JOINN Laboratories (China), Xi Luo, is also the chief financial officer of CanSino Biologics,[106] a Chinese pharmaceutical company that developed China's first coronavirus vaccine in partnership with AMMS.[107]

Yet JOINN's most troubling connection to China's military is Shusheng

Geng, who worked for AMMS's Institute of Pharmacology and Toxicology. Geng was previously a "research collaborator with high-level People's Liberation Army (PLA) scientists, who are considered key contributors to China's biowarfare program."[108] In December 2021, the US Commerce Department added AMMS and eleven of its research institutes to the Entity List, "thereby prohibiting exports, reexports and in-country transfers of American technology."[109] This status means the US government believes AMMS has been "acting contrary to the foreign policy or national security interests of the United States."[110]

When ChinaSF recruits risky Chinese companies like JOINN, more than the Bay Area is affected. The negative impacts can spread across the country. In 2022, JOINN Laboratories purchased 1,400 acres in Levy County, Florida, for $5.5 million, with plans to build a primate quarantine and breeding facility.[111] The sale was one of the largest recent Chinese purchases of US land.[112] The company planned to perform scientific experiments on lab monkeys at the site despite the land's zoning for rural residential housing or forestry. Their intention to build a primate quarantine and breeding farm came amid a global shortage of lab monkeys and soaring prices: "According to Chinese media reports, the price of an experimental monkey in China has risen from more than 40,000 yuan (about $5,500) to more than 120,000 yuan (about $16,600) in less than two years, prompting contract research organizations (CROs) to scramble for lab monkey resources."[113] The purchasers wanted the property in Florida to help remedy this problem. Not long after the purchase, a spokesman from Florida Governor Ron Desantis's office spoke out against it: "The governor has been consistently opposed to the Chinese Communist Party (CCP)'s growing influence in Florida, and this proposed facility is a prime example of the type of activity that we are acting to prohibit."[114] Soon thereafter, DeSantis signed a series of bills banning Chinese citizens from buying agricultural land in Florida.[115] Another alarming fact is JOINN's close connection to a Hong Kong company called Biorichland LLC, which owns the fifty-three-acre property in San Francisco where JOINN and several other Chinese biotech companies operate.[116] ChinaSF cofounder Skip Whitney—a close ally of Newsom—sold the property to Biorichland through his real estate brokerage firm, Kidder Mathews, which is an official financial sponsor of ChinaSF (and a substantial Newsom donor). Whitney claimed that the purchase provided "a Seal of Approval by the Chinese Government for investment in the Bay Area" and "a bridge for Chinese pharmaceutical companies who want to come."[117]

Biorichland is wholly owned by Zhou Fengyuan, the son of JOINN founders Feng Yuxi and Zhou Zhiwen. According to Hong Kong Stock Exchange filings, Biorichland is "primarily engaged in real estate management in California."[118] What's never been reported, however, is that in 2013, Biorichland was licensed by the Federal Communications Commission (FCC) to use a private radio network for all its operations. In its official FCC application, Biorichland mentioned nothing about real estate, but instead reported, "We are a pharmaceutical research facility, and we will use radios to better coordinate our activities."[119] Of course, this raises plenty of security-related questions, but even more disturbing is the "special conditions" waiver that Biorichland received for its license. According to the waiver, "Antenna structures for land, base and fixed stations authorized for operation at temporary unspecified locations may be erected without specific prior approval of the Commission."[120] So it's fair to ask: Does the company intend to set up radio towers on the land they purchased in Florida? Have they already begun erecting them? The technology available and the CCP's history make this oversight alarming.[121]

One of the City of San Francisco's most inexcusable moves came on October 14, 2017, when it signed a memorandum of understanding (MOU) on "friendly cooperation" between the City and Chinese company Kweichow Moutai Co., Ltd., which is the largest liquor company in the world. Since 2018, the state-owned business has been ranked as China's most valuable company, with an estimated worth of over 1 trillion yuan (US $145 billion).[122] Kweichow produces a unique blend of grain alcohol called Moutai, which Chinese government officials so highly regard that for decades it has been known as the national liquor of the CCP. In 1949, when the CCP first gained power, Premier Zhou Enlai "personally endorsed" Moutai as the official drink for state banquets, and eventually the CCP forcibly took over the company and made it a state-owned enterprise. Until the 1980s, Moutai had been "reserved exclusively for Communist Party leaders, senior government officials and their relatives."[123]

Several corruption scandals involving bribery by CCP officials have marred Kweichow Moutai's history.[124] In 2010, the former general manager of Moutai was sentenced to death for accepting millions of dollars in bribes.[125] Again, one must ask an obvious question: why would San Francisco sign an MOU agreeing to "friendly cooperation" with a corrupt Chinese company known for producing the official liquor of the CCP?

Details of the MOU reveal what "friendly cooperation" means: establishing a branch office in San Francisco to increase Moutai sales and expand their North American market share, to advise Moutai on how to market new US products, to assist in expanding Moutai brand recognition and influence, and to schedule events each year in San Francisco to officially celebrate Kweichow Moutai Day throughout the city. Although the MOU claims the mutual goal is to enhance cultural exchange and "develop win-win collaborations," the memorandum is heavily one-sided, with the city getting nothing tangible in return for doing Moutai's bidding.[126] Kweichow Moutai's chairman, Yuan Renguo, "facilitated the delegation's visit" that resulted in the signing of the historic MOU.[127] Less than two weeks later, shares in Kweichow Moutai jumped to a new all-time high. Still, within a couple of months, Yuan was forced to step down from the company and has since been arrested and given a life sentence in China for accepting over $17 million in bribes while serving as Moutai's chairman.[128] Shockingly, none of the above warning signs stopped California's public employee pension fund from investing in the company. By 2020, the California Public Employees' Retirement System (CalPERS) owned nearly $24 million in Kweichow Moutai shares.[129] The sad truth is that CalPERS has invested in most of the problematic Chinese companies discussed in this chapter, including Suntech, Trina Solar, ReneSola, and JOINN Laboratories. But CalPERS wasn't the only California pension to invest in Moutai. By 2023, the California State Teachers' Retirement System (CalSTRS) had surpassed CalPERS, purchasing nearly $27 million in Moutai shares.[130]

What was the golden ticket that gave these corrupt foreign companies access to state-level California funds? When you consider how little San Francisco received in return for bringing in and propping up a corrupt liquor company with strong ties to the CCP, you're left with the question that maybe something like bribery—which seems to be Moutai's modus operandi—could explain why the City would ever sign such a lopsided MOU.

Records obtained through a records request from San Francisco's Office of Economic and Workforce Development reveal several noteworthy findings about ChinaSF that have never been made public. The first revelation has to do with the number of jobs created. From its inception, ChinaSF has been promoted as a program that would create many local Bay Area jobs through direct Chinese investment, but the data seems to reveal otherwise.[131] From 2008 to 2018, ChinaSF was responsible for bringing in $5.1 billion in foreign investment, but those billions only created 788 jobs.[132] To put into perspective how measly this number is, one only needs to compare it to the national average. For the years ChinaSF was bringing in Chinese investment, the average rate of job creation per million dollars of pledged capital in the U.S. was around 2. What this means is that the $5.1Billion of foreign investment that ChinaSF brought in should have created more than 10,000 jobs.[133]

The job-creator claim looks even more suspect when you analyze ChinaSF's annual reports. For instance, in its report for July 2016 to June 2017, ChinaSF claims to have recruited seventeen companies that brought in $2.1 billion of Chinese investment that created 106 jobs. However, fifty of those jobs came from just one company (Vcanbio), and 80 percent of all the jobs came from just five companies that only brought in around $170 million. This means the other twelve businesses combined, brought in roughly $2 billion but generated fewer than thirty jobs.[134]

If you break the numbers down even further, you'll discover an astonishing fact: $1.75 billion of investment came from just two Chinese electric scooter companies: Mobike and OFO.

How many total Bay Area jobs did this $1.75 billion investment create? A total of three.[135]

ChinaSF records also reveal funding sources that have never been publicized. We know that ChinaSF has been busy over the years cohosting events, traveling to conferences and seminars, and recruiting Chinese companies, while managing four offices in China and one in San Francisco. Running an international outfit of this kind requires substantial cash, but ChinaSF has never clearly explained where its money comes from. Despite initial claims that all funding would come from the private sector, researchers at Tampere University reported in 2013 that 30 percent of ChinaSF's budget had come from the city of San Francisco.[136] The rest came from private individuals and companies who paid annual fees based on their membership category, which was tiered into silver, gold, and platinum levels.[137] In 2013, ChinaSF touted some of these sponsors on their website and in press releases, including Deloitte, BlackRock, Wells Fargo, Cisco Systems, Lennar Urban, and East West Bank.[138]

However, no one seemed to notice when an infamous Chinese company became their top financial sponsor in 2016. This might be because the US government has long identified that company, Huawei Technologies, as one of China's most dangerous tech companies.[139] According to an internal report, ChinaSF hosted two events in 2016, headlined by Huawei, which led to Huawei establishing a new research and development office in San Francisco.[140] The amount of money Huawei funneled to ChinaSF is unknown, but it's worth noting that in 2016, Huawei generated more than $75 billion in revenue, so they had plenty of cash to flash around.[141]

Before becoming ChinaSF's top sponsor, Huawei was at the center of countless scandals. In 2003, Cisco sued Huawei for theft of its technology.[142] In 2004, a Huawei employee was caught spying on a competitor's technology at a US trade show.[143] In 2005, the Rand Corporation issued an alarming report revealing a close working relationship between Huawei and China's military. In 2007, founder Ren Zhengfei lied to the FBI about

Huawei's dealings with Iran—a breach of US sanctions.[144] In 2008, the US government blocked Huawei from buying a portion of a US tech firm that sells antihacking software to the US military, due to concerns that the Chinese might use it to spy.[145] That same year, leaked documents revealed that Huawei had covertly helped build North Korea's wireless mobile system. In 2010, the Committee of Foreign Investment in the United States (CFIUS) blocked Huawei's purchase of California tech company 3Leaf, and Motorola filed suit against the company for stealing technology.[146] In 2013, the Department of Justice (DOJ) indicted Huawei for wire fraud and theft of trade secrets and revealed that the company had been "offering bonuses to employees who succeeded in stealing confidential information from other companies."[147]

Why would a nonprofit operating out of the mayor's office accept funding from a Chinese company with such a fraudulent and dangerous past?

Since then, Huawei has been found guilty of stealing trade secrets from a California company, banned from selling telecommunications equipment in the United States, banned from most US universities, and blacklisted by the US Department of Commerce.[148]

When ChinaSF held a ceremony in 2010 to announce the opening of its Beijing office, board member Keyong Ren—a director at the state-owned China Construction Bank—gave a presentation in which he admitted that investments in US companies would be contingent on "obtaining exclusive China market right of proprietary technology," and he confirmed to attendees that this "would involve US companies handing over their secret formulas."[149] This echoed the advice of ChinaSF cofounder Vincent Lo, who was known for advising Chinese companies to buy minority stakes in Bay Area companies because the payoff was "direct dibs on what the company comes up with."[150] In other words, a clean steal. No espionage required.

The payment processing company China UnionPay has also been an official financial sponsor of ChinaSF.[151] This is alarming given that China UnionPay is a Chinese state-owned entity with close ties to the CCP and "is often seen as an arm of Chinese state policy."[152] UnionPay has been used by organized crime groups and drug traffickers all around the world, including the Chinese Triads, which consist of a global network of crime syndicates operating in conjunction with Chinese secret fraternal societies that were founded hundreds of years ago.[153] Alvin Chau was a member of the notorious 14K Triad and the boss of a junket operator who "brokered the gambling activity of Chinese high-rollers" at casinos in Macau. He was busted when investigators caught him using China UnionPay to launder more than $1 million of drug-trafficking proceeds per day through Macau's Suncity Casino.[154] In 2023 he was sentenced to eighteen years in prison for racketeering and illegal gambling and was forced to pay over $800 million in restitution.[155]

During his final days as mayor, after being elected lieutenant governor, Newsom telegraphed his intention to continue exploiting China SF by laying out a plan that would cleverly expand the program to the state level.

> As China is one of the most important international trading partners for our great State of California, it will be important to take proactive steps in building a productive relationship. (I plan to use ChinaSF as a basis for the exploration of a state model for international economic development with respect to China.) ChinaSF's sustained growth and progress will be key in maintaining San Francisco's status as the premiere North American gateway. Furthermore, together with ChinaSF Board members and partners, ChinaSF can be an important model demonstration of the proactive thought leadership necessary to build a mutually beneficial relationship with Chinese business and government.[156]

Newsom had figured out a new blueprint for hauling in Chinese money and business with very little oversight, and he wasn't about to waste his efforts.

In less than a year, Newsom's former communications chief in the mayor's office—Darlene Chiu Bryant—was named ChinaSF's new director.[157] Bryant had traveled with Newsom on his first trip to China in 2005 and witnessed the planning and formation of ChinaSF. Nicknamed locally as "the Fixer" for any Chinese businesses "wanting to make hay in San Francisco," Bryant was a perfect fit for Newsom, allowing him to keep close ties with Chinese companies.[158] In July 2011, Lieutenant Governor Newsom published a report entitled *An Economic Growth and Competitiveness Agenda for California,* in which he recommended creating "a China presence for California within 180 days, building on existing efforts of [various entities and] ChinaSF."[159]

Newsom's 180-day prediction was a bit optimistic, but in less than two years, on April 11, 2013, California Governor Jerry Brown officially opened the new California-China Office of Trade and Investment (CCTO) to "serve as a hub for California companies interested in entering or expanding in China…and Chinese companies seeking investment opportunities in California." Like ChinaSF, the CCTO claimed it would be funded entirely by private sources. In a strange move, however, the office was required to be staffed and operated by the Bay Area Council, a San Francisco group that had worked closely with Newsom and ChinaSF over the years.[160] In its first annual report, the CCTO stated that one of its goals was to develop "a network…with the ChinaSF office in Beijing."[161]

By late 2018, ChinaSF had expanded and evolved into an actual 501(c)(3) nonprofit called GlobalSF that was registered in California a few weeks after Newsom was elected governor.[162] ChinaSF's director, Darlene Bryant, also took over the reins at GlobalSF and continues to oversee ChinaSF as an initiative of the new nonprofit. With this move, ChinaSF became an official partner of California's newly formed China Trade and Investment Network, which operates directly out of Governor Newsom's Office of Business and Economic Development (also known as "GO-Biz").[163] Somehow, stealthily, Gavin had managed to drag his signature program along with him as he ascended state politics, and then embed it into the operational structure of California's bureaucracy.

During his tenure as lieutenant governor, Newsom's interest in China went beyond promoting ChinaSF. He was now ready to pursue personal business across the Pacific, so he got to work. A few months after his 2011 swearing-in, Newsom's wine company, PlumpJack Management Group, applied to register the trademarks PlumpJack and CADE with the Chinese government's trademark office.[164] These trademarks are the names of two of Newsom's vintage wines and the source of much of his wealth.[165]

A year later, in March 2012, Newsom led a wine-tasting dinner at the T8 Restaurant in Shanghai featuring both of these wines. The expensive event was titled "American Fine Wine Dinner: CADE & PlumpJack Wines," and tickets cost 788 yuan ($100+) per person. An advertisement for the event announced:

> There's ample representation of European, Asian, and South American wines in Shanghai, but you don't often see too much in the way of American vintages showcased around town, that makes this one something special. Two Napa Valley boutique wineries—CADE and PlumpJack—are at T8 for a special one-off wine tasting dinner led by Mr. Gavin Newsom on March 15.[166]

T8, which Condé Nast listed as one of the top fifty new restaurants in the world when it opened, was one of the first fine-dining restaurants established in Xintiandi, the flashy entertainment district in Shanghai developed by ChinaSF cofounder Vincent Lo and his company, Shui On Group.[167] Lo's prestigious Shui On Club members receive special discounts when dining at T8.[168]

Gavin's "special one-off wine tasting" at the esteemed T8 came when wine exports were making a major breakthrough in China. In 2010, US wine exports to China—90 percent of which comes from California—saw a 27 percent increase in revenue, and during the first eight months of 2011, $35.7 million of US wine was shipped to China, up 20 percent from the year before. California's wine industry had been dubbed the "Sleeping Tiger" in China for years, but was now wide awake and on the prowl, looking to target China's growing middle class.[169] Newsom's enterprises were no exception.

At the time, ChinaSF was helping US wineries develop strategies to break into the untapped Chinese wine market, including one label owned by a former ChinaSF intern who credits the program with helping him find interested Chinese partners.[170] As a tip of the hat to his friends across the Pacific, Newsom constructed an office and laboratory at one of his wineries using recycled shipping containers from China, a feature found nowhere else in Napa Valley.[171]

Newsom partners with the Hong Kong distributor Jebsen Wines and Spirits (JWS) to sell his CADE and PlumpJack wines in China.[172] JWS is a subsidiary of Jebsen & Co. Ltd, an international trade company founded in Hong Kong in 1895 by the Jebsen family of Denmark. In 1963, the new communist state of China expelled Jebsen and many other foreign "capitalist" companies, but shortly thereafter the company was readmitted to operate.[173] Now, with offices scattered all over mainland China, it serves as the gateway for more than two hundred foreign luxury brands seeking to build up market share in China.[174] In 2011—the same year Newsom trademarked his wines in China—his financial disclosures revealed that he was a partial owner of Jebsen & Co. and received income from the company.[175]

Newsom may have connected with Jebsen through his friend and ChinaSF codirector Vincent Lo. In addition to being a major investor in Lo's signature company, Shui On Land, Jebsen & Co.'s current chairman, Dr. Hans Michael Jebsen, serves with Lo on the Business School Advisory Council of The Hong Kong University of Science and Technology (HKUST). Jebsen and Lo also serve as members of the Hong Kong Trade Development Council (HKTDC). One thing both men have in common is their hearty support of China's Belt and Road Initiative (BRI), also known as One Belt, One Road (OBOR).[176] Started in 2013 by Chinese President Xi Jinping, BRI is a strategic foreign economic policy initiative created to "expand China's global economic reach and influence" by investing in infrastructure, transportation, manufacturing, and other technologies in countries around the world. BRI investments are primarily sponsored by the Chinese government to help secure access to foreign sources of agriculture, energy, and strategic commodities.[177] In 2017, the CCP incorporated BRI permanently into the party's charter.[178]

US experts say that China's BRI undercuts the "operations and principles of global institutions" and allows China's military to benefit from civilian infrastructure projects. The US government has ordered strong sanctions against several Chinese state firms building military infrastructure in the South China Sea to meet BRI objectives.[179] China's BRI has also been accused of "debt-trap diplomacy" to exploit developing countries and for implementing projects that "rely on financing schemes that involve access to natural resources."[180] In 2020, *Forbes* magazine summed up BRI by stating that Xi's signature initiative had "nearly become a euphemism for wasteful spending, environmental destruction and untenable debt."[181] Even worse, the US Department of Homeland Security (DHS) claims that Chinese Triads running drug operations "have plied their ill-gotten gains into Belt and Road projects," and crimes such as bribery and fraud have been woven into the operations of BRI since its inception.[182] Even Vincent Lo's company, Shui On, has admitted that "it's company policy to use triads" for large construction projects.[183] The Global Initiative against Transnational Organized Crime published a report detailing "the opportunities that increased connectivity provided by the BRI may afford organized crime networks at a time when illicit trade is already expanding dramatically worldwide, and criminal networks are seeking ever more favourable pathways for illicit trade."[184]

In May 2017, the *South China Morning Post* published an interview with Vincent Lo and Hans Michael Jebsen in which they both praised China's BRI. "I see One Belt, One Road as such a tremendous opportunity for Hong Kong and for the world," Dr. Lo stated. "I hope we can build a platform to ensure that international resources interested in One Belt, One Road will come through Hong Kong." Jebsen noted that BRI "is a positive thing whether in this, or in any other, part of the world." Lo added, "I think other countries can study what China has done."[185]

Newsom's close relationship with two prominent Hong Kong business-men promoting China's BRI is concerning and raises several questions:

Does Newsom support the goals of China's BRI?
Does Newsom coordinate California policy to better align with China's BRI?
Is San Francisco just another stop on China's ever-expanding Belt and Road empire?

In 2018, *China Daily* reported that ChinaSF was also "exploring ways to take part in the Belt and Road Initiative, proposed by China, and to tie the San Francisco Bay Area to the Greater Bay Area of the Pearl River Delta in China."[186]

Some might argue that this claim is untrustworthy because the Central Propaganda Department of the Chinese Communist Party owns the *China Daily* newspaper. But Newsom and ChinaSF can't make that argument because they're the ones who recruited *China Daily* to the Bay Area. In a 2008 press release, Newsom announced, "China Daily's decision to open its West Coast Operations Office in San Francisco demonstrates that our city is increasingly becoming the center of gravity for Chinese companies, including important media organizations like China Daily."[187]

Close analysis of available data reveals that most descriptions of ChinaSF by government and media have been vacuous and misleading. Essentially, ChinaSF is the branded name of a complex bureaucratic mirage used as cover to legitimize the massive transfer of Bay Area technology, property, and wealth to China while streamlining the establishment of Chinese business in the United States. It's the secret elixir Newsom concocted to help transform San Francisco into the primary entry point and hub of China's BRI in the United States. On the surface, the flurry of MOUs, press conferences, ribbon cuttings, and so forth—propped up by reassuring proclamations from chambers of commerce and government officials like

Newsom—cohere into what may look like an innovative job-generating public-private partnership.[188] But the deeper you probe into who's funding ChinaSF, who's failing to vet all the Chinese companies coming in, and who's making money off the deals—you discover there's no reasonable public accountability structure in place, not enough records for the public to review, and no clear explanations for why the San Francisco mayor's office has a right to engage in risky subnational business schemes in some cases with People's Republic of China criminals and shady Chinese firms who have exploited and damaged the US economy and fleeced American citizens with their fraudulent schemes.

CHAPTER FOUR

The California Way

T HE 'CALIFORNIA WAY' MEANS rejecting old binaries and finding
new solutions to big problems," Newsom declared in his March 2022
State of the State speech. "Take climate policy, for example...California
has no peers," he said, before ticking off what the state has done to battle
emissions and transitioning into what he cast as its economic and educational successes.

> Look, I think all of us here can at least agree: People have always looked
> to California for inspiration. And now, in the midst of so much turmoil,
> with stacking stresses and dramatic social and economic change, Cali-
> fornia is doing what we have done for generations, lighting out the ter-
> ritory ahead of the rest, expanding the horizon of what's possible. We
> know that government cannot be the entire solution, but we also know
> that government has always been part of the solution. By creating a
> platform for people and the private sector to thrive.[1]

"That's the California way," he concluded repeatedly throughout the
speech.[2] To hear Newsom tell it, one might think California was in a state
of nirvana, with low crime and affordable energy, where residents were all
housed and highly employed, and public education was excellent. But nothing could have been further from the truth.

It was two years after the onset of the pandemic. Most states had declared
an end to their COVID lockdowns and restrictions and were trying to get

their economies and the lives of their citizens back to normal. But Governor Newsom was still clinging to his COVID powers after more than twenty-four months of ruling by fiat, deploying unilateral executive orders to lock down the state and keep it restricted in an unprecedented expansion of the governor's power. At the time of the remarks, gas and grocery prices had spiked to record highs, with the state's taxes on fuel hitting the highest in the nation, and the state's homeless population, already the highest by far in the nation, had increased by at least 22,500 during COVID.[3]

Police and cities across the state were struggling to respond to a new public scourge: roaming bands of masked thieves barging into department stores and luxury brand shops and taking as much as their arms and bags could carry out. Few areas of California were spared. In late 2021, mobs of looters had hit two stores on Rodeo Drive in Beverly Hills: Louis Vuitton and Saks Fifth Avenue.[4] But the problems plaguing California during COVID didn't spring forth out of the blue; they were decades in the making, as Newsom, Harris, and their predecessors who came to power in San Francisco in the early 1990s relentlessly pushed the entire state leftward.

How did the once Golden State of dreams and opportunity become a bastion of far-left social experiments that have failed the state and have residents leaving in droves?

(It sounds like modern conservative folklore, but it also happens to be true: so many people left California in 2021 that U-Haul says it actually ran out of trucks to rent, and the top destinations for those trucks were Texas, Florida, Tennessee, South Carolina, and Arizona.)[5]

It didn't happen overnight but over the course of forty years.

Ronald Reagan's iconic years as governor of California in the late 1960s to mid-1970s epitomized the American West's gritty narrative of stubborn self-determination and endless possibilities. In many ways, his life story embodied the rest of the country's image of what California had long stood for and cemented it for a generation.[6]

The Illinois native with a sunny disposition rose from humble beginnings to become a sports announcer and then ventured out West to break into Hollywood, riding his fame and vows to crack down on radical left-ist movements into the governor's mansion and all the way to the White House.[7] Yet since the former B-list actor who confronted communism and led a Morning in America revival left the political stage, the Golden State's political hue morphed from deep magenta to cobalt, with the shift rapidly accelerating over the last decade. Despite the reverence many Republicans hold for Reagan, critics on the right blame him for signing an immigration reform bill in 1986 that provided amnesty to 3 million illegal immigrants for paving the way for more amnesty bills and making California, along with the rest of the country, a magnet for more illegal migration.[8]

Over the past 40 years, the influx of illegal immigrants and the gen-erations of legal children born to them has helped cement California as a solidly blue state.[9] Only two Republicans, career politician Pete Wilson and Hollywood megastar Arnold Schwarzenegger, have captured the gov-ernor's mansion in the last thirty years.[10] Except for one year in the mid-1990s, Democrats have maintained complete command and control of the state legislature for more than four decades. In 2018, the party won veto-proof supermajorities in both houses of the California legislature.[11]

While traditional Democratic strongholds in the Rust Belt and the South shifted red and helped elect Donald Trump in 2024, California is now a one-party state largely ruled by entrenched political dynasties from San Francisco whose personal and professional behavior often undercuts their purported progressive aims of helping the less fortunate. Most states don't regard their top elected official holding their position as an inherited right, but such is the way of current California politics, a folksy mix of pre-vailing progressive wisdom and voter apathy that often turns a blind eye to personal immorality, political corruption, extremist gurus, and even dangerous cults, as this chapter will later chronicle. Such scandals have routinely torpedoed political careers in other states; in California they are simply tolerated for the sake of raw party power and because of the public's general disinterest in politics and policy and the atrophy of local news out-lets because of now anemic newspaper readership.

In 2010, Californians readily gave seventy-one-year-old Jerry Brown his job back. Brown had last served in 1983, after two unsuccessful runs for the Democratic presidential nomination and a failed Senate bid, campaigns in which he was mocked nationwide as "Governor Moonbeam" for his liberal policies on the environment and push for a state space program.[12]

It wasn't always this way. For much of the last century, Los Angeles and San Diego, the largest urban hubs in Southern California, had enough aviation, defense-related businesses, and military bases to politically balance the liberal influence of Hollywood and Latino voters, who in California have tended to vote Democratic despite their Catholic heritage and more traditional social values.[13] But several factors have pulled the entire state to the far left: military base closings after the end of the Cold War; the flight of tech, aviation and other businesses to states with lower taxes; amnesty and sanctuary policies that opened the floodgates to illegal immigration; and San Francisco's liberal contagion spreading south.[14] Elon Musk has moved most of his SpaceX and Tesla operations to Texas after public feuds with Newsom.[15] In 2024, he announced plans to move X.com's headquarters to the Lone Star State as well.[16]

From 1910 through the 1930s, the inverse dynamic was taking place. Two civil leaders, Harry Chandler, a real estate investor and publisher of the *Los Angeles Times*, and Harry Culver, founder of Culver City, used their money and influence to entice aircraft manufacturers and carriers to the region, marketing the benefits of Southern California's climate, lower construction costs and abundance of workers eager to join the new industry.[17] The Lockheed brothers readily left Northern California and headed south to set up an aircraft production firm in 1916. It would grow into the aerospace behemoth Lockheed Martin with the help of the British Royal Air Force, an early client, and during World War II when demand for bombers, fighters, and transport planes spiked. In the 1920s, Donald Douglas, Jack Northrop, and Howard Hughes quickly joined the Los Angeles–area aerospace manufacturing boom, which solidified the region as a center of aircraft production.[18]

San Francisco, by contrast, had long been an unruly town of sailors and shipping prospectors and slums. In less than a decade, in the mid-1850s, the gold rush transformed it from a village of eight hundred to a booming metropolis of fifty thousand people who had flocked to the city by the bay from all over the world in hopes of striking it rich.[19] Chinese immigrants started arriving in the city before California joined the United States, driven by severe poverty in southern China, where a series of famines and floods had killed millions of people. They found work in railroad construction, mining, and agriculture and eventually helped build the city's Bay Area rapid-transit light-rail subway system.[20]

Before the late 1970s tech boom, the city's economy included a mix of shipping, banking, real estate, and textile manufacturing without a dominant anchor industry. Into this post–World War II cultural vacuum of the 1950s slipped a group of writers and artists, including Jack Kerouac and Allen Ginsberg, who met at Columbia University in New York City and moved west to San Francisco, as the Manhattan Institute noted in its *City Journal* article, "Native Son: the problem of Gavin Newsom."[21]

The group dubbed themselves the Beat Generation and embraced a nonconformist brand of bohemian hedonism, rejecting materialism and pursuing spiritual quests through Western and Eastern religions while experimenting with psychedelic drugs and sexual freedom.[22] Archetypal members of that era's counterculture were goatee-wearing men in berets who frequented European-style coffeehouses, recited poetry, and played the bongos.[23] The influence of the beatniks and the counterculture mecca they created in shaping San Francisco's and the entire state's culture and politics was pivotal. By 1967, the so-called Summer of Love, tens of thousands of young people had converged on San Francisco, its surrounding suburbs, and scenic woodsy open spaces to take their place in the hippie revolution.[24] The movement spawned a patchwork of counterculture communes across Northern California and Oregon, where thousands of young people dropped out of society and headed back to the land, setting up small communities where they eschewed materialism and embraced free love, and, in most cases, experimentation with all types of drug use—marijuana and psychedelics, including mushrooms and LSD.[25]

Meanwhile, Bill Malone, the state Democratic party boss who chaired the California Democratic Party after World War II and ran it like a patronage political machine, was beginning to lose power by the early 1950s. A new generation of San Francisco Democrats was rising and coalescing around a loose alliance of labor interests, racial minorities, and activist students while balancing business interests prevalent in their moneyed class.[26] A US Senate investigation into organized crime tarnished Malone's reputation while ushering in a new era of accountability. While not on par with the Mafia kingpins the probe took down in other areas of the country, more than a dozen Malone associates, including Malone's brother, were implicated in financial scandals.[27]

The downfall gave rise to a new Democratic era. Philip and John Burton, brothers and charismatic Democratic lawmakers, ushered in a uniquely California version of limousine liberalism to the city of San Francisco and the state.[28] The brothers, with their brash style and razor-sharp political instincts, were the leaders of a type of bourgeois liberalism—socially progressive and bent on expanding government and public works but operating from a moneyed, elite, and established San Francisco upper crust.[29] Gavin Newsom's grandfather quickly shifted loyalties away from the self-made Irishman Malone to this world of enlightened oligarchs. The movement's leaders included former Republican-turned-Democrat Pat Brown. Brown, also an Irish Catholic, grew up working and spending time in his father's cigar store, which doubled as a gambling shop. During high school, Brown was a debate champion and held twelve student government offices before skipping undergraduate college and moving right to law school, and then immediately running for public office.[30]

Brown ran his first campaign as a Republican for state assembly but lost badly. After the Great Depression dimmed his faith in corporate America, he switched parties. He became a New Dealer, embracing President Franklin Delano Roosevelt's big government approach to building the nation's economic recovery around big deficit-spending investments in public works.[31] After another unsuccessful campaign for district attorney in 1939, he ran again in 1943 with the slogan "Crack down on crime, elect Brown this time." In a surprise political upset, Brown soundly defeated the incumbent, Matthew Brady, and began his political rise as a pro-labor but center-left champion.[32] Brown based his successful 1958 campaign for governor on promises of "responsible liberalism," support for labor, and building out the state's infrastructure. Once elected, he went to work building highways, universities, and a sprawling aqueduct water network to help the booming agriculture industry in the state's dry central valley.[33]

In this way, San Francisco's new liberal ruling class was influenced by the emerging counterculture, but it did not rise from it, as the *City Journal* opined. The same political dynasties that occupied its mansions and private schools and ran its charities and galas pulled the political strings, though their trust-fund children often crossed in and out of the movement's sex-and-drugs subcultures.[34] The new nonconformists clashed with the buttoned-up Eisenhower-era World War II generation, and the cultural shift corresponded with civil rights–era protests, student sit-ins, and mass riots in the streets against the Vietnam War in California and throughout the nation. Brown had remained popular, easily defeating Richard Nixon in 1962, but the unrest across the state—Watts riots in 1965 and student protests at the University of California, Berkeley—created an opening for Ronald Reagan, a well-known Hollywood B-list movie star and gifted communicator with a more conservative law-and-order message. Reagan built his campaign around two main themes: "to send the welfare bums back to work" and to "clean up the mess at Berkeley." Reagan won in a landslide.[35]

If California in the 1960s was romanticized by the Summer of Love, nonconformity, and idealism, the 1970s was the reality check, when high-flying ideas about human nature gave way to petty, venal, and often ruthless forces. Waves of violent clashes between police and antiwar and civil rights protesters led to several slain officers in San Francisco. In Oakland, the Black Liberation Army, a paramilitary offshoot of the Black Panther Party, carried out several acts of terrorism and vigilante justice in the early 1970s. Domestic turmoil was beginning to consume California and the rest of the country, with outrage and bitterness emanating in part from the assassinations of President John Kennedy in 1963 and Senator Robert Kennedy and Martin Luther King Jr. in 1968.[36]

An FBI terrorism expert described the Bay Area during that time as the "Belfast of North America," comparing the bombings and shootings to the violence in Northern Ireland.[37] Peace-and-love flower power suddenly had a dark side, with tolerance of communes and cult leaders and far-left activists morphing into violence in the name of social change. The Black Panthers, the Manson family, the Symbionese Liberation Army, and the Weather Underground, a violent offshoot of Students for a Democratic Society, were all hell-bent on force to achieve their various left-wing goals.[38]

Reagan reacted to the student protests by swiftly working with the University of California Board of Regents to oust its president, Clerk Kerr. Two years later, he sent the California Highway Patrol and 2,200 National Guard troops to occupy the city of Berkeley when students tried to take over vacant land the university had purchased for dormitory construction.[39] A group of hippies decided to turn the area into a park where they could congregate without normal city laws and other restraints, an early precursor to the Capitol Hill Autonomous Zone, or CHAZ, Seattle's police-free neighborhood that ended in violence and disorder amid the pandemic in 2020.[40]

After a month, the university stepped in to clear the property and began clashing with "take-back-the-park" protesters.[41] Reagan declared martial law, and a military helicopter doused the campuses with tear gas. The clashes led to the death of one student when police opened fire with bird shot and buckshot, and dozens more were injured. The Berkeley student newspaper labeled the incident "Bloody Thursday," a precursor to the Kent State shootings a year later, but conservative supporters rallied around Reagan, drowning out the criticism.[42] Reagan survived a successful recall campaign and was reelected with 52.8 percent of the vote. He ultimately decided to opt out of a third term as he focused on national politics.[43]

Brown's son, Jerry, serving as secretary of state at the time, then stepped into the breach, eager to win back the seat his father lost to Reagan. Brown won by just two percentage points against GOP State Controller Houston

Flournoy. Republicans attributed the defeat to anti-GOP sentiment that had swept the nation. The election came just ninety days after Nixon resigned from office amid the Watergate scandal.[44] The unrest and state-wide support for stopping it threatened to undermine the new liberalism taking hold in San Francisco. But the Burtons, Browns, Newsoms, and other like-minded elites dug in, morphing into an oligarchy that embraced social change and most liberal causes—even some radical cults—while internally working to prevent the counterculture warriors and anarchists from gaining footholds in any elected offices.

The most bizarre and cautionary episode during the tumultuous period came from the communist cult called the Peoples Temple. This so-called church was not openly violent like Charles Manson or the Weather Underground but taught the divinity of socialism with Jim Jones, its charismatic but sociopathic founder, exercising severe levels of control over the church's members. Jones, with his raven hair, clergyman's collar, and dark sunglasses (worn to disguise his reddened, drug-addled eyes), directed his top lieutenants to blackmail, threaten, and intimidate members into signing away their rights, even their paternity, to the church, endangering the custody of their children should they decide to leave the cult.[45]

In reality, the Peoples Temple was not a church at all. It started as a purported offshoot of Pentecostalism, but Jones soon transitioned to worshipping communism. Once the Peoples Temple had moved to California in 1972, Jones disparaged all forms of Christianity and religion of any type, and his lectures were full of left-wing spiritual gibberish. Some of his more bizarre themes: "God is Socialism, and I am Principle Socialism, and that's what makes me God. But Socialism is more than just in a personal form. The deity of Socialism is impersonal and ever-present."[46]

While its theology was nonexistent, Jones drew members with his progressive platitudes, which promised to break down racial barriers and reduce systemic iniquities, attracting a predominantly black congregation that the white preacher later ruled with callous cruelty.[47] When Willie Brown first met Jones, the future mayor of San Francisco was still serving as speaker of the state assembly. Jones, a political refugee of sorts from rural

Indiana, struck up a friendship with Willie Brown, immediately recognizing him as a conduit for opening doors to the state's Democratic establishment. Jones was soon meeting with everyone across the Democratic establishment, from Governor Jerry Brown and Jane Fonda to First Lady Rosalynn Carter.[48]

Brown's ready support gave Jones an air of legitimacy as he publicly and privately lauded Jones. Governor Brown, Willie Brown, and several other elected Democrats attended a large dinner in Jones's honor in 1976. Willie Brown, serving as master of ceremonies, introduced Jones, stating, "Let me present to you a combination of Martin Luther King Jr., Angela Davis, Albert Einstein...Chairman Mao."[49] Jones appears to have enjoyed a transactional relationship with Brown, gaining legitimacy from his connections to top Democrats and liberal celebrities.[50]

It was helpful for Brown, too. He knew Jones could deploy thousands of fanatical far-left followers to the ballot boxes. At Brown's direction, Jones, wearing a clergyman's white-and-black collar, readily mobilized his followers for George Moscone's closely fought candidacy for mayor of San Francisco, which Brown was running at the time. The Temple is credited with handing Moscone, whose name now graces San Francisco's convention center, the electoral victory, though his opponents accused Jones of stuffing the ballot box. As the newly elected mayor, Moscone then appointed Jones to the city's Housing Authority Commission (he balked at a less powerful post). Jones soon became chairman, making him the largest landlord in San Francisco.[51]

Under pressure to investigate the election interference allegations, newly elected District Attorney Joseph Freitas, a Moscone ally who engineered Peoples Temple support for his election, appointed an investigatory committee, tapping Tim Stoen, a member of the Peoples Temple, to run it. Stoen said he found no election fraud and was later hired by the district attorney's office. (Stoen, several years later, left the cult and engaged in a multiyear custody battle with the church over his young son.)[52]

Brown continued to regularly appear at Temple events and dinners, fawning over Jones in speeches and official letters.[53] The Temple also mobilized to back Harvey Milk's 1977 supervisor campaign. Milk, the first openly gay man elected to public office in California, was a brash and outspoken gay rights activist in the Castro District. The San Francisco neighborhood had become a magnet for gay men and lesbians in the late 1960s and '70s.[54] Milk lost several campaigns for city supervisor and another for California state assembly but was elected with the help of the Peoples Temple. The city also had just reorganized its election process to choose representatives from neighborhoods rather than via citywide ballots.[55]

Perhaps because of their disdain for biblical tradition, the Peoples Temple was seen as one of the most gay-friendly churches in the region.[56] But by that time, the complaints around the Peoples Temple, including that Jones was drugging and secluding members who questioned him, had grown to a clamor. Several high-profile members defected, and an increasing number of adherents decamped to Jones's commune in a remote corner of Guyana. The press could no longer ignore it.[57]

As questions about Jones reached the authorities in Guyana, Brown again served as a character witness for Jones. "Rev. Jim Jones is that person who can be helpful when all appears to be lost, and hope is just about gone," the powerful California politician wrote Prime Minister Forbes Burnham. "Having him as a resident in your country can only be a plus no matter how short or long his stay."[58] The Jonestown outpost in Guyana would end in tragedy nearly one year after Brown wrote his letter. When Representative Leo Ryan, who represented a nearby Bay Area congressional district, made an investigatory visit to Jonestown, he was murdered by members of the Temple on an airstrip when some Temple defectors tried to flee the compound with him.[59]

Jones then ordered his brainwashed flock to down a cyanide-laced drink, something they had rehearsed many times before. The mass suicide spawned the pop culture reference to being brainwashed—"drinking the 'Kool-Aid.'" All 918 members of the congregation perished. Nearly three hundred were children.[60]

Just nine days later, San Francisco was reeling from another tragedy. Former San Francisco Supervisor Dan White showed up at San Francisco

City Hall and murdered Moscone in the mayor's office, shooting him in the head at close range, not more than an hour after Willie Brown had left a meeting with him.[61] White was angry that Moscone was not planning to reappoint him to the supervisor position he had recently resigned from because of its low salary. After shooting Moscone, he went to his former office where he found Harvey Milk. He fired rapidly on his fellow supervisor, killing him instantly.[62]

White fled the scene. Dianne Feinstein, another fellow supervisor, was the first to find Milk's deceased body. When trying to find his pulse, her fingers instead found a bullet wound in his throat. Directly after the assassination, Feinstein assumed the role of mayor and went on to become California's first woman US senator and its longest-serving senator until her death in 2023.[63]

In other cities across the country, such public tragedies would have spurred multiple resignations and sweeping accountability measures. Anyone who had publicly thrown their credibility behind a cult leader responsible for the mass suicides of more than nine hundred people would face instant condemnation from the press, as well as from their constituents and other elected leaders.[64] But after the counterculture-fueled violence of 1978, the elite political establishment tightened its hold on power, putting an abrupt end to any encroachment—at least when it comes to elected office—from the far left's radical elements. While this close-knit group of highly educated, intermingled members of San Francisco's oligarchy often paid lip service and at times symbolically embraced far-left activists, they imposed an insider-only system of loyalty.

Willie Brown, buoyed by his popularity as a civil rights fighter for minorities and the gay community, only amassed more power in the state assembly. In the years following the Jonestown mass suicides, Brown was never held to account for his role in boosting Jim Jones and welcoming him into the upper echelons of San Francisco's political community. Instead, he enjoyed several political promotions, becoming speaker of the assembly just three years after the Jonestown tragedy. In fact, Brown's long service in the assembly and political connections made him one of the most powerful state legislators in the country.[65]

During his three decades in the legislature, he worked to defeat the Three Strikes Law, led efforts to increase AIDS research funding, and raised awareness about South Africa's apartheid, all the while directing state funds to San Francisco, especially for public health and mental health.[66] He also galvanized support for more public spending on public schools, holding up the state budget for more than two months in 1992 until Governor Pete Wilson, a Republican, added another $1.1 billion for education.[67] At one point, Willie Brown was such a dominant force in the state legislature that he nicknamed himself the Ayatollah of the Assembly, estimating that he personally helped raise close to $75 million to help elect and reelect state Democrats.[68]

Even though the legislature was quickly shifting blue, millions of voters across the state still had some power to stop the increasingly bloated government budget. The same year of the violent upheaval in San Francisco, voters passed Proposition 13, a state constitutional amendment severely limiting the legislature's ability to raise property taxes. California legislators then started increasing every other type of tax—income, excise, and sales taxes—to fund the massive public projects and special interest payouts of its ever-expanding budget required.[69]

Throughout the early 1970s, the hippies and their love for open spaces helped foster the environmental movement, and an antigrowth ideology took hold. In 1969, environmental forces across the state were still level-headed enough to push out David Brower, a talented mountaineer and wilderness guide, as the head of the Sierra Club over his absolute opposition to nuclear power and dams, including the Glen Canyon Dam across the Colorado River.[70] A decade later, the Berkeley-born Brower's extreme preservationist attitudes dominated the Sierra Club and the ruling liberal establishment. Despite earning his living working for the world's largest oil magnate, Bill Newsom joined the Sierra Club's board, at one point acquiring a pet otter from one of his colleagues. Gavin Newsom recalled how as a boy, the pet otter, which was named Potter, slept curled up under his bed.[71]

Jerry Brown quickly became a leader in the environmental movement, sponsoring the first-ever tax incentive for rooftop solar and repealing the "depletion allowance," a tax break for the state's oil industry.[72] When Brown ran a losing presidential primary challenge against Jimmy Carter in 1980, he promised to increase funds for the space program as a "first step in bringing us a solar-powered satellite to provide solar energy for this planet."[73] Brown's 1980 campaign epitomized California Democrats' embrace of environmentalism as their best attempt at a secular New Age religion: "Protect the earth, serve the people, explore the universe."[74]

Even as the ruling class began to shift leftward in certain areas, the state's majority of more centrist voters repeatedly tried to rein them in. In 1983, Jerry Brown opted to run for Senate instead of governor but lost to Republican San Diego Mayor Pete Wilson. Voters then narrowly chose George Deukmejian, also a Republican and a vehement Brown critic, as governor. Deukmejian was overwhelmingly elected in 1986.[75] In 1990, Wilson succeeded Deukmejian as governor, and voters passed a constitutional amendment to impose term limits on state legislators, partly in response to Willie Brown's stranglehold on the job. Brown then opted to run for San Francisco mayor and handily won.[76]

Known for his wheeling and dealing, Brown's eight-year tenure as mayor was marred by repeated allegations of corruption. The FBI spent five years investigating Brown and his tight-knit network of appointed officials and supporters, including Charlie Walker, a buddy of Brown's who decades earlier had served time in San Quentin for fraud. The probe into Walker came up short, though Walker's daughter was one of fourteen people who eventually pleaded guilty to federal charges related to the sale of Section 8 vouchers at the city's housing authority.[77]

Kamala Harris, who had been involved in a very public affair with Brown, as we noted previously, ran for San Francisco district attorney with his backing, never mentioning the federal corruption investigation nor opening her own investigations into aspects of it once elected. During the same election, Brown was term-limited out as mayor and was busy backing Newsom, his well-connected protégé, as his successor. Newsom handily won the first balloting in November 2003, taking 42 percent of the vote. But the runoff proved far more difficult against upstart Supervisor and Green Party candidate Matt Gonzalez. As the election day grew closer, the local power structure was so stressed about a series of polls showing the race a dead heat that Newsom's backers hauled in the heaviest hitters they could find.[78]

San Francisco developer Walter Shorenstein, who once owned 25 percent of the city's buildings, sent a private plane back east to pick up President Bill Clinton, who held a rally for Newsom.[79] Appalled at the prospect of a far-left Green Party mayor, Chinese business interests endorsed Newsom as a more centrist alternative. Julie Lee, an influential Chinese community organizer, power broker, and prolific fundraiser, came to Newsom's aid. Lee, who ran the three-thousand-member-strong San Francisco Neighborhood Association, also spoke out on Newsom's behalf on her nightly radio show. (Lee would later be convicted in a public corruption scheme—see Chapter Three for more details.)

While younger Chinese voters often view themselves as progressive, as a larger voting bloc Chinese Californians tend to pursue more moderate, business-friendly policies compared to those of the more liberal white, black, and Hispanic populations. In the early 2000s, 60 percent of San Franciscans approved a ballot initiative that outlawed panhandling, and many of the Left denounced it as too onerous on the poor while the Chinese community generally approved of it.[80]

In the end, Newsom edged out Gonzalez by just 6 percent despite outspending him ten to one.[81] The closer-than-expected win left an indelible impression: it rocked Newsom's confidence in the more centrist liberal-establishment model passed down to him, while at the same time permitting him to forge an allegiance with his Chinese constituents, even those like Rose Pak, a powerful community organizer who had direct links to China's repressive communist regime and others with unsavory gang ties.[82]

As outlined in Chapter 2, "Growing Up Getty," Newsom followed his grandfather's footsteps into San Francisco politics. Newsom became the youngest-ever member of the San Francisco Board of Supervisors via an appointment from Willie Brown.

Though a political neophyte, in 1998 Newsom already had his sights on the White House, telling a reporter he wanted to be president of the United States. Back then, critics argued that he was nothing more than a Willie Brown puppet. Because he had no experience, he owed everything to Brown and could not cross him.

Shortly after he was sworn in, Newsom found out just how short his leash would be. His first day on the job, Newsom sharply questioned Mayor Brown's plans for a stadium complex for the 49ers, which would require a $100 million bond measure but was aimed at staving off the team's threat to leave the city. Brown labeled Newsom's independence as political naivete.[83]

"Those are rookie mistakes," Brown told the *SFGate*. "It's not a matter of his changing his mind; it's a matter of fully understanding the facts."[84] The board would soon unanimously vote in favor of Brown's pet project. The heavy-handed smackdown followed by their consistent work in tandem led some Democrats to disparage Newsom publicly as an appendage of Brown.

After serving five years as a supervisor, Newsom won his mayoral race in 2003, promising to operate as a "social liberal" and a "fiscal watchdog." Shortly after taking office, he urged the city clerk to issue nearly four thousand same-sex couples marriage licenses in violation of state law. It was a smart move, aimed at winning fealty from the city's liberal base, many of whom had just voted for his opponent in the hard-fought mayoral race. But the flouting of public law went beyond the Democratic Party's norms and status-quo comfort zone. Obama, who was running for Senate in Illinois at the time—and who embraced gay marriage himself in 2012—reportedly went to great trouble to avoid taking a photo with Newsom.[85] Obama has denied the claims, but Newsom has hinted that they are true.[86]

Not to be politically outmaneuvered, Harris, who was serving as San Francisco district attorney, performed one of the first same-sex unions in the United States during the city's so-called Winter of Love. To hear Harris tell it, her role in officiating one of the first same-sex couple unions in the country was somewhat spontaneous. She was heading to the airport but decided to check out all the commotion at City Hall, where long lines of gay and lesbian couple had showed up to have their relationships formally recognized as marriages by the state. After being sworn in, she and other local officials began performing unions in every "nook and cranny" of City Hall, she recalled. "I was delighted to be a part of it."[87]

Newsom's move to break the law and start marrying same-sex partners in the city sparked a legal battle in the state—that Newsom and the gay couples would ultimately win, albeit with a few bumps along the way. In 2015, the Supreme Court extended the federal right to marry to same-sex couple in a 5-4 decision.

It was a time of quick ascendency for both Newsom and Harris — with both owing their rapid political success to former San Francisco Mayor and California political kingmaker Will Brown.

Bay Area Democratic circles are notoriously small and overlapping, and for decades orbited around Brown. Newsom had several points of entry into San Francisco's tony political in-club—his father's Getty connections along with those of his aunt by marriage, Nancy Pelosi, as well as Brown. But Harris, the Oakland-born daughter of two immigrants—had just one—"da mayor." Brown mentored both and gave both their first political commissions.

But Harris's relationship with the political power broker, several years her father's senior, was far more *personal*.

They dated in the mid-1990s when Brown was openly separated from his longtime wife, Blanche Vitero. While leader of the California State Assembly, then-Speaker Brown placed Harris on two high-paying, part-time boards: the Insurance Appeals Board and the Medical Assistance Commission, positions that paid her more than $400,000 over five years, according to *SF Weekly*.[88] Brown also bought Harris a BMW to help the barely thirty-year-old shuttle between her six-figure day job as a prosecutor with the Alameda County district attorney's office, her board meetings, and her evening appointments on the San Francisco cocktail circuit.[89]

The couple split up in 1995, which astounded those "who found Kamala the perfect antidote to whatever playboy tendencies still reside[d] in the mayor-elect's jaunty persona," according to the *San Francisco Chronicle*'s Herb Caen.[90] Brown backed Harris in her successful run for San Francisco district attorney general, but she has repeatedly tried to shake off the cloud he created over her entire political career, including in that 2003 race.

Harris at the time called Brown an "albatross hanging around my neck."

"His career is over; I will be alive and kicking for the next forty years. I do not owe him a thing," she told *SF Weekly*, vowing, "If there is corruption, it will be prosecuted."[91]

But those statements don't line up with the facts.

Eight years after taking over City Hall, Brown's machine boosted Harris's ascent and ultimately successful challenge to her former boss, San Francisco District Attorney Terence Hallinan. Harris was miffed he had passed her over for a promotion, so much so that she resigned and took a job at the San Francisco city attorney's office. And Brown was reportedly none too pleased with Hallinan's decision to investigate corruption allegations against members of Willie Brown Inc. In 2003, Brown's machine provided Harris with a campaign manager, a blue-chip fundraiser—even an independent expenditure arm, and, of course, a Rolodex of donors, all of whom helped her smash through a voluntary campaign spending cap. The act eventually earned her campaign a record $34,000 campaign fine, according to Peter Schweitzer.[92] And allegedly as part of Brown's operation, city employees spent work hours as campaign "volunteers" for both Harris and Newsom, who were vying to succeed Brown in City Hall that year.

Yet Harris's affair with Brown and his well-documented patronage has continued to cast a pall over her record—especially because the garrulous ninety-year-old will not stop publicly undermining her. Last summer after Democrats pushed Biden aside and attempted to anoint Harris, Brown ominously publicly fretted that Harris had "the Hillary syndrome"—that "people don't like her," *Politico* reported.[93] Since Harris became vice president, her former boyfriend and political benefactor has often said that if Harris ever becomes president, "she'll deport my ass."[94]

While Brown delivered a full-throated endorsement of Harris in a midsummer interview with the *San Francisco Chronicle*, he also made news by suggesting she would tap Newsom for a cabinet position. "I can't imagine a new President Harris not including Mr. Newsom in some aspect of her administration," he remarked.[95] Those comments were far off the Democratic Party talking points, which at the time were focused on trying to balance Harris's reputation as a San Francisco liberal with a more centrist white male running mate from Pennsylvania, the Midwest, or the South. Harris eventually chose Minnesota Governor Tim Walz, whose liberal record has been cited as a top liability in many post-mortem critiques of her failed campaign.

During her time as California attorney general, Harris also ignored repeated urgings to prosecute Pacific Gas and Electric (PG&E) and Southern California Edison for several deadly disasters traced to old and decaying equipment and the California Public Utilities Commission (CPUC) for internal corruption. While Willie Brown was still assembly speaker, a lobbyist accused PG&E of helping steer a contract to one of his legal clients while the utility was seeking action on a legislative matter worth billions. After he left office, Brown served as a highly compensated PG&E lobbyist or consultant for a decade while Harris was weighing whether to prosecute the utility and CPUC.

Throughout her career, Harris has been riddled with accusations that her prosecution of cases was selective and that she often went after the little guys while protecting powerful friends and donors.

In 2015, she ignored a detailed request from her San Diego office to investigate supplement maker Herbalife for flouting a standing court order regarding its nutrition and ingredient claims—a matter that had caught the attention of other state attorneys general and the Federal Trade Commission (FTC).[96] The connection? Her new husband, fellow attorney Douglas Emhoff. Emhoff was a lead partner at the law firm Venable in Los Angeles. Herbalife—among other supplement makers—was a major Venable client.[97] Despite receiving more than seven hundred complaint letters from consumers detailing Herbalife's predatory practices, Attorney General Harris failed to act.[98] A year later, the FTC negotiated a $200 million settlement with Herbalife on deceptive advertising practices, among other illegal actions outlined in a memo from Harris's San Diego office. In 2020, the Justice Department fined the company $122 million for violating the Foreign Corrupt Practices Act with its dealings in China.

During her failed 2024 election, Harris ran a series of ads stating that, as attorney general, she stood up to big banks accused of predatory lending amid the mortgage crisis of the late 2000s. But her record is far more complex. While she worked closely with former President Joe Biden's son Beau, the then-attorney general of Delaware, to negotiate a $25 billion national settlement, California's portion evaporated into thin air after it got to the state.

California Governor Jerry Brown quickly diverted the $331 million the state received in compensation for victims to pay off state budget shortfalls that had occurred before the housing crisis.

Harris's unwillingness to stand up to Brown on behalf of victims has been a point of contention for years. She needed Brown's endorsement for her Senate race and didn't want to rock the boat. The move has been criticized by some minority groups that should be natural allies, such as the National Asian American Coalition (NAAC), for letting them down. In the case of the NAAC, they charged that Harris left them and other victims high and dry when Brown snatched the funds to prevent his own political crisis and fill the budget deficit.

Harris initially spoke out against Brown's diversion of the funds, but then never said anything about it again. "While the state is undeniably facing a difficult budget gap, these funds should be used to help Californians stay in their homes," Harris said in a statement in 2012. "I plan to work with the governor and legislature toward a balanced budget that honors our obligations to California's homeowners."[99]

She remained silent on a subsequent court battle that began in 2014—after she left the attorney general's office—for the last year and a half while serving as senator, and during her presidential bid in 2024.

That reticence has critics arguing that Harris hasn't demonstrated the same political courage she boasts of deploying against the banks to stand up to Brown, Newsom, and other prominent Democrats in the California legislature.

Prominent state Republicans also called on Harris to take a stand on the redirection of the mortgage settlement money, which California courts deemed illegal three times. "If [Harris] is going to be a champion for the underserved and the victims of the housing crisis who lost funds designed to help them, that she helped secure, then she should have been out front on the issue," California State Senate Republican leader Shannon Grove said in an interview with us.

The failure to stand up for—or even meet with minority victims of the housing crisis—is a misstep the media never forced Harris to truly address during her failed bid to succeed Biden.

Even during the height of the 2024 presidential campaign, the media also never held her to account for response to the infamous Jussie Smollett hoax, when the former *Empire* star faked his own hate crime by paying two men to stage a "homophobic" attack against him, which included draping a noose around his neck.[100] Smollett claimed that the paid actors he'd hired were Trump supporters who yelled, "This is MAGA country" during the attack.[101]

Within days—and long before there was a verdict in the case—Kamala Harris publicly defended Smollett when she tweeted, "@JussieSmollett is one of the kindest, most gentle human beings I know. I'm praying for his quick recovery. This was an attempted modern-day lynching. No one should have to fear for their life because of their sexuality or color of their skin. We must confront this hate."[102]

As of this writing, Harris still hasn't deleted her tweet, even though Smollett was eventually found guilty of felony disorderly conduct and filing false reports and sentenced to 150 days in jail.[103] During his hearing, Cook County Judge James Linn told Smollett, "You're not a victim of a racial hate crime, you're not a victim of a homophobic hate crime. You're just a charlatan pretending to be a victim of a hate crime, and that's shameful."[104]

The timing of the hoax was fortuitous. Just a few weeks prior Kamala Harris and Cory Booker had introduced a bill that made lynching a hate crime.[105] Sure enough, it eventually became enshrined in law, after Harris rushed to describe Smollet's false attack as a "modern-day lynching."[106]

During Harris's speech at the 2024 Democratic National Convention, the former prosecutor said: "Every day, in the courtroom, I stood proudly before a judge and I said five words: Kamala Harris, for the people. And to be clear—and to be clear, my entire career, I've only had one client: the people."[107] But in 2011, when the Supreme Court ruled that California's dangerous and overcrowded prisons had devolved into a form of "cruel and unusual punishment" and that the only solution was to release some of their low-risk inmates, Attorney General Harris fought the ruling on behalf of Governor Jerry Brown. "I have a client, and I don't get to choose my client," she told the critics.

When asked by an LGBTQ+ advocacy group why she composed a brief that sought to deny gender affirmation for trans prisoners, Harris said, "I had clients, and one of them was the California Department of Corrections."[108]

Yet eight years later, it was an entirely different story. In 2019, when Harris was seeking support for her abbreviated presidential campaign from the LGBTQ+ community, she attended the National Center for Transgender Equity Action Fund conference and bragged that she worked "behind the scenes" when she was California attorney general to change the state's law to support taxpayer-funded gender transition surgeries for prisoners.

"When I was attorney general, I learned that the California Department of Corrections, which was a client of mine—I didn't get to choose my clients—that they were standing in the way of [gender-reassignment] surgery for prisoners," she said. "And there was a specific case. And when I learned about the case, I worked behind the scenes to not only make sure that transgender woman got the services she was deserving...I made sure they changed the policy in the state of California so that every transgender inmate in the prison system would have access to the medical care that they desired and need."

She quickly added that she knew, at the time, that she was making history in California, but looking back believed it was the first such law in the country "where [she] pushed for that policy in a department of corrections."[109]

Harris has long claimed to be a champion of the LGBTQ+ community, an obvious necessity to win elections in gay-friendly San Francisco. In 2007, in her role as district attorney, she and two other city officials launched an awareness campaign against gay rape and to "encourage victims to seek support services and report the crimes," according to a district attorney's office press release. Harris announced the campaign at a press conference on the steps of City Hall and touted it as "the first campaign of its kind sponsored by a district attorney anywhere."[110]

Years, later, in 2020, then-Governor Newsom signed a bill reducing penalties for sodomy with minors by expanding judges' discretion regarding pedophile sex offender registration in certain statutory rape cases. The bill expanded the state law that already provided judges with such discretion in cases of "voluntary," but illegal, vaginal sex between a minor aged fourteen to seventeen and an adult within ten years of the minor's age. The bill broadened that discretion to also apply in cases of "voluntary" oral and anal sex with the same-age parameters.

In 2019, as a presidential candidate, the pro-LGBTQ+ Human Rights Campaign (HRC) touted her policy agendas as "one of the most substantive" of any candidate in the field. "She attended the HRC-CNN [-sponsored] Power of Pride Townhall, where she discussed her in-depth agendas to combat HIV/AIDS among black and brown people and reduce violence against transgender and gender non-conforming community, particularly black transgender women," the HRC said in a press release in the summer of 2019.[111]

Still, Harris notably declined to prosecute one heinous alleged case while serving as San Francisco district attorney that would have helped protect gay men from contracting AIDS. A thirty-one-year-old man who was HIV-positive was allegedly victimizing closeted gay men by responding to personal ads for sex, according to Doug Eckenrod, retired deputy director for California State Parole, a division within the California Department of

Corrections, who was serving as a sex offender investigator for the state at the time.

In a lengthy interview, Eckenrod told us that this man was a convicted pedophile, having been found guilty of felony sodomy of a person under fourteen years old, and at the time was living in Contra Costa County, east of San Francisco. He said the felon wasn't allowed, under his parole terms, to travel to a different county without notifying the state parole board but had done so several times.

When Eckenrod responded to the parole violations by arresting the convicted felon at his home, he conducted a forensic search of the man's computer and phone and discovered a prostitution website account in which the man was actively prostituting himself, targeting gay men in San Francisco County.

The man allegedly told him he was making the frequent trips into San Francisco to respond to ads for sexual encounters with married but closeted gay men.

Eckenrod told us that this individual provided what he called a clear confession, but because the crimes had occurred in San Francisco, it would be up to Harris's office to determine whether to prosecute. When Eckenrod contacted the district attorney's office, he was encouraged that a deputy district attorney was interested in the case. But after that official consulted office management, and possibly Harris herself, the attorney called him back to let him know they would not be prosecuting the case. The convicted felon would go on to break his parole terms and be returned to prison two additional times, before being released after severing the statutory maximum for his felony pedophile conviction in 2013, according to a response from the California Department of Corrections and Rehabilitation to our public records request.

Attorney General Harris also faced sharp criticism for her handling of the 2007 Moonlight Fire, which ravaged sixty-five thousand acres in the California Sierras. A lead investigator with the California Department of Forestry and Fire Protection (Cal Fire) was found to have repeatedly lied about the fire's origins, destroyed notes, and collaborated with US Forest

Service investigators to falsify reports, all in an effort to shift the blame—and the financial burden—onto private landowners. A California judge deemed the investigation so "corrupt and tainted" and the abuses so "pervasive" and "egregious" that he dismissed it and ordered sanctions. During the case it was uncovered that Cal Fire had illegally funneled nearly $4 million of state funds into a hidden slush fund. When California legislators asked Attorney General Harris to investigate the misuse of public funds, she declined, citing a conflict of interest because Cal Fire was her "client."[112]

I think you see the pattern. *We the people* are not Kamala's *client*. Never have been.

Kamala's true client is the Permanent Political Class, and the group of elites was extraordinarily successful in promoting her to become vice president, one step away from the leader of the free world. But to reach the pinnacle of US politics and attain the White House, Harris would have to face the most diverse group of voters she ever had, and these individuals, the American people, have no allegiances to Washington's or California's powerbrokers. Quite the opposite, in fact, many hold them in utter contempt. Harris's ultimate downfall can be attributed to her patronage-fueled rise and just how untested she remained as vice president.

Back in the mid-2000s while Harris was quickly moving up the political ladder, Newsom's mayoral tenure was marked by other now-familiar governing priorities. He vowed to fight homelessness, taking an unapologetic housing-first approach, which is based on the progressive notion that housing is a right that all people are entitled to have, even if it's provided by taxpayer funds through the government free of charge. Despite his pledge to his campaign pledge to be a "fiscal watchdog," his very first action as mayor was to propose a $100 million bond measure to build single-occupancy housing units for homeless people.[113] Six months into his tenure he broadened his vision, vowing to "end" homelessness in the city by rolling out a ten-year plan that promised to provide three thousand new apartments, not just shelter beds aimed at providing a temporary Band-Aid to the problem.[114]

"We're moving toward a goal and desire not to manage but to end home-lessness," he said.

Fast-forward twenty years, and we can see just how futile Newsom's adherence to housing-first policies has been. According to Politifact, during Newsom's time as mayor his sweeping homelessness initiatives had zero impact. Despite all the spending, those living on the city's streets increased from the first available report during his tenure, from 2005, which shows a total of 6,248 homeless in the city until January 2011, Newsom's final month in office, when the number was 6,455.[115] That was a paltry increase compared to the epidemic of homelessness occurring statewide and in San Francisco as Newsom rose in the ranks, and he and nearly every other top Democratic leader in the state continued down the housing-first path. From 2014 to 2020, California's homeless population would explode by 42 percent, compared to a near 10 percent decline around the rest of the nation during that time.

Newsom's time as Mayor was also marred by scandals early on, several involving women and alcohol after his marriage to Guilfoyle ended in divorce, as we mentioned in Chapter 2, "Growing Up Getty." Still, New-som's political ambitions were so unbridled that in 2009 he launched a short-lived challenge to Jerry Brown. After several months, Newsom aban-doned the race in the face of paltry poll numbers, opting to run a successful campaign for lieutenant governor. Newsom has described that stretch in his life, operating in the large shadow of Governor Jerry Brown, as eight years of political purgatory. During that time, Newsom managed to write a book, entitled *Citizenville*, in which he argued for government that kept pace with technological changes elsewhere in our society, offering a vision for a far more transparent, efficient, and even entrepreneurial government.[116]

"We simply cannot have a government that relies on bureaucracy and maintaining the status quo," he wrote.[117]

Looking back, however, Newsom has achieved nothing resembling his book's vision. Quite the opposite, in fact. In addition to adding to the exploding deficit—which at last count as of the writing of this book was an estimated $46.8 billion, according to Democrats' figures—as well as his failures on homelessness, crime, and cost of living, Newsom presided over the worst fiscal scandal in the state's history. During the COVID pandemic, outdated technology at the state labor department and bureaucratic bundling wreaked havoc on the ability of unemployed residents to get their COVID unemployment checks and led to shocking levels of fraud, as we will discuss in detail in Chapter 9.

And Newsom can hardly blame the pandemic for his failures to innovate and usher in a new era of ethics and transparency, as his book promised. After eight long years in Brown's shadow, Newsom quickly moved to consolidate power and steer benefits to political donors and friends.

In 2023, Newsom directed $630,000 in taxpayer dollars to Equality California, an LGBTQ+ group fighting alongside state Superintendent of Public Instruction Tony Thurmond against school boards' efforts to oppose policies prohibiting teachers and public school administrators from telling parents if their child is gender-transitioning and their ability to object to diversity-oriented curricula.[118] Immediately after Trump's 2024 win, a California progressive group rebranded its website to rally activists and deep-pocketed donors against "authoritarianism." The organization, "We Are California," is an arm of the California Calls, which uses its nonprofit and political advocacy subsidiaries to organize voters to approve tax hikes. Wealthy funders include Facebook Founder Mark Zuckerberg's Chan Zuckerberg Initiative, the anti-police Akonadi Foundation, and the Tides Foundation, a progressive dark-money group. The group's list of partner organizations includes immigrant rights groups, such as Coalition for Humane Immigrant Rights, which has received millions of dollars in federal grant funds used to help illegal immigrants resettle in California.[119]

Newsom also made no bones about using the governorship to promote his wife's documentary film nonprofit, which advocates for "gender-justice," equality, and inclusivity.[120]

On taking office, Newsom quickly announced the creation of the taxpayer-funded Office of the First Partner for his wife, Jennifer Siebel Newsom, and planned to staff it with at least two women making six-figure salaries.[121]

Newsom, through his much-touted "California Way," has no qualms about engaging in ethically dubious fundraising schemes to further his political ambitions and passions. During his first four years in office, Newsom actively solicited donations from state vendors and state employees and their affiliated political action committees, according to a detailed 2022 report by Open The Books.[122]

The report cited 979 state vendors who gave $10.6 million in political donations to Newsom during the 2010, 2018, recall election, and 2022 election cycles. The donations appear to have paid off, with the same companies reaping $6.2 billion in state payments over the same period.

While Newsom was taking money from state contractors, his wife was soliciting donations to her filmmaking charity, the Representation Project. Several corporations with contracts of business pending before the state provided five- and six-figure donations to Siebel Newsom's charity. These donations also helped pay Siebel Newsom a total of $1.5 million in salary from 2013 to 2021, and helped The Representation Project give $1.6 million to her private company, Girls Club Entertainment since 2012, Open The Books found, citing IRS 990 returns.[123]

Open The Books also uncovered how Siebel Newsom produces the "gender-justice" films and then hawks them to public schools in all 50 states, and appears to harness her organization's connections to reap the licensing fees for their screenings, although the fees schools actually pay for the films remains unclear. The first partner though her Representation Project has released four films, complete with lesson plans. The companion curriculum also advises teachers and administrators that children may need to see a school counselor after watching the films and completing the accompanying assignments, which sensitize them about social privilege, oppression, and gender equality. In blatant political advocacy, the film's accompanying curricula include a discussion with Governor Newsom commenting within the films and pressing viewers to gather with friends and vote for politicians that support a "care economy" that "embraces universal human values."[124]

Several of Siebel Newsom's movies, *The Mask You Live In*, *Fair Play*, *The*

Great American Lie, and *Miss Representation,* warn teachers to have counselors and therapists on hand to respond to students' reactions to the films.

Some parents have complained that the movies contain pornographic material inappropriate for the eleven-year-olds (such as an animated upside-down stripper with tape over her breasts) who were forced to watch it. Those intended for fifteen-year-olds also drew complaints for images of nearly naked women being slapped, handcuffed, and brutalized—images taken from porn sites.[125]

Siebel Newsom's films and the Representation Project lesson plans also promote nonbinary gender identification. The curricula accompanying *The Mask You Live In,* includes a "genderbread person," whose "gender expression" and "sexual attraction" and "gender identity" exist on a spectrum that can be mixed and matched.[126]

While conservative outlets have questioned the propriety of the Newsoms' pulling in revenue from public schools and the content of the films, most of the media outlets in the state have offered nothing but praise. Apparently, it's all part of the "California Way," an innovative means of indoctrinating children to embrace gender transitions and fluid gender identity.

But by now, schools and the state education system should be on notice that parents aren't likely to take this spoon-fed far-left curricula lying down. Powerful union forces succeeded in keeping California students out of the classroom longer than in any other state, and the parents awakened to the reality that teachers and educators did not always have their children's best interests in mind. By mid-2022, voters across the state were in full revolt against the "California Way."

Protracted COVID lockdowns decimated local businesses, and record fentanyl overdoses proved too much to bear even for voters in the nation's most liberal city. In February 2022, fed-up San Francisco parents recalled three of the city's school board members over their decision to keep schools shuttered and students in virtual learning for more than a year, while wasting time renaming forty-four school sites whose monikers, according to these board members, were linked to racism and sexism.[127]

Voters then turned their sights on San Francisco District Attorney Chesa Boudin, the son of two Weather Underground leaders convicted of murder, who had been raised by Bill Ayers, the group's far-left militant cofounder.[128] Boudin came to office on promises that he would no longer prosecute lower-level "quality of life" crimes like soliciting sex, public urination, recreational drug use and lower-level theft, and he followed through despite a backlash.[129] In 2022, Boudin was recalled, with 55 percent of voters in the most liberal city in the nation backing his removal.[130]

Current Mayor London Breed, who also criticized the school board and Boudin, appointed Brooke Jenkins, who worked in the district attorney's office until resigning to back Boudin's recall, to replace Boudin.[131] Over the last two years, Jenkins has been busy trying to clean up a corruption mess at San Francisco City Hall that has snared several officials first appointed by Brown and Newsom.[132] Jenkins is following the lead of federal prosecutors, who first cracked open the corruption scandal amid the first months of the COVID pandemic.[133]

Ongoing investigations by the district attorney's Public Integrity Task Force and the FBI have led to indictments, guilty pleas, and convictions of more than a dozen city officials, contractors, and prominent local business executives.[134] The prosecutions have snared several key city officials whose tenures date back to Brown's and Newsom's stints as mayor on various corruption charges, including wire fraud, bribery, and kickbacks. The FBI has been investigating top city officials since 2018 through wiretaps and undercover officers.[135]

On everything from ideologically driven education to failures in curbing crime, the "California Way" has sparked backlashes from voters in recent years. After the US Supreme Court in 2011 forced California to address the problem of its overcrowded prisons, the state could have built more prisons. Instead, Democrats in the legislature predictably decided to empty them out. The state prison population has dropped from 160,000 in 2011 to around 96,000 today, with Newsom releasing tens of thousands of prisoners during COVID purportedly to prevent the virus's deadly spread across the state's correctional institutions. But the COVID excuse was entirely misleading.

Eckenrod, who served as the pandemic liaison between the California prison system and its health care division but said he spent most of his time interacting with Newsom's office, told us there was no reason to release the prisoners because the prison population had a much lower death rate from the virus than the outside population in the summer of 2020 when Newsom was contemplating the first set of prisoner releases. He was in charge of tracking the numbers and analyzing them so he informed his superiors that the numbers didn't show an increased risk of remaining in prison, but they simply shrugged it off. "We were expecting Doom's Day inside the prison population," Eckenrod told us. "And we told the public that's why we released so many prisoners. But it was a lie. You were more likely to die as a released inmate into the community. We were increasing their risk by releasing them."[136] Since 2020, the California Department of Corrections and Rehabilitation has reported 95,574 COVID-19 cases with 263 deaths, or a .275% death rate of those who contracted COVID and were not released while having it. The current U.S. Centers for Disease death rate is 1.16% for the entire United States as of the first week in December 2024, meaning that released California prisoners are nearly 400% more likely to die from COVID after being released from prison and residing in the United States.[137]

Asked for a comment, Newsom's office referred me to the CDCR, which disputed Eckenrod's assertions. Albert Lundeen, a CDCR spokesman, argued without providing proof that its "actions to reduce the prison populations saved lives, especially for populations at risk of COVID."

Newsom's administration released these prisoners with no plan, resources or ability to manage the prison population's transition back into the community, Eckenrod added. A series of criminal reform measures, including Proposition 47, which lowers felonies to misdemeanors as long as thieves steal less than $950 in goods, are coddling criminals and have led to spikes in violent and nonviolent crime alike. They're also shunting the burden of housing the state's criminals onto municipal jails. The curtailed incarcerations have simply become pit stops in the life of criminals—and "catch-and-release" policies governing the detention of illegal immigrations also turn deportation into a merry-go-round.[138]

Riverside County District Attorney Michael Hestin put it starkly: "Our system of justice has become a literal revolving door."[139] He lays the blame squarely on the state's shift from imprisonment to rehabilitation over the last decade.

Newsom remains committed to prisoner rehabilitation even though the state wasn't tracking recent recidivism rates until this year when a CalMatters investigation faulted the state for failing to do so.[140] Newsom also continues moving forward with plans to turn San Quentin prison into a rehabilitation center. Between fiscal years 2013–2014 and 2018–2019, the state allocated $1.6 billion to prisoner rehabilitation, yet it can't say whether the programs curbed ex-cons' criminal activity. It's a rather disturbing omission considering that tens of thousands of California felons have been rearrested after serving a fraction of their sentences during the past decade. A spokeswoman for the California Department of Corrections and Rehabilitation (CDCR) wouldn't address the lag in data when contacted. Likewise, the CDCR has not explained to multiple news outlets, nor to us, why recidivism statistics from Newsom's tenure are unavailable.[141]

Are the released criminals responsible for the sharp rise in crime? No one in California knows. In 2014, California launched an ambitious program for parolees as a way to implement its criminal justice reforms. Newsom took those even further in 2023, dubbing his updated rehab program the "California Model."[142] One state rehab program known for its acronym, STOP, is ostensibly overseen by the CDCR and costs taxpayers $100 million annually, but the state has little to show for the expense. CDCR doesn't keep track of how many parolees are participating in STOP, or how much of a program a participant completes, for example. And details, including the names and addresses of the private entities providing the services, are often outdated or incomplete, *CalMatters* found.[143]

Even more alarming are California laws that allow convicted felons to provide housing and rehab for former prisoners.

Take the 2019 case of Attila Colar, an ex-con who served time for engaging in multiple elaborate schemes defrauding California after winning a state contract providing homes for parolees. He was sentenced to seventeen years in prison in October 2023 after being convicted on forty-four felonies, including conspiracy, bank fraud, wire fraud, aggravated identity theft, making a false statement to a bank, destruction of property, and witness tampering.

Colar, fifty-one, ran a company that provided housing for participants of halfway house for a STOP program aimed at helping parolees get back on their feet. But instead of helping others to rehabilitate their lives, he used his tenants' names and false identities to pocket $1 million in COVID relief money. He also allegedly physically abused residents, parolees in the program, and others with mental health disorders living on fixed incomes, according to the original indictment.

That's not where the scandal ends. Four companies rife with conflicts of interest held all STOP contracts, according to the *CalMatters* investigation. Two boasted officials who previously led the corrections department, for instance—creating a different type of revolving door in California's criminal justice system. And some vendors had eyebrow-raising arrangements with housing facilities.

For instance, some reentry home managers leased facilities from their own executives. And still others had suspended business licenses or revoked nonprofit status. Yet the CDCR follows through on little—if any—mandatory oversight of the contractors and their hundreds of subcontractors

Apparently, the "California Way" means no accountability: as the complete absence of rehabilitation tracking and oversight shows, justice rarely reigns in one-party towns or states. Still, the liberal policies that had been piling up in San Francisco and across the state for decades crossed several red lines—at times even for the city's mostly progressive residents. Many voters have finally had enough of the "California Way," but the damage has been done, and turning the situation around will take real leadership and a wholesale rejection of the progressive policies that got us here.

CHAPTER FIVE

State of Deception

I N OCTOBER 2023, ARMED Food and Drug Administration agents arrested Chinese national Jia Bei Zhu outside of a secret chemical laboratory Zhu was operating in Reedley, California.[1] Earlier in the year, the lab had been raided by local, state, and federal agents after complaints about suspicious unlicensed activity. Investigators were shocked to discover more than eight hundred biological agents at the site, many of which were potentially infectious bacteria and viral pathogens, including chlamydia, hepatitis, herpes, HIV, malaria, and possibly Ebola—none of it properly stored.[2] Thousands of dead and dying mice were found in inhumane conditions, along with various blood and tissue samples used to produce tens of thousands of COVID-19 and pregnancy testing kits.[3] One of the lab owners was a biotech company called Universal Medtech International (UMI).[4]

Frank Gaffney, who served as assistant secretary of defense under Ronald Reagan and founded the Center for Security and Policy, questioned whether the Reedley lab might have been involved in biowarfare. In an August 2023 article, Gaffney stated that "Communist Chinese appear to have covertly established a toxic waste dump and/or laboratory with the inherent capability of producing biological weapons in proximity to a key US military facility—and a lot of Americans—in central California."[5] Gaffney argued that the facility was "either an actual biowarfare lab or could rapidly be used as such." He continued: "Freshly manufactured biological agents are more lethal. And, if the lab's expensive, genetically modified mice or other means delivered such agents to a key Navy base nearby, it could be devastating to our Pacific fleet's combat capabilities." During a webinar hosted by the foreign policy interest group Committee on the Present Danger of China (CPDC) titled "Chinese Carry-Out: A CCP Biowarfare Lab in California?" Gaffney interviewed CPDC president Brian Kennedy, who observed that "what we see up in Reedley looked to me...like a high desert meth lab version of the Wuhan Institute of Virology...a knockoff...that they were going to operate in the United States."[6]

Initially there was public outcry over the government's lack of transparency and truthfulness about the biolab, but eventually the investigation uncovered Zhu's true identity—a still-at-large fugitive in Canada and "a serious fraudster."[7] In 2016, a Canadian court issued a $330 million judgment against him for the extensive theft of an American cattle company's intellectual property, which he was using to develop a workable platform to help him enter the Chinese dairy market.[8] To avoid paying one of the largest judgments ever issued in Canada, Zhu illegally fled across the US border and made his way to California where he used pseudonyms, counterfeit documents, and other tools of deception to continue his fraudulent work.[9]

For years, UMI's clandestine laboratory flew below the public's radar, but its California operations couldn't have been a secret for everyone. In 2019, shortly after Newsom became governor, his GO-Biz office (shorthand for the Office of Business and Economic Development) signed a $360,000 tax credit agreement with UMI which required the Chinese firm to file periodic reports with the state about their business operations and financial holdings.[10]

These days in California, so many Chinese criminals run fake businesses that law enforcement is constantly surprised by what they find. In 2017 when FBI and Homeland Security raided the office of the California Investment Immigration Fund in San Gabriel Valley, they uncovered a multifaceted transnational fraud scheme orchestrated by Chinese American attorney Victoria Chan.[11] For years, Chan had exploited the federal EB-5 visa program, which allows foreign nationals to obtain US residency green cards by investing at least $500,000 in American businesses that create ten full-time jobs.[12] Operating under the guise of her fake company, California

Investment Immigration Fund (CIIF), Chan amassed over $50 million from one hundred Chinese investors who used seventy-two different bank accounts to wire the money.[13] Some of the investors turned out to be criminals who'd been placed on China's 100 Most Wanted fugitive list.[14]

Victorian Chan pledged that the EB-5 funds would be expended on legitimate CIIF development projects; instead, the cash was secretly spent on personal luxuries, including million-dollar homes and high-priced vehicles for her father, Tat Chan, who played a central role in the scheme.[15] Photographs of project sites taken over several years showed no signs of construction, and no permits had ever been pulled. In many cases, cash was illegally refunded to investors who never met the program's job creation requirements. Over the course of a decade, Chan submitted around 130 fraudulent visa applications.[16]

Eventually, Chan pleaded guilty to charges of visa fraud, wire fraud, and international money laundering.[17] Authorities seized and forfeited nine of her properties that were worth a combined $30 million, and the California bar quickly disbarred her from practicing law in the state.[18] Yet somehow, despite facing a potential forty-five-year prison sentence, she was sentenced to only one day in jail.[19]

Now if this were the whole story it would be disturbing enough, but in 2015 the Chan clan was entangled in a different clandestine operation that the media never reported. This scheme began on April 13, 2015, the day after Hillary Clinton announced she was running for president. At 5:39 p.m. that day Victoria Chan sent an email to Clinton's campaign manager, John Podesta, using his faculty email address at Georgetown University, where he was a visiting law professor.[20] She wrote:

Hi John,
I represent a business association that would like to campaign for Hillary votes from Americans living abroad in China.
    Please advise how we can go about doing this?
Thank you,

Victoria Chan
Attorney at Law
Harris Law Group USA

An email this brief, direct, and informal suggests that Victoria Chan and John Podesta already knew each other. Podesta then forwarded the email to Clinton's campaign finance director, Dennis Cheng.[21] (Both of these emails are still publicly archived at WikiLeaks.com for anyone to view.)

We don't know if Podesta or Cheng ever responded to Victoria Chan's request to campaign for Hillary in China, but we do know that nearly $30,000 was eventually donated to Hillary Clinton's campaign from individuals who listed Victoria Chan's post office box address as their own. Each member of the Chan family donated the maximum of $2,700, including Tat's girlfriend Fang Zheng. But six other unidentifiable names using Victoria Chan's address also donated the maximum to Clinton.[22] These suspicious donations were never mentioned in Chan's criminal case, but they raise the question of whether Chan funneled $30,000 from her fraud scheme into Clinton's campaign and then used different names in Federal Election Commission filings to hide that she was the true source.

Even worse, Hillary's campaign also accepted donations from one of China's most wanted criminal fugitives—Jin Xu, a former communist leader from Wuhan who fled China to avoid charges there of embezzlement and bribery. Xu was still on China's most wanted list at the time Hillary's campaign accepted his donation.[23]

As a whole, California's elected officials have consistently failed to mitigate the Chinese criminal threat to the Golden State. But nobody has failed more in this regard than Governor Gavin Newsom. In September of 2022, amid concerns over Chinese land acquisition across the country, Newsom vetoed a state bill (SB 1084) that would have barred foreign governments and state-owned enterprises from "purchasing, acquiring, leasing or holding interest in California lands" and would have required the California

Department of Food and Agriculture (CDFA) to compile an annual report on foreign ownership of agricultural land, water rights, and other assets.[24] The bill was authored by Democratic Senator Melissa Hurtado, and it passed the assembly 75–0 and the senate 37–0, signifying a rare bipartisan agreement on the dangers the bill sought to prevent. It was widely expected that Newsom would support the popular bill, but in his official veto message Newsom offered this unconvincing reason for rejecting it:

> Federal law requires foreign governments to report interests in agricultural land to the United States Department of Agriculture (USDA), and USDA compiles this information annually into a public report. The additional data reporting required by this bill is beyond CDFA's purview and would create new and arduous responsibilities for the department.[25]

In a nutshell, Newsom offered two excuses, both of which were disingenuous.

The claim that it would be too "arduous" for the state of California to keep track of the data is especially bogus. In October 2023, Newsom signed a "first-in-the-nation" climate bill that would require large California corporations to disclose their "carbon footprints" and "climate-related" financial risks—a data-collection effort far more complex and expansive than tracking foreign ownership of agricultural property.[26] That same month, Newsom also signed a law that would force venture capital firms to annually disclose diversity data on "the race, disability status and sexual orientation" of employees, which would be compiled into annual reports by the government.[27] In other words, government data collection is easily funded and achieved if it's for the oppressive monitoring of Californians; meanwhile, foreigners get a pass. Moreover, if Newsom really believed that it's dangerous to let foreign governments purchase California farmland, he would be prepared to do all the "arduous" data collection needed to prevent it.

Newsom also used the excuse that the USDA already tracks foreign ownership of farmland at the national level, which should suffice. Here

Newsom is referring to the Agricultural Foreign Investment Disclosure Act (AFIDA), which requires "foreign persons who acquire, transfer, or hold interests in agricultural land to report such transactions and holdings to the Secretary of Agriculture" where they can be officially approved and archived.[28] But part of the reason the bill was brought forward in California is that the USDA has a well-documented history of failing to properly enforce AFIDA measures. According to a 2022 report by the US-China Economic and Security Review Commission, no legitimate enforcement measures are in place to track lack of reporting or false reporting. The report describes the absence of enforcement protocol as follows :

> It is unclear to what extent USDA conducts field assessments or tracks changes in land use or ownership after the initial paperwork is filed. Chinese firms may easily circumvent current reporting requirements under the Agricultural Foreign Investment Disclosure Act and could repurpose the purchased land with little concern of repercussions from USDA due to the lack of enforcement measures in place. Without the proper collection of land data, it will be increasingly difficult for the US government to monitor and consider any potential risks to national security."[29]

As one expert put it, "These corporations can set up a domestic corporation in Delaware, fill out a W9, then bypass reporting at all."[30] It's really that simple.

When it was revealed that a Delaware-registered company known as Flannery Associates spent nearly $1 billion dollars in 2023 purchasing fifty-two thousand acres of Northern California farmland—some of it near Travis Air Force Base—the author of the vetoed bill, Hurtado, held a press conference in which she stated: "Since the start of the pandemic, I have witnessed an increase in agricultural land sales purchased by private interests. The $1 billion transaction near the air force base is extremely concerning, especially since California had the ability to be proactive by passing Senate Bill (SB) 1084."[31] Hurtado went on to say that the bill "would have increased transparency on agricultural land transactions, enhanced our understanding on the present status of foreign ownership of agricultural land, and put Californians in control of their food supply chain by preventing foreign governments from purchasing agricultural land."[32]

Newsom's insufficient reasons for vetoing the bill raise the question of what else might have motivated his decision. When you consider that for many years he was the one prying open the floodgates for unvetted Chinese ownership of California property (see Chapter 2), it's reasonable to conclude that if he had signed the bill, it would have damaged some of the relationships that he'd been building in China and possibly thwarted any future plans of Chinese collaboration he had in mind.

Another possibility: dozens of California vineyards are foreign owned, several by Chinese companies. Is it possible that Newsom didn't want to cause any problems for his fellow vineyard owners by cutting off business or letting the state probe their ownership status?

For instance, Newsom owns Odette Estate Winery, which is in the historic Stag Leaps District of Napa Valley. Less than two miles away is Quixote Winery, which is owned by a subsidiary of the Chinese state-owned firm Jilin Yatai Group Company Ltd.[33] In 2008, the two wineries held an event together called "Plumpjack Quixote Winery."[34] If Newsom had signed the bill, companies like the state-owned Yatai Group could no longer purchase California wineries.

Another vineyard is owned by Penny Ching, the wife of Chinese spy Xuehua (Edward) Peng, who was busted and sentenced to prison in 2020 for acting as an agent of China's Ministry of State Security (MSS).[35] Would Newsom want to rustle those feathers?

China Oceanwide Holdings, another state-owned Chinese conglomerate, paid $41 million through a US subsidiary for a 180-acre ranch in Sonoma County to establish a winery.[36] The president and chairman of Oceanwide, Zhiqiang Lu, is a member of the Chinese People's Political Consultative Conference, a United Front group that officially advises the Chinese Communist Party (CCP).[37] Oceanwide was initially recruited to the Bay Area through Newsom's signature ChinaSF program—a clear sign that Newsom vetoed the bill because he actually wants *more* Chinese companies buying California property.[38]

Another ChinaSF recruit, Z&L properties—a China-based developer whose owner, Zhang Li, pleaded guilty in 2023 to bribing a public official and whose company paid a $1 million fine—was able to purchase the historic Richmond Ranch, which SiliconValley.com described as "3,654 acres of pristine hills, vales and fields in southeast San Jose" where people can "experience a lifestyle akin to the rural California of the 19th Century."[39] All of it was zoned for agricultural use.

As one might expect, none of these Chinese companies are listed in the USDA's AFIDA database of foreign-owned agricultural land, despite Newsom's assurance that the data is federally tracked.[40] Instead of protecting and informing the citizens of his own state by approving a unanimously bipartisan bill, Newsom chose to embolden the corrupt foreign actors working tirelessly to manipulate and defraud their way into California.

Investigative journalist Peter Schweizer has pointed out that "Newsom has a history of shielding the CCP from legitimate criticism while cultivating ties with the CCP."[41] For example, when Newsom was San Francisco mayor, the torch rally for the Beijing Olympics was planned to run through San Francisco and other parts of the Bay Area. News of the plan prompted activists upset with China's human rights abuses to organize a rally to protest the relay. But at the last minute, Newsom did a "switcheroo" and completely changed the relay route, which, as Schweizer recounts, left "thousands of protestors and supporters at one end of San Francisco while the torch passed through the other side of town."[42] At the time, the president of San Francisco's Board of Supervisors, Aaron Peskin, declared that "Gavin runs San Francisco the way the Premier of China runs his country—secrecy, lies, misinformation, lack of transparency, and manipulating the populace. He did it so China can report they had a great torch run. It's the worst kind of government—government by deceit and misinformation."[43]

In February of 2020, Congressman Jim Banks, a Republican from Indiana, sent a letter to Gavin Newsom demanding an investigation of California's Public Employee Retirement System (CalPERS) and its chief investment officer, Yu Ben Meng, for suspicious investment decisions and possible ties to the CCP.[44] In his letter, Banks wrote:

> Secretary Pompeo was correct when he said China knows that it won't get concessions from [the Trump] administration, so it has pivoted to exploiting state and local governments. Unfortunately, China found success in California. CalPERS has been funneling retired public servants' savings to companies that abuse human rights and supply the Chinese military. And it has done so at the behest of its CIO, Yu Ben Meng, a man enlisted in China's Thousand Talents Program—which has been described by the FBI as one of China's "non-traditional espionage" programs. This poses a national security risk to every region of the United States.[45]

Banks went on to explain how unusual it is for a public pension to invest in "companies [the United States has] blacklisted, that make Chinese military equipment or are responsible for technologies like Hikvision, which is the equipment that is used by the Chinese for surveillance on the Uyghur Muslim population."[46]

In response to the scandal, a former chairman of the US-China Economic and Security Review Commission posed a serious financial question: "Doesn't being sanctioned represent an asymmetric material risk to the share values and corporate reputations of these companies, and if so, are California's public employees being properly protected as investors?"[47] Overall, CalPERS has invested at least $3 billion in Chinese companies that are adversarial to the United States, and as Banks put it, "It is happening right under Gavin's nose."[48]

One of the disreputable companies CalPERS invested in is China Communication Construction Company (CCCC). In 2018, *Bloomberg* published a scathing article on CCCC that revealed countless examples of "fraudulent bidding practices, corruption, environmental violations, mistreatment of workers, national security concerns, and even a role in building Chinese military bases on reefs in disputed areas of the South China

Sea."[49] The *Bloomberg* report argued that while there are many companies that have been accused of bribery and environmental degradation as they operate abroad, "the number and scope of allegations involving CCCC set it apart."[50] None of this mattered to the state of California.

Prior to serving as CIO for CalPERS, Meng had been recruited by the Thousand Talents program to serve for three years as the director of China's State Administration of Foreign Exchange (SAFE), a regulatory bureau that functions as an administrative arm of the People's Bank of China, and thus is politically required to carry out the policies of the CCP.[51] So regardless of whether Meng was a card-carrying member of the CCP when he was overseeing SAFE, his leadership only served to sharpen the spear of CCP foreign expansion.

Ask yourself: why would the largest US public pension fund hire a high-level CCP strategist to direct their investment decisions and manage their approximately $400 billion in assets? CalPERS even made Yu Ben Meng the highest-paid state employee in California, with a salary topping $1.5 million. Was it Meng's recent work history in China that most impressed the CalPERS human resources department?

After being criticized for the fund's investments in Chinese companies, very little was done to resolve all the questions surrounding Meng's leadership until an anonymous ethics complaint was filed against him with California's Fair Political Practices Commission (FPPC) in August 2020. The complaint alleged that Meng had approved a $1 billion investment in a private equity company controlled by the Blackstone Group, a financial firm in which he was personally a shareholder. Meng's financial disclosures show that he held as much as $100,000 in Blackstone stock when he okayed the deal. Soon after the complaint was filed, Meng resigned, and the FPPC opened an investigation.[52]

Four years later, in November 2024, Meng was charged with two conflict of interest violations for his Blackstone stock purchases and fined $10,000.[53]

When a government watchdog entity with "fair practices" in its title takes four years to resolve such an issue, shouldn't that be a flashing red light that there's a systemic public accountability and disclosure problem in the state?

In early 2024, the governor and his lobbyist allies sparked a public backlash over the lobbyists' use of nondisclosure agreements (NDAs) in the final negotiations of the state's fast-food labor law, which required most fast-food restaurants to pay their employees a twenty-dollar minimum wage. The powerful Services Employees International Union (SEIU) required fast-food representatives to sign NDAs during the final dealmaking meeting that produced a rushed bill that lawmakers approved within the final days of the 2023 legislative session.

Republicans accused Newsom and the SEIU of engaging in a cover-up.

"NDAs have no business in the legislative process," GOP Assemblyman Bill Essayli said in an X.com post. "The people have a right to know when Gavin Newsom's major donor gets his Panera businesses exempted from a minimum wage bill. But NDAs between big business and labor unions shielded the negotiation process from the public." He added, "When trying to pass a bill to ban NDAs to stop this corruption, the Elections Committee today silenced me, cut my mic, and killed the bill." And he insisted, "What are big lobbyists @CalChamber trying to hide? Why won't Democrats in the Assembly stop the use of NDAs?"[54]

Just a few months later, the Democratic-controlled assembly blocked a bill that would ban the use of NDAs in the state's lawmaking process.

State Democrats' proclivity for concealment also applies to Newsom's soft-on-crime policies. In 2019, it took six unanimous rulings by the California Supreme Court to reject Newsom's repeated efforts "to keep secret the files the Governor submits in support of his requests for the Supreme Court's consent to grant clemency to twice-convicted felons."[55] If you're going to release dangerous recidivist criminals back onto the street, including dangerous violent offenders, the last thing you want is the people in the street to find out. Retired California Senior Assistant Attorney General Ron Matthias, who specialized in homicide appeals during his career, stated:

> If it were up to Newsom, the public would learn nothing more
> about those prisoners and their claimed rehabilitation, and nothing

whatsoever about the suffering they inflicted on their victims and other details of their crimes...Newsom's unrelenting efforts to keep the public in the dark have forced crime victims, the media, and prosecutors to file motions to unseal just to keep themselves and the public minimally informed about what he and (indirectly) the court are up to...Any governor who genuinely cared about transparency and open government would submit all disclosable information to the court in publicly accessible form at the outset of the clemency-approval process. Newsom's hide-the-ball tactics prove that he does not.[56]

When Newsom was mayor of San Francisco, he presided over the darkest era of government transparency in San Francisco history—thanks in part to his newly elected district attorney, Kamala Harris. In 1999, San Francisco voters overwhelmingly supported the passage of the Sunshine Ordinance, which was created to bring more transparency to local government by giving citizens better access to public records and public meetings.[57] In 2011, San Francisco's Ethics Commission convened a civil grand jury to investigate how well the Sunshine Ordinance was being followed.[58]

The result was a report titled *The Sleeping Watch Dog*, which, among other insights, revealed this extraordinary fact: from 2004 to 2010, each case where the Sunshine Ordinance Task Force confirmed that records requests had been denied in violation of the ordinance had been dismissed.[59] Not a single action was taken against any government employee who refused to comply. Kamala Harris, who was district attorney at the time, was responsible for enforcement of noncompliance. She obviously cared very little about the ethical mandate, given that her own district attorney's office had repeatedly failed to comply. As a final act of defiance, one of the last things Harris did as district attorney was violate open-government law by refusing to provide her opponent in California's attorney general election with public records requested from her campaign.[60]

Harris has a long and dirty history of hiding information from the citizens she represents. In 2021, *Forbes* dubbed Vice President Kamala Harris the least transparent politician in the nation. Harris earned this distinction for failing to provide records in response to requests under the Freedom of Information Act for payroll information from the vice president's office. This refusal to comply is remarkable, given that all federal executive agencies, all fifty states, and over eighty thousand local governments are legally required to provide payroll data. A watchdog group called Open The Books repeatedly requested this data from Vice President Harris to no avail and claims she's the only elected official in the entire country, at any level, who does not provide it.[61] Despite being denied the records, Open The Books compiled enough data from other sources to determine that by July 2024, 92 percent of her original staff were no longer employed. Such a high turnover rate is unsurprising given Harris's reputation as an alleged "soul-destroying" bully who runs a "toxic workplace."[62]

It may seem like nitpicking to condemn Harris for something as relatively insignificant as failing to release payroll data, but consider this: when Harris was California attorney general, the deputy director of community affairs in her Los Angeles office, Brandon Kiel, was arrested for his involvement with a secret fake police group known as the Masonic Fraternal Police Department.[63] Ostensibly created to protect all the Masonic grand masters in Southern California, this quasi-police cult claimed to be over three thousand years old and used fake ID cards, uniforms, and vehicles to fraudulently carry out their covert work. Kiel's father-in-law was the leader of the group and went by the name of Supreme Sovereign Grand Master David Henry X.[64] His typical attire included flamboyant top hats, gold cuffs, and Masonic aprons covered in esoteric symbols.[65]

Kiel allegedly referred to himself as the chief deputy of the Masonic Fraternal Police Department in letters he sent to police departments requesting to set up meetings.[66] A Santa Clarita Valley police officer once confronted Kiel in fake-cop mode and asked whom he worked for. Kiel gave the officer a business card from the Department of Justice (DOJ) showing that he worked out of Kamala Harris's office.[67] During an undercover operation, Kiel allegedly told a disguised detective that the California DOJ "was well aware and supportive of the Masonic Fraternal Police Department."[68] All charges against Kiel were eventually dropped, and believe it or not, within a couple of years he was hired by Realtor.com to run background checks on their employees.[69]

For Californians who lived through Harris's political rise from San Francisco district attorney to California attorney general to US senator to vice president, her arrogant lack of transparency is just business as usual. In one infamous case, while Harris was serving as San Francisco's district attorney, her office "violated defendants' rights by hiding damaging information about a police drug lab technician and ignoring demands to account for its failings."[70] The Superior Court judge issued a harsh ruling which argued that prosecutors at the "highest levels" had violated defendants' rights and failed "to fulfill their constitutional duty to tell defense attorneys about problems surrounding Deborah Madden, the now-retired technician at the heart of the cocaine-skimming scandal that led police to shut down the drug analysis section of their crime lab."[71]

When Harris took over as district attorney, San Francisco was in the midst of a scandal after the revelation that the local archdiocese had nearly a century's worth of records documenting sexual abuse complaints against more than forty former and current priests who were never prosecuted for their crimes. Responding to similar revelations in other cities, district attorney's offices began filing lawsuits against abusive priests whose sins had long been covered up, but not Kamala. As Peter Schweizer reports in *Profiles in Corruption*, "During her decade-and-a-half tenure as a chief prosecutor, Harris would *fail to prosecute a single case* of priest abuse, and her office would strangely hide vital records on abuses that had occurred despite the protests of victims group."[72]

Why would a district attorney with a background as a sex crimes prosecutor fail to investigate the biggest sex abuse scandal in the city's history? Schweizer offers a plausible reason: "According to San Francisco election financial disclosures, high-dollar donations to Harris's [district attorney] campaign began to roll in" after her competitor, Terrence Hallinan—who at the time served as district attorney—was threatening to prosecute some of the long-hidden priest abuse complaints.[73]

Victims told the *Intercept* that her treatment of their cases baffled them:

"In her seven years as district attorney, Harris's office did not proactively assist in civil cases against clergy sex abuse and ignored requests by activists and survivors to access the cache of investigative files that could have helped them secure justice."[74] Attorney Rick Simons has represented multiple victims of clergy abuse, and he claimed that Harris was notorious for refusing to respond to public records requests and that her office even refused to release records of investigations into priests who had already been tried, convicted, jailed, and released. He believes that Harris's penchant for secrecy "shows a pattern and practice and policy of ignoring the rights of children by one of the largest institutions of the city and county of San Francisco, and in the Bay Area."[75]

Joe Piscitelli, a director of the Survivors Network of Those Abused by Priests who's been repeatedly denied records, denounced the actions of Harris's district attorney's office and said, "They're full of shit. You can quote me on that. They're not protecting victims. They're protecting the [priests]."[76]

In California, the fight for government transparency is a never-ending uphill battle. Media group *CalMatters* reports that government agencies "have plenty of confidentiality tools at their disposal" to block the public's access to records: "The California Public Records Act itself has enough disclosure exceptions to fill an oil tanker."[77] This deliberate lack of disclosure can be found across the entire bureaucratic spectrum in California, from the Department of Education to the Department of Cannabis Control.[78] In 2024, the state watchdog Truth in Accounting ranked California third from last when it comes to financial transparency.[79]

Tragically, even the State Bar of California is notorious for its secrecy and opaque maneuvers. In one of the longest public record battles in state history, the bar fought for eleven years against a UCLA professor's request for demographic data about people seeking to become attorneys.[80] And recent audits have found, among other problems, that the state bar consistently hides the fact that it lacks the required reserve of money in its client security fund to compensate all the victims of dishonest California attorneys.[81] In 2023, a scandal erupted when news broke that the State Bar Association had taken no action on multiple complaints made against one of the most powerful, politically connected attorneys in California—Tom Girardi—who routinely entertained and showered lavish perks on the state investigators.[82]

For decades, Girardi had been stealing from his clients—allegedly embezzling over $18 million—without ever being held responsible.[83] Over 150 complaints rolled in before the state bar took action, and the total eventually grew to over two hundred.[84] A lawsuit filed against Girardi argued that his firm operated "the largest criminal racketeering enterprise in the history of plaintiff's law" that played out "like a tale out of a Grisham novel."[85] In August 2024, Girardi was found guilty by a jury on four counts of wire fraud related to his embezzling scheme and faces 14 years in prison. At time of writing he is still awaiting sentencing.[86]

After the guilty verdict was announced, US Attorney Martin Estrada issued a strong condemnation: "Tom Girardi built celebrity status and lured in victims by falsely portraying himself as a 'Champion of Justice'. In reality, he was a Robin-Hood-in-reverse, stealing from the needy to support a lavish, Hollywood lifestyle. Today's verdict shows that the game is up."[87] UCLA legal ethics Professor Scott Cummings further observed that the "problems revealed by the Girardi scandal are at bottom problems of the corrupting influence of wealth and power, that influence gains its scope to the fullest degree when allowed to fester under the cloak of secrecy."[88] For decades, the millions Girardi donated to politicians provided him ample cover. Gavin Newsom was a big recipient, pulling in more than $90,000 from the now-disbarred attorney.[89]

Single-party dominance in California naturally leads to a more secretive legislative process, particularly when it comes to the state budget. In 2020, auditors for the nonprofit organization Open The Books made record requests to all fifty states asking for their line-by-line vendor payments, and California was the only state that refused to provide it, forcing Open The

Books to file a lawsuit. Initially, California Controller Betty Yee claimed she was unable to locate the payments and refused to produce a single transaction out of the fifty million the state had made the previous year. In court filings, Yee even condescendingly referred to vendor payments as being of "limited public interest"—an insult to taxpayers given that these are arguably some of the state's *most* important public records. Yee also claimed that fulfilling the records request would cause an "undue burden" for her agency, even though it's a central part of the job.[90]

Forbes magazine asked the question on everyone's mind: "Are you beginning to think that the entire California state payment system is designed to hide waste, fraud, corruption and taxpayer abuse?"[91] After a decade-long legal dogfight to get the records, Open The Books accomplished "what the governor, controller, attorney general, lawmakers, a Superior Court judge, and state bureaucrats refused to do. [They] opened the books on California's line-by-line state expenditures." These transactions are now searchable at www.openthebooks.com/california-state-checkbook/.

You'd think that a governor would be alarmed and upset by the widespread lack of disclosure in his state, but of course Newsom likes to keep secrets, too. When he stopped publicly disclosing his official schedule and travel plans in early 2023, the *Sacramento Bee* published an editorial piece titled "California governor won't share his schedule. Is Newsom secretive or elitist?" Of course, the answer to this headline is that he's both.

As the *Orange County Register* put it, "No one employs the anti-transparency, limited-access strategy better than Gavin Newsom."[92] Tactics included "failing to respond to requests for comment, only communicating via email (to avoid surprises), refusing to make subject matter experts available, refusing to provide a name for a quote and slow walking or refusing to respond to public records requests as required by law."[93]

In 2022, Newsom and his staff earned widespread ridicule even in the state's mostly liberal press corps for refusing to disclose the governor's whereabouts for days until finally sharing that he was in Montana spending time with his in-laws. The choice of location venue raised eyebrows because Montana is among the twenty-two red states for which Newsom banned state-funded and state-sponsored travel, citing policies he said were discriminatory to LGBTQ+ people.

Foreign influence poses a major threat to higher education in California. No state hauls in more foreign funding for its universities, but little is publicly known about the donors.[94] The foreign gift database for the Department of Education (DOE) reveals that over the past thirty years nearly $7.4 billion dollars flowed into California's institutes of higher learning from foreign sources. That's over eight times more than what Florida received. Unfortunately, the DOE's current rules only require donations of more than $250,000 to be reported, and universities only have to provide the DOE with the name of the foreign country where the funds originated. There's no requirement to report the names of the individuals or organizations who donated. What this means is that California's universities have been flooded with more than $7 billion dollars of anonymous foreign cash—a large enough sum to dramatically impact the state's higher education system by giving unnamed foreigners some level of control.

California universities have received more foreign cash from China—$577,738,657—than from any other country. Stanford University is the biggest beneficiary, and they have repeatedly tried to stonewall disclosing the sources of the funding. A 2020 DOE investigation unearthed more than $64 million from China that Stanford concealed during the previous decade.[95] In total, Stanford has received nearly $1.6 billion in foreign gifts, with more than $132 million coming from China. It's a shame that Stanford isn't required to disclose exactly who gave all that money, especially when you consider that Stanford once hired a Chinese neuroscience researcher, Dr. Chen Song, who had worked for China's military (PLA). An FBI investigation uncovered Song's hidden PLA affiliation, and in February 2021 a grand jury indicted Dr. Song on charges of visa fraud, obstruction of justice, and destruction of documents. Without explanation, prosecutors dropped the entire case against her a few months later.[96]

California higher ed is plagued with all types of fraud. When news first broke in 2021 that fake student "bots" at California community colleges were perpetrating COVID-19 relief scams, it seemed like just another bureau-cratic failure story from the COVID era, when tricksters of all stripes were scrambling for a slice of federal aid. But a few months later a *Los Angeles Times* headline grabbed everyone's attention: "More than 65,000 fake students applied for financial aid in wide community college scam."[97]

Very soon thereafter someone with the title of interim vice chancel-lor of digital innovation and infrastructure announced that California's 116-campus community college system needed $100 million for security upgrades because analyses had determined that 20 percent of the traffic on its main web portal was "malicious and bot-related."[98] The perpetrators turned out to be anonymous cybercriminals with a sense of humor: many of them registered fake students with names like Donald Trump, Barack Obama, Carl-Carl, and the cleverly absurd ALLOFTHEABOVE.

As more layers of the scam were peeled back, an alarming picture emerged. It turned out that these hackers had likely siphoned up to $900 million each semester in financial aid and COVID relief. Part of this stag-gering sum was funneled to thousands of fake student bots, which were, in a sense, "attending" community college classes in California. The situation was so dire that a "bot-sleuthing professor" became an unexpected hero, cutting through the bureaucratic fog to quantify the problem.[99] With Cal-ifornia's Office of the Inspector General stepping in, even more disturbing details surfaced. This wasn't just a simple scam; it was a full-blown mali-cious fraud ring. Some fake accounts were reportedly being operated by victims of human trafficking who were coerced into posing as students and applying for loans.

In the face of such elaborate deception, government officials have not always been forthcoming about what really happened, who got paid, who's responsible, or how they plan on ending this threat. In January 2024, 25 percent of the state's community college applicants were still suspected fake bots.[100]

"Who walks away from $16,000 of casino chips?"

That was the question that triggered the colossal downfall of Los

Angeles City Councilman José Huizar and helped crack open an investigation into the ever-sprawling network of public corruption that's seeped into every corner of LA. Huizar, who's now serving a thirteen-year prison sentence for racketeering and tax evasion, was gambling at the Palazzo casino during a secret 2016 trip to Vegas when a casino employee recognized him and asked to confirm his identity.[101] Huizar refused and abruptly exited the casino, leaving behind a $16,000 pile of casino chips. This type of behavior from an elected official was suspicious enough that the FBI was given court approval to set up wiretaps and search Huizar's emails and texts.[102] What they discovered was alarming.

Huizar's casino chips had been supplied to him as a bribe from Chinese billionaire Wei Huang, an ambitious investor who at the time had plans to build the largest skyscraper west of the Mississippi in downtown Los Angeles.[103] For years Huang had funded Huizar's all-expense-paid trips to Las Vegas (twenty in total) that included "flights on a private jet, luxury hotel villas with private pools, tens of thousands of dollars in gambling chips, Rolls-Royce car services, expensive food and alcohol, private casino hosts, and prostitutes."[104] Huizar used false names on flight manifests to hide his tracks. Investigators found that Huang paid Huizar bribes totaling more than $1 million and fronted him $600,000 in collateral for a bank loan that Huizar used as hush money to settle a sexual harassment claim brought by a previous aid.[105]

For Huang and his company Shen Zhen World, *pay-to-play* was the only viable option for getting things done in Los Angeles. Councilman Huizar held all the key positions on committees that approved development projects, and it was his district where Huang desired to build. Huang's right-hand man, Ricky Zheng, once explained to a jury that their strategy was simple but effective: "You give, give, give until one day you have a big ask."[106]

Former LA City Administrator Miguel Santana told the *New York Times* that a scandal like this was almost inevitable. "The depth of power that a council member has around development in their own districts almost facilitates the level of corruption that took place," he said.

But Huizar wasn't just exploiting his position as representative of Council

District 14 (CD-14) in exchange for a series of favors. In a plea agreement, Huizar admitted that from 2013 to 2020 he was the leader of a criminal ring called the CD-14 Enterprise, whose members were primarily lobbyists, consultants, and other city officials. Under the guise of governance, members of the CD-14 Enterprise "raised and solicited funds from developers and their proxies with projects in CD-14 to be paid to Huizar's desired accounts and political action committees" in exchange for official acts.[107]

US Attorney Martin Estrada called it "one of the most wide-ranging and brazen public corruption cases ever uncovered in this district...Angelenos deserve better than being used for the personal enrichment of politicians grifting the system and foreign investors whose currency is corruption."[108] IRS Special Agent Tyler Hatcher said that Huizar "leveraged his position to enrich himself and his close allies in a mafia-style organization."[109]

In August 2024, the New York Times reported that over the past decade, "576 public officials in California have been convicted on federal corruption charges," including more than fifty political figures in Los Angeles and San Francisco since 2019.[110] These numbers are so shocking that it's almost as if these cities have become miniature Mafia states. Prosecutors and political analysts argue that the "heavy concentration of power at Los Angeles City Hall, the receding presence of local news media, a population that often tunes out local politics and a growing Democratic supermajority in state government have all helped insulate officeholders from damage."[111] The *New York Times* argues that "the arrival of large-scale investments from China"—which brought Chinese investors trying to navigate the state's byzantine process for political approvals—intensified the problems.[112]

When elected officials plan to run roughshod over the concerns of their own citizens, they need to hide as much damning evidence as possible. When they reach their hands into the public coffers, they would rather it be in the dark. Journalist and former press secretary Bill Moyers put it this way: "Secrecy is the freedom zealots dream of: no watchman to check the door, no accountant to check the books, no judge to check the law. The secret government has no constitution. The rules it follows are the rules it makes up."[113] In other words: It's just the California Way.

CHAPTER SIX

Bleeding the Beast

THE GRAND HAVANA ROOM in Beverly Hills was a perfect spot for Lieutenant Governor Newsom to haul in lots of cash for his governor race. At the center of the renowned members-only cigar club a large glass-walled room holds hundreds of humidor lockers made from Spanish cedar with brass nameplates that read like a who's who list of Hollywood elites.[1] Over the years deep-pocketed stars like Milton Berle, Robert De Niro, Jack Nicholson, Bruce Willis, and Danny DeVito, to name a few, would gather around the club's mahogany tables to socialize and smoke rare cigars.[2] Arnold Schwarzeneggar has been a dedicated member since the club's inception—a natural fit given his background in Hollywood and politics. When Beverly Hills proposed a law in 2019 to prohibit the sale of tobacco products, Schwarzenegger penned a letter to the city lobbying for the Grand Havana Room to be exempt. Referring to the club as a "character-defining institution" that had become his personal "home away from home," Schwarzeneggar wrote with genteel confidence that he trusted the city would "recognize the fundamental difference between elite lounges like the Grand Havana Room and convenience stores and gas stations."[3] The difference was that rubbing elbows with elite club members had become essential to the business models of many prominent executives. Well-heeled friends in high places always come in handy but especially in the Golden State, which is replete with moneyed celebrities and tech execs. The Grand Havana Room is a good place to find them.

Yet it was a relatively unknown lawyer named Edgar Sargsyan who decided to organize a 2016 fundraiser at the Grand Havana for New-som's campaign for governor. Sargsyan was an Armenian businessman and recently licensed California attorney who liked to mingle at the club with Los Angeles's upper crust, which is where he first befriended Arnold Schwarzeneggar in 2014. The pair were known for buying each other expensive luxury gifts. Once, after purchasing Schwarzeneggar a $1,500 glass of Macallan 25 scotch and literally giving him the ring off his finger, Sargsyan was gifted a handcrafted watch made from the metal of an Austrian tank and a ring emblazoned with the official California seal.[4]

Sargsyan had also forged relationships with other politicians like Kevin de León, and even Barack Obama, who made a cameo appearance at New-som's fundraiser.[5] As expected, the Grand Havana event was a success. Sargsyan and his entourage of friends—which included several members of law enforcement—partied with Gavin Newsom, and the aspiring governor hauled in hefty campaign funds.[6] What everyone failed to realize (or chose to overlook) was that Sargsyan was living a double life as a world-class fraudster, and that all his newfound wealth and success came directly from his involvement in organized crime. To fully understand how a guy like Sargsyan came to be throwing a ritzy fundraiser for a California campaign for governor, we need to look back twenty years to when he first made his way to the West Coast.

According to media reports, when Edgar Sargsyan arrived in California he was broke and jobless and sleeping in his car behind a Del Taco in Glendale. Despite having a law degree from a university in his home country of Armenia, the twenty-three-year-old spoke no English, so he took a job as a "capper" in the Armenian community that required him to haul in LA clients for Armenian attorneys in exchange for a finder's fee. During this time Sargsyan met a crooked lawyer who trained him in the clever arts of fraud and exploitation of local bureaucracy.[7] Before long Sargsyan was running a sizable identity-theft mill straight out of his apartment that brought in a fortune from credit card fraud alone. In one scheme, young Edgar purchased names and social security numbers from international student-exchange programs and secretly built up the students' credit ratings, then took out loans and racked up large charges in their names.[8] The truth is, Sargsyan had become a midlevel California con man who preyed upon his own ethnic community. All of that would change the day he became a US citizen.

To celebrate the occasion, Sargsyan threw a party at The Boulevard restaurant in Beverly Hills, where a friend introduced him to Lev Aslan Dermen, the alleged boss of the Armenian Mafia in Los Angeles whose nickname was The Lion.[9] Over the years, Dermen's illicit endeavors brought in loads of money, and he was often seen rolling through the streets of Los Angeles in his armored SUV with an entourage of black-clad bodyguards, many of whom were off-duty LAPD officers.[10] Despite past run-ins with every level of law enforcement, Dermen had navigated the gauntlet unscathed, a remarkable feat that he used to help shroud himself in an aura of invulnerability.[11]

The Lion was always heavy with cash, so he bought a mansion in Bel Air down the street from Beyoncé, an office in Beverly Hills, and luxurious waterfront villas in Istanbul, Turkey. He was known to have a strong affinity for Bugattis, Lamborghinis, mega yachts, and private jets. Some claim that Dermen had a lethal one-of-a-kind gold ring that he could use to prick skin and inject poison during a handshake.[12] Clearly, Sargsyan was impressed by the Lion. In less than a month he started dabbling in Dermen's underworld empire, and the big bucks started rolling in.[13]

Dermen owned a vast network of gas stations that he used as a business front to hide his true moneymaking operation: biofuel fraud on a mind-boggling scale involving illicit actors on several continents.[14] Dermen's biggest scheme was a partnership he formed with a polygamist Mormon in Utah named Jacob Kingston. The unlikely pair hailed from opposite worlds, but they had one thing in common: a well-honed talent for plundering the public coffers through fraud and manipulation. Kingston and his family operated on the outskirts of Salt Lake City where they lived an isolated life with strict social rules, but over the years they started to act like a quasi-corporation controlling a web of companies that have been investigated for crimes ranging from tax evasion, welfare fraud, and labor law abuse. According to prosecutors, Kingston and his clan had been running these gambits for so long that they coined an official term for it: "bleeding the beast."[15]

Dermen and Kingston devised an elaborate plan to defraud the US government by claiming tax credits for biofuel that did not exist. Using a byzantine network of international shell companies and reams of forged documents, together, according to according to the Department of Justice (DOJ), they "shipped millions of gallons of biodiesel within the US and from the US to foreign countries and back again to create the appearance that qualifying renewable fuel was being produced and sold. They also doctored production and transportation records to substantiate...fraudulent claims for more than $1 billion in...renewable tax credits."[16]

Over $100 million of their illicit proceeds were sent to companies in Turkey, where they also met with President Erdogan.[17] In one stunt, they rotated barge loads of falsely labeled biofuel in a circle pattern between ports in Texas and Louisiana, which scored them tax credits on the same load more than a dozen times.[18]

Sargsyan's primary role in the biofuel scheme was to launder Dermen's money through California real estate, which sometimes involved showing up at a gas station with $500,000 in cash and buying it on the spot. Within two years he'd raked in more than $10 million from these deals, which he spent on a Beverly Hills penthouse, a Sherman Oaks mansion, and a private jet. He invested half a million dollars in a pornography company and sunk $150,000 into a Sharon Stone movie. Sargsyan also paid for expensive cosmetic hair surgery and porcelain veneers for his teeth, which likely served him well when he finally decided to become a lawyer—the gangster way, of course—by paying a smart attorney a lot of cash to take the bar exam in his name.[19] For $140,000, Sargsyan became a fake Beverly Hills lawyer, complete with a phony law office with polished hardwood desks and framed photos of himself shaking hands with politicians like Barack Obama, Bill Clinton, and Jerry Brown.[20]

This is the same office where Gavin Newsom met with Sargsyan for his own friendly photo on the day of the cigar lounge fundraiser. In it, Sargsyan points to the wall, insinuating that after Newsom gets elected, his framed photo will join the others. The visit must have been important, because according to *Los Angeles Magazine*, "Newsom's convoy shut down South Rodeo Drive for the visit when he stopped by the Pillar Law Group—the law firm from which Sargsyan ran an identity theft and credit card fraud ring—to have lunch in 2016. At the time, Sargsyan was presenting himself as an attorney to the then-lieutenant governor."[21] After the photo op, the pair headed over to the Grand Havana Room where Sargsyan had organized the Newsom campaign event.[22] Sargsyan texted a recap to his friend (whom we later learn was a dirty FBI agent), writing, "We had lunch and talked about everything, including Levon."[23]

At this point, the bogus lawyer must have felt like all the hustling and the swindling were finally paying off. He had somehow managed to fake his way into California's upper echelon. But things quickly went south for Sargsyan when he did the unthinkable and double-crossed the Lion by siphoning off millions from the biofuel scam and stealing one of his jets.[24] When Sargsyan learned that Dermen had uncovered his transgressions, he was convinced he would soon be a dead man, so he ran to the Feds and started talking.[25]

When all the dust had cleared, Lev Dermen was found guilty by a jury of multiple counts of fraud and money laundering and sentenced to forty years in prison. Jacob Kingston of Utah was sentenced to eighteen years, and both men were forced to pay hundreds of thousands in restitution. The IRS declared their crimes an "unprecedented fraud against the United States and its citizens and is one of the most egregious examples of tax fraud in US history."[26] But as Kingston's own lawyer admitted, it was really a "simple fraud. The government is just writing these million-dollar checks, $5 million checks, $20 million checks, just because you gave them some paperwork that shows maybe you made biodiesel."[27] The message was clear that large, clueless, unmotivated bureaucracies with out-of-date technology and poorly designed programs are sitting ducks for the underworld masterminds who, if left unchecked, will continue to bleed California's wealth and resources.

After their investigation the DOJ noted that "throughout the scheme,

Dermen falsely assured Jacob Kingston that Kingston and his family would be protected by Dermen's 'umbrella' of corrupt law enforcement and immune from criminal prosecution."[28] This umbrella consisted of three dirty cops: Felix Cisneros, a Department of Homeland Security special agent; Babak Broumand, an FBI special agent; and John Balian, a Glendale narcotics officer whom Sargsyan bribed with black market cannabis that Balian sold through his daughter's dispensary.[29] This is the same crooked trio that was seen partying with Gavin Newsom at Sargsyan's cigar lounge fundraiser.[30] All three are now in prison. The FBI agent, Broumand (whom Sargsyan once used to obtain liquid Demerol for a Qatari prince), was sentenced to six years for accepting $150,000 in bribes from Sargsyan in exchange for sensitive FBI data that benefited the criminal ring.[31] In a creative attempt to hide the bribes, Broumand funneled the cash into a lice-removal hair salon called Love Bugs LLC that was owned by his wife, Mailana Mavromatis, a licensed attorney. Despite being charged with a felony, Mavromatis has not been disbarred.

So what happened to Sargsyan, the figure at the center of this whole fiasco? He got the lightest sentence of all: six months in prison for two counts of bribery. Such a weak punishment for a deeply entwined member of the Armenian Mafia raises questions about whether Sargsyan's relationship with Gavin Newsom may have helped his cause. In addition to the cigar-lounge fundraisers, California campaign records show that Sargsyan and his have wife donated a combined $60,000 to Newsom campaigns. Sargsyan also donated $15,000 to Newsom anonymously through a company called ARCA Capital.[32] When news of the donations broke, a spokesperson for Newsom's campaign said the governor had donated all of Sargsyan's donations to a charity. However, a review of California's campaign finance database shows that Newsom's campaign refunded $15,000 directly back to Sargsyan, and there is no clear indication that Gavin has donated the remaining $60,000 to charity.

When newspapers in Belize reported that their minister of security, John Saldivar, had also received a substantial $50,000 campaign donation from Lev Dermen, the reaction was much different. Saldivar had been accused of taking bribes from Dermen, but never charged, and when he resigned from office he swore that he'd only accepted campaign donations and nothing else.[33] Nevertheless, in 2022 the US State Department banned Saldivar and his family from traveling to the United States because of his alleged involvement in "significant corruption."[34] Meanwhile, Newsom, who also took a substantial amount of Dermen's dirty money via Sargsyan, gets a pass.

Most of the people defrauded by Sargysan were other Armenian Americans who lived in and around Los Angeles. This isn't surprising, given that the highest concentration of Armenian Americans in the country live in an area stretching from West Hollywood to Pasadena that's been federally mapped as the 30th congressional voting district.[35] For the past three decades, any politician running to represent this district in Congress must win over the support, and more importantly the votes, of Armenian Americans. Since 2000, the district has been represented by Adam Schiff, who learned early on how to master the art of identity politics to win elections. When he ran for Congress in 2000, the city of Glendale had been a Republican stronghold for decades. But in this election the tides dramatically turned, in part because Schiff's Republican opponent, James Rogan, was widely targeted for defeat by Democrats due to his prominent role in the Senate trial to impeach Bill Clinton. Some have tried to chalk up Schiff's victory solely to this backlash, but it really boiled down to who was a better friend to Armenian American voters.[36]

At one point in the race, the two candidates were playing 140 ads per day on the Armenian cable channels.[37] Rogan's costly mistake was working a last-minute deal that allowed a bill to be removed from the House floor that would have officially recognized the Armenian genocide.[38] Scholars who have studied this incident claim that, in response, "the Armenian American community in southern California expressed their anger with the Republican Party by voting for Adam Schiff, and sending a strong message that there were consequences for political backroom deals."[39] Schiff had already passed a California bill that officially recognized the hundred-year-old event as genocide, out of frustration that the US government had refused to do so at the federal level, and he had utilized state funds to finance a documentary on the Armenian genocide. In the end, Schiff's victory made it clear that the Armenian community was no longer going to support a candidate in their district who didn't crusade for official recognition of an Armenian genocide. Since then, Congress has passed resolutions recognizing the Armenian Genocide (2019) and President Joe Biden issued a statement in 2021 formally acknowledging the events of 1915 as genocide.[40]

During the 1990s, leading up to Schiff's 2000 congressional win, the *Los Angeles Times* and other California media consistently reported on the rise of Armenian gangs in Schiff's voting district. These criminal groups have committed numerous violent crimes such as drug trafficking, gunrunning, kidnappings, drive-by shootings, bombings, murder, extortion, auto theft, vandalism, and so forth. Armenian gangsters also have been known for their prowess in fraud and complex financial crime. In 2001, an FBI special agent in Los Angeles said that "Armenian organized crime syndicates are flourishing in the county and focusing their efforts on lucrative white-collar crime. In particular, these syndicates are heavily involved in identity theft and various types of related immigration, insurance, medical and credit card fraud."[41]

Racketeering was another growing problem.[42] Sargeant Steve Voors of the Los Angeles County Sheriff's Major Crimes Bureau declared it "one of the fastest-growing organized crime problems in California."[43] In 2001, there were already more than 450 known Armenian American organized crime members and associates. The problem was so bad that cities like Glendale began holding public gatherings to work on "conflict resolution" related to Armenian gang activity.[44]

In 1999, Armenian gangsters defrauded nearly $1 Billion from California's Medi-Cal system, "making it one of the largest frauds against a state in American history." The pilfered cash was, astonishingly, more than double the annual $450 million budget of the entire Republic of Armenia at that time.[45] The FBI alleged "massive criminal activity by storefront businesses that sent millions of dollars in phony claims to the state medical poverty program for crutches, adult diapers, prescriptions and other supplies and services." These fake medical supply stores proliferated so fast that they became "as numerous as hamburger joints and fried chicken emporiums," with most of the fraud taking place in Armenian neighborhoods in Schiff's district.[46]

The *Los Angeles Times* reported that Schiff had previously received a complaint from local chamber of commerce members who were concerned that eight new unneeded medical supply stores "sprang up within a year," but it is unclear whether Schiff took any action.[47]

In 2005, a House bill came to the floor that would have expanded the role of the federal government in fighting gang violence by upping mandatory sentences and creating an anti-racketeering statute similar to the one used against Mafia dons to prosecute criminal street gangs."[48] One might assume this would be a no-brainer vote of support from Schiff, who knew better than anyone that his political operations were headquartered in a hot spot of Armenian organized crime. But Schiff voted no on the bill, claiming, without evidence, that it would just sweep more juveniles into prison.

In 2010, a "vast network of Armenian gangsters" headquartered in Schiff's district was arrested for defrauding Medicare on a massive scale by creating hundreds of phantom health-care clinics all across the country where they used stolen identities to create fake bills for patient care that was never administered. The criminal enterprise raked in $163 million before being caught, making it the largest Medicare scam of all time. Over seventy Armenian mobsters were nabbed.[49]

US Attorney Preet Bharara described the sophisticated criminal network as "a veritable fraud franchise" that "puts the traditional Mafia to shame."[50] The FBI noted "the diabolical beauty of the Medicare fraud scheme...was that it was completely notional...the whole doctor-patient interaction was a mirage...but the money was real, while it lasted."[51]

We know the money was real because one of the gang leaders, Pogos Satamyan, donated $10,000 of the illicitly gained funds to the Democratic Congressional Campaign Committee (DCCC) just a few months before he was arrested. Despite calls for the donation to be returned to the Medicare program, the DCCC kept the dirty money.[52]

A year later, Schiff introduced legislation to modify the standards for Medicare fraud investigations, but not in the way you might think.[53] Given that he represented a district that was the hub of the greatest Medicare fraud in history, one would assume that Schiff would have requested more comprehensive audits to help prevent and punish Medicare fraud. Instead, his proposed bill sought to ease the burden on hospitals that were being audited for Medicare fraud by limiting the number of documentation requests that investigators could make. The bill never passed, but Schiff had made it clear that he was willing to leave the door open for fraudsters, even if it meant endangering his own constituents.[54]

Keep in mind that Schiff knew how to play identity politics the "California Way"—by promising key constituent groups what they wanted, even if he couldn't really deliver. During his political career Schiff passed two bills that gave California survivors of the Armenian genocide the right to bring lawsuits against insurance companies for unrecovered insurance claims for the years 1915 to 1923, the period during which the Armenian diaspora contends that genocide was committed against them by the Ottoman Empire.[55] When a federal court struck down one of the laws in 2009, claiming that it "amounted to unconstitutional meddling in US foreign policy," Schiff was angry and declared that the ruling was just "another injury to victims of genocide."[56]

It's been disputed whether these bills were constitutional or not, but what's clear is that the ensuing legal settlements filed to recover the claims have been fraught with mismanagement, corruption, and fraud. In March of 2022, a *Los Angeles Times* investigation revealed that over the years since Schiff passed the legislation that established the right of Armenian genocide survivors to bring lawsuits, only 8 percent of claims submitted worldwide by Armenians had been approved in the largest $17.5 million lawsuit brought against French Insurance company AXA:

> Armenians who stepped forward to collect on ancestors' policies in the settlement with the French insurer had their claims rejected at an astonishing rate of 92 percent, court records show. Applicants were

denied despite offering convincing evidence such as century-old insurance records, birth certificates, ship manifests, hand-drawn family trees and copies of heirloom Bibles.

"It was for us blood money—blood of the people killed in the genocide," said Samuel Shnorhokian, a retired French businessman who served on a court-approved settlement board and has tried for years to persuade the FBI and other agencies to investigate. "We never thought there would be misappropriation of funds."[57]

In addition to funneling money to fake and nonexistent charities, some of the AXA settlement money was used by one attorney, Vartkes Yeghiayan, to pay his daughter's law school tuition.[58] Two unidentifiable men who never applied for settlement compensation—one in Iraq and one in Syria—each received around $500,000.[59] And $750,000 that was supposed to be diverted to Armenian religious organizations never arrived.[60] Inexplicably, $100,000 was transferred to the Vatican Bank in Rome.[61] Fingers were pointed and lawsuits were filed between many of the lawyers and administrators who worked on the claims, each accusing the other of wrongdoing.

Some of the Armenian attorneys involved with the settlements have been investigated by the California Bar and two had their licenses suspended. Many of them and their family members have donated to Schiff's campaigns. Most famous of these is Mark Geragos, a defense attorney who has represented notorious clients such as Michael Jackson, Jussie Smollett, Colin Kaepernick, Winona Ryder, and Michael Avenatti.[62] In 2024, Hunter Biden became his newest celebrity client. Geragos rose to prominence after he represented Susan McDougal in the Whitewater scandal and is arguably the best-known Armenian lawyer in America.[63] Geragos was also Lev Dermen's longtime personal attorney, and had successfully defended him against past charges of fraud and assaulting a cop.[64]

In 2001, Geragos signed on to help handle the Armenian genocide insurance litigation amid skepticism that claims from ninety years ago could succeed. The lawsuits eventually hauled in $37.7 million—a huge windfall for the lawyers, but not so much for the clients. As pointed out earlier in this chapter, only a small percentage of the settlement money ever made it to family survivors. Despite this unfortunate fact, in a 2017 interview, Geragos said that out of all his legal achievements, he was most proud of his work on the Armenian genocide settlements.[65]

In 2022, the LA Times did a deep dive into the problems plaguing the genocide settlements and reported, among other things, that Geragos transferred $450,000 of the settlement funds—part of the $3 million earmarked "to advance the interests of the Armenian community"—to an Armenian Apostolic Church diocese in Glendale where he'd served as general counsel for over twenty years. Geragos later brought a defamation lawsuit against the newspaper accusing it of "conducting a broadside fishing expedition… trying to see what dirt, if any, they could find on him." In early 2024, the judge dismissed his lawsuit and ordered Geragos to pay the *LA Times* $218,000 in legal fees. Two years earlier the California bar had announced that Geragos and his law partner Brian Kabateck (another big Schiff donor) were under investigation for their mishandling of the settlement funds.[66] The status of that investigation is unclear.

Geragos was also a longtime board member at Armenia Fund, a transnational charitable organization established by Armenian presidential decree in 1992 to serve the humanitarian needs of the Republic of Armenia and help its citizens better connect with the global Armenian diaspora.[67] Geragos frequently hosted galas and presided over fundraising telethons in Los Angeles aimed at raising money for the fund from Armenian Americans in California.[68] He was known for assuring donors their money was not being misused by claiming standard audits had been performed and insisting that he had seen the results of the funded projects firsthand.[69] But critics have argued that the Armenia Fund "has a long history of corruption, criminality, and even abetting military affairs."[70]

For instance, according to an investigation by The National Interest, in 2013 money raised from the annual Armenian Fund telethon was misused to purchase luxury vehicles and pay off personal loans for members of a separatist regime in Karabakh. The investigation also claimed that in 2007 some of the cash raised by the Armenia Fund was used to construct a windsurfing resort on the beaches of Lake Sevan for the wife of a former Armenian president.[71] Yet somehow, none of these dubious activities slowed Adam Schiff's support of the scandal-ridden group.

Throughout his political career Schiff has publicly endorsed the Armenia Fund and held meetings with its leaders and helped raise millions of dollars for its projects. During the 2017 annual telethon, Schiff even released a personal video encouraging Armenian Americans in California to donate to the fund. Tragically, those who took Schiff's advice were in effect swindled, because a year later the Armenia Fund director, Ara Vardanyan, was arrested and charged with embezzling approximately $41,000 from the fund to feed his online gambling addiction, and for creating and signing fraudulent furniture contracts with secondary schools so he could pocket the money.[72] And the person overseeing the Armenia Fund's finances, Gagik Khachatryan—known for turning a blind eye to corruption while serving as head of state revenues for the Armenian government—had his $60 million Los Angeles mansion confiscated in 2024 by US prosecutors who claimed it was purchased with bribe money.[73] It has been alleged that roughly half of the Armenian government's military expenses for the 2020 Nagorno-Karabakh Conflict came from the Armenia Fund, which, if true, should disqualify the group from tax-exempt status in the United States.[74]

One of the Armenia Fund's biggest annual donors was the Lion himself, Lev Dermen.[75] Another megadonor was Lev's brother, Grigor Termendjian, who was also charged in 2023 with money laundering and conspiring to defraud the IRS by concealing $38 million of taxable cash.[76] Are we supposed to believe that Geragos and Schiff were completely unaware that they were cheerleaders for a disreputable operation?

Former Beverly Hills lawyer Berj Boyajian founded and incorporated the Armenia Fund in California and for years served alongside Geragos as president of the fund. He was also appointed to the Armenian Insurance Settlement Board to evaluate claims, and for more than a decade he helped divvy out settlement payments around the globe. As it turns out, Boyajian signed and endorsed over $300,000 worth of checks meant for heirs of genocide victims and deposited them into his law firm's bank account.[77]

He also transferred $150,000 to an LA jeweler in the form of a bridge loan (which Boyajian claims was paid back) to procure a diamond for his good friend (and now disbarred attorney) Tom Girardi, who wanted to give his young wife, Erika, a new sparkly ring.[78] He even endorsed a $24,000 check made out to the wife of his best friend, former state legislator Walter Karabian. Eventually, Boyajian pleaded no contest to a felony and a misdemeanor charge, and is no longer eligible to practice law in California.[79] It's worth asking how Boyajian ever got appointed to either of these groups.

Another lesser-known Armenian lawyer involved in the settlement controversies was Arthur Charchian of Glendale. He was later convicted in a different case and pleaded guilty to laundering half a million dollars through his client trust accounts with twenty coconspirators who used fake Republic of Armenia passports to open bank accounts and hide the millions it stole from the IRS. Soon after, Charchian was investigated by the California bar and banned from practicing law in California.[80] At the time he was arrested, Charchian had been running a website called wildfireclaims.com that purported to represent victims who brought lawsuits for wildfire damage.[81]

Charchian also had political connections. As former president of the political group Southern California Armenian Democrats (SCAD), Charchian was an ally of Schiff and Newsom, with SCAD holding events and offering endorsements for both during his tenure.[82] In 2014 Schiff attended a Christmas Ball at an Armenian church where he presented Charchian an award for his professional accomplishments as an Armenian American.[83] Charchian had also been appointed chairman of the Los Angeles Design Review Board and a member of the state's Physician Assistant Board, where he served until his conviction.[84] Shortly after, an LA Times opinion piece raised an astute question: "Does this current revelation into Charchian's willingness to break the law not bring into question any decision in which he participated during his term on the Design Review Board?"[85] Despite his criminal background and sketchy ethics, the state of California continues to approve Charchian's license to own a property that houses multiple cannabis companies controlled by another controversial Armenian businessman—Garib Karapetyan, aka the Pot King of Sacramento.[86] At a 2016 Armenian genocide event at a Glendale museum, Charchian told BBC reporters that he had considered running for political office but decided against it because he believed that bigoted stereotypes would be used to attack him "only knowing that [his] last name ends in '-ian.'" He explained, "It's a disability that we carry as Armenians."[87]

Tragically, it was criminal behavior like Charchian's subsequent fraud that helped blow up this stereotype, to the point where recently many Armenian Americans have been unfairly discriminated against because of it. In November 2023, the Consumer Financial Protection Bureau ordered Citibank to pay $26 million in fines for discriminating against Armenian American credit card applicants between 2015 and 2021.[88] A Citi spokesperson told CNN, "Regrettably, in trying to thwart a well-documented Armenian fraud ring operating in certain parts of California, a few employees took impermissible actions" such as targeting common Armenian surnames ending in -ian and -yan for denial.[89] Some Citibank employees referred to these applicants as more likely to commit fraud or being part of the "Armenian Mafia." According to Lev Dermen's attorney Mark Geragos, the term "Armenian Mafia" is racist hyperbole, even though this is the term used by federal investigators.[90]

This chapter's focus on Armenian organized crime is not meant to further demonize or misrepresent Armenians as inherently criminal or unethical. The purpose is to highlight the way political elites and law enforcement in California have enabled and benefited from mobsters and dangerous international criminals who continue to drain taxpayer resources and distort the democratic process. The "Armenian Mafia" is just one of many crime groups that have similarly infiltrated California business and politics, such as the Chinese Triads, the Mexican cartel, Hell's Angels motorcycle gangs, and more.[91]

Andy Khawaja, a shady businessman born in Lebanon, was another big Schiff donor who helped push the Armenian genocide legitimacy campaign.

In 2018, Schiff's campaign received $136,500 from employees of Khawaja's crooked West Hollywood business, Allied Wallet Inc. According to the *Daily Beast*, prior to settling charges brought by the FTC in 2019, Allied Wallet was a lesser-known payment processing company that for years had "functioned as a sort of credit card processor for fraudsters, swindlers, and rip-off artists bilking the public out of more than $100 million. It was the go-to company for Ponzi and pyramid scheme operators, phony debt collectors, coaching and education scams, and other fraudulent activities."[92] The FTC's probe revealed that "Khawaja's company had helped pornographers, shady debt collectors and offshore gamblers access the international banking system, often by using dummy foreign corporations and fake websites to disguise the underlying business."[93] In one fraudulent scheme, Allied Wallet helped a phone-sex business catering to rape fantasies and diaper fetishes funnel their transactions through a fake home-cleaning company to avoid scrutiny by credit card companies.[94] Internal documents obtained by the AP show that even Allied Wallet's own staff "deemed the underlying business activities to be 'very, very illegal.' "[95]

Despite Andy Khawaja's sketchy background, on June 26, 2018, Democratic Senator Chuck Schumer of New York inexplicably appointed him to the US Commission on International Religious Freedom (USCIRF).[96] As the *Epoch Times* noted, "There is nothing in Khawaja's USCIRF biography that connects him with specific religious institutions or international religious advocacy groups."[97] In less than a year on the job, Khawaja used his position at USCIRF to coauthor an exclusive article with publisher Harut Sassounian of the *California Courier* titled *"Remembering Genocide, Preventing Disaster."*[98] The article sought to "underscore the urgency of drawing upon the lessons of the Armenian Genocide in order to help prevent continued atrocities."[99] Sassounian, who owns the *Courier*, is a friend of Adam Schiff's and was the person responsible for getting Schiff to nominate the pope for the 2016 Nobel Peace Prize.[100] The same month he published the article, Khawaja and Allied Wallet were forced by the Federal Trade Commission to pay a $110 million judgment for knowingly processing fraudulent transactions.[101]

In December 2019, Khawaja was fired from his USCIRF position after he was indicted with seven others affiliated with Allied Wallet for helping orchestrate "a conspiracy to channel millions of dollars in illegal campaign contributions" from a foreign entity to several 2016 political campaigns, including Hillary Clinton's and Donald Trump's.[102] In addition to Khawaja, three other individuals associated with the fraud scheme—including Khawaja's Latvian model girlfriend and a now disbarred Armenian attorney from Glendale—illicitly funneled over $35,000 in straw donations to Schiff's 2016 political campaign. All the money used to run this scheme ultimately came from Lebanese lobbyist George Nader, a convicted pedophile and child sex trafficker who many believe is a foreign spy.[103] For anyone concerned about the threat of foreign interference in US elections, consider this revelation from the DOJ: "Nader and Khawaja further concealed the scheme by surreptitiously communicating through an encrypted messaging system with coded language about the transfer of funds and their hosting of and attendance at fundraising and campaign-related events."[104] Khawaja was charged with "two counts of conspiracy, three counts of making conduit contributions, three counts of causing excessive contributions, thirteen counts of making false statements, thirteen counts of causing false records to be filed, and one count of obstruction of a federal grand jury investigation."[105]

Khawaja's associate, Glendale attorney Rudy Dekermenjian, pleaded guilty in 2020 to excessive, conduit contributions totaling $50,000 into US election campaigns.[106] The money was illegally funneled from Khawaja (with 5,000 ending up in Schiff's campaign).[107] On the same day, Dekermenjian also pleaded guilty in a separate case for "defrauding a bank into processing more than $5 million in credit and debit card payments for a student loan debit relief merchant that had previously been terminated by the bank's risk department and his attempt to obstruct a federal grand jury proceeding."[108] Previously he had worked with the Armenian National Committee of America (ACNA) and formerly clerked with Judge Dickran Tevrizian, who served as mediator in several of the genocide insurance settlements.[109] Dekermenjian is perhaps most famous for flying Lindsay Lohan in his private jet to one of her DUI court hearings to make certain she would be on time.[110]

Khawaja was a friend of Gavin Newsom's as well. In December 2016, Newsom received $56,000 in campaign contributions from Allied Wallet, but unlike the donations to Schiff and others, for Newsom there's no name listed in the employer section of his campaign data for the contribution; instead, the company name "Allied Wallet" is listed in the section where the contributor's name should go.[111] Perhaps this has confused journalists who've failed to report on the questionable donation.

It's worth noting that despite being propped up politically by the Armenian voters in his district, Adam Schiff has chosen to live over 2,600 miles away from them in Potomac, Maryland, one of the richest cities in the country.[112] Schiff may own a small condo in Burbank, but photos from social media show that he actually lives and raises his family in a 3,500-square-foot Maryland home; and Schiff designated this Maryland home as his primary residence for tax purposes as late as 2009, and multiple times (2009, 2010, 2011 and 2013) claimed the Maryland home as primary when refinancing his mortgage.[113] In April 2024, California Congressman Chris Bish issued a report claiming that Schiff may have also committed election fraud and voter fraud by claiming on official documents that he was a citizen of both California and Maryland.

Schiff's close connections to some of the most notorious fraudsters in California history raise the question of whether he operates in the same manner as the company he keeps. Until California's political class disentangles itself from the myriad criminal groups that target the state's bloated bureaucracy as an easy beast to bleed, citizens of the Golden State will continue to be victimized. The more that Schiff and Newsom and other California politicians continue to shake hands and make deals with lords of the underworld and accept illicit money into their campaigns, the more they endanger the rest of America, as these ruthless gangsters will feed off their success to seek out politicians in other states to bribe, extort, and control.

CHAPTER SEVEN

Up in Smoke

O NCE THE EVIDENCE WAS FOUND, it was a simple open-and-shut case of gross corporate negligence. A rusty, broken metal hook caused eighty-five people to perish in the Camp Fire of 2018, the most deadly and destructive blaze in California history. Steel c-hooks support insulators, which hold thousands of pounds of high-voltage jumper conductors in position on massive electric towers. In rural areas, these enormous steel structures hold up transmission lines that crisscross the state and cluster in urban areas, then spread outward like essential veins and arteries carrying the lifeblood of civilization: light and power. In this case, all the equipment was owned by Pacific Gas and Electric (PG&E), a massive utility company that provides gas and electricity to 5.2 million homes in the northern two-thirds of California.

An investigation by state regulators found that the hook in question was nearly one hundred years old. High winds often ripped through the valley, causing constant swaying, and the metal-on-metal friction bore a groove in the hook that continued disintegrating until it snapped on November 8, 2018. What took place afterward was nothing short of apocalyptic. When the hook broke, the jumper conductor fell and struck the tower. The resulting short circuit sent sparks into the vegetation below, igniting an inferno that raced across eight miles of dry trees and vegetation, encompassing the now unfortunately named foothill town of Paradise, incinerating everything in its path. Before the fire, Paradise's history was more promising—it was home to the largest gold nugget ever found, a whopping fifty-four pounds.

The uncontrolled blaze burned through nineteen thousand buildings, 90 percent of the town's structures—fourteen thousand of which were homes. The few tree-lined exit routes became tunnels of fire full of dense, choking smoke. Frantic residents trying to flee were stuck in paralyzed lines of traffic, while propane tanks exploding around them added to the sense of panic and doom. The evacuation was further complicated because the town of Paradise is a popular retirement community in Butte County with a population that skews older with limited mobility.

Some residents who managed to escape by car said it felt like a war zone. Many ran out of gas and ditched their vehicles amid the swirling embers. Four people weren't so lucky. They got stuck in steep terrain on a ridge double-sided by canyons and were later found incinerated in their cars. The Butte County Sheriff's Office brought in family members to identify the dead through DNA samples.

Most of the charred and leveled structures were homes, but the blaze also destroyed schools, churches, restaurants, hospitals, and other small businesses. An entire town and thousands of dreams and livelihoods were utterly immolated. And the devastation was not contained to Butte County. Nearly 175 miles away, the blanket of toxic fumes was so thick and expansive that it obscured the San Francisco skyline. For two weeks, record-high levels of dangerous particulate matter choked the Bay Area. Alcatraz Island and cable cars shut down as Bay Area residents tried to flee to anywhere with better air quality—Pismo, Reno, Oregon, or Southern California.[1] A year and a half before the COVID pandemic would hit, California residents were donning surgical masks to protect themselves from the toxic pollutants spewing from the fire.

Many Paradise residents couldn't afford to leave for clearer horizons. Thousands of families whose homes were demolished were forced to squat in Walmart parking lots, church lawns, or anywhere they could set up tents. At least a thousand were still looking for housing six months later, and many property owners resorted to living in trailers on the lots that once held their homes but that now contained only ashes. When COVID hit, hundreds of people remained in these tight rudimentary living quarters, stuck with Newsom's strict stay-at-home policies. They were waiting for their restitution payouts from PG&E, which were delayed while the company's bankruptcy deal was negotiated.

It took a year and eight months of investigations by the Department of Forestry and Fire Protection (Cal Fire), the California Public Utility Commission (CPUC), and state prosecutors for PG&E to plead guilty in June 2020 to eighty-four counts of involuntary manslaughter. The utility admitted to causing the Camp Fire through reckless and criminally negligent lack of maintenance of its transmission lines.

"Our equipment started that fire," PG&E CEO and President Bill Johnson stated at a court hearing. "I wish there was some way to take back what happened or to take away the impact, the pain that those people have suffered," he said. "But I know that can't be done."[2] Sadly, the investigations proved that the Camp Fire was completely preventable. Detailed reports showed that the utility failed to maintain or replace the c-hook and never thoroughly inspected the tower. And it wasn't an isolated incident. The investigations found a pattern of inadequate inspection and maintenance of PG&E's transmission towers, which the utility's internal reports failed to document. In federal court filings, the utility acknowledged that in the late 1980s it had conducted tests of c-hooks used in connecting insulators and power lines to transmission towers but could not say whether it had followed up. However, it noted two other occasions where hooks failed in the ten years leading up to the Camp Fire.[3]

The mountain of evidence against PG&E was damning enough, but the utility's ongoing self-enrichment by executives and other employees has further infuriated wildfire victims and consumer rights groups. PG&E executives and other employees received hundreds of millions of dollars in bonuses in part for purportedly meeting safety goals during the same years preceding the fires that state regulators cited as showing chronic poor equipment inspection and maintenance practices. Executives had received the bonuses in 2015 when two people died in a different wildfire tied to its equipment. In 2019, incentive payments were sent to ten thousand employees despite angry opposition from a legal team representing wildfire victims.

Such a long and checkered history of negligence and greed creates the obvious question: where is the oversight?

Despite decades of court determinations against PG&E and guilty pleas for several wildfires, the last two governors, Gavin Newsom and Jerry Brown, and many other prominent Democrats who help run the state repeatedly blamed climate change as the deadly blaze's main culprit. While drier weather patterns no doubt made the vegetation more combustible, Cal Fire investigations found that most of the destructive blazes resulted from PG&E negligence. Consumer watchdog groups and wildfire victim advocates have also begged to differ with those blaming climate change, pointing to PG&E's executives' greed and focus on profits.

In fact, a much broader corruption problem fueled the back-to-back years of deadly wildfires that still threaten California every fall: PG&E's power and influence depend on politicians' willingness to either look the other way or come to the utility's rescue when it's in a legal or financial jam. There has been no shortage of financial and legal scandals for PG&E over the last two decades.

The state's politicians have been all too eager to bail out the utility, and it's not hard to see why. PG&E spent nearly $5 million lobbying at the federal level and $2.4 million at the state level in 2020 and 2021 alone. It spreads its largesse to key spheres of influence around the state, donating to politicians' reelection campaigns, nonprofits tied to them or their wives, and numerous galas and charities for the state's philanthropic elites.

Politicians and charities across the state readily accept the funds even though they've long known that PG&E is a bad actor. It's been more than a decade since the utility was found at fault for a "litany of failures" in the 2010 gas line explosion in San Bruno that charred an entire neighborhood, killing eight and injuring fifty-eight people.[4] Two days after that announcement, the largest utility in California was back to business as usual, sponsoring a charity baseball game near San Francisco's financial district. Ed Lee, the city's mayor at the time, threw out the first pitch.

"PG&E is a great local company who gets it," Lee remarked at the event.[5]

A year later, a 2012 audit by the CPUC found that PG&E diverted more than $100 million in funds for gas-safety operations—money collected from customers over fifteen years—and spent it for other purposes, including profit for stockholders and bonuses for executives.[6]

But the San Bruno failures pale in comparison to the statewide spate of destruction that ensued due to PG&E's negligence. A *Wall Street Journal* investigation found that from June 2014 to 2017, PG&E equipment was responsible for igniting more than 1,500 fires. That's more than one fire a day on average. In 2017 and 2018 alone, wildfires sparked by PG&E's equipment or failure to trim vegetation near its electric lines killed more than 130 people and destroyed more than 27,000 homes. In 2019, a federal judge in San Francisco castigated the utility for pumping out $4.5 billion in dividends to its shareholders while letting its tree-trimming budget wither.[7] At the time, PG&E was already under probation for its negligence in the 2010 San Bruno gas pipeline explosion. During a probation hearing, Judge William Alsup directed a federal monitor to randomly inspect its tree-trimming program.

"I'm not cutting you any slack," Alsup said.[8]

When PG&E attorneys complained that they couldn't possibly keep track of all the trees next to power lines that needed trimming, the judge offered no mercy.

"That's a problem of your own making," he said. "A lot of money went to dividends that should've gone to your trees. Get square with the people of California who depend on you to do the job safely."[9]

Judge Alsup also declared that the decision on whether PG&E violated the terms of its probation would lie with him, not the CPUC. The commission is supposed to provide state utility oversight, but so far it's proven to be too close to the utilities it supervises to hold them accountable, and for years has been plagued by its own corruption scandals. Despite the negative press, PG&E didn't become an instant political pariah. Instead, the deep-pocketed utility continued to cozy up to politicians and well-connected lobbyists, serving as a cash cow for the political class.

SCRB Strategies—a well-connected political consultancy firm that has changed its name and personnel several times in recent years and now goes by Bearstar Strategies—received more than $1.1 million from PG&E in 2018 for research and consulting.[10] The firm helped run campaigns for Newsom, Jerry Brown, Kamala Harris, and Ed Lee. Willie Brown, California's longest-serving speaker of the state assembly—and who also tapped Newsom to succeed him as San Francisco mayor—has readily acknowledged being on the PG&E influence-peddling payroll for more than a decade. He also wasn't shy about why he agreed to trade on his high-flying career in California politics to help rebuild the utility's tarnished reputation: lucrative lobbying and consulting contracts.

During PG&E's initial bankruptcy considerations in 2019, Brown told the New York Times he had recently approached Newsom with a vague message that the company paid him to deliver. He wouldn't provide details about their discussions but made no bones about what was driving his decisions to represent the utility's interests in Sacramento.

"I hope that they call me because every call generates an invoice," he told the paper.[11] Willie Brown has plenty of company. Some of the most powerful politicians in the state worked overtime to save PG&E when its very existence was hanging in the balance. In late 2019, after several years of deadly wildfire seasons, Newsom appeared to have had enough and lashed out at the massive utility.

"It took us decades to get here," Newsom said during a press conference. "Make no mistake. We will get out of this mess, and when we do, we will hold PG&E accountable to a degree they have not been held to before."[12]

Newsom had just toured the charred remains of wineries, homes, and other property ravaged by another destructive blaze, the Kincade Fire, which scorched eighty thousand acres in Northern California and was still raging at the time of the governor's remarks. A PG&E transmission tower had broken near the origin of the massive blaze.[13] Days after Newsom's comments, both the San Francisco Chronicle and the San Jose Mercury News issued blistering editorials condemning PG&E's practices, with the *Chronicle* calling on the CPUC to impose "the serious regulatory attention [the utility] should have been subject to many years ago."[14]

Newsom said decades of mismanagement and prioritizing executive bonuses and shareholder profits over the safety of PG&E's grid had led to a crisis in the state. The Kincade wildfire clobbered California's wine country during September when many grapes were still awaiting harvest. Smoke damage ruined one-third of California's wine grapes that year, and several historic wineries were destroyed or heavily damaged. All told, the state's wine grape crop came in at 3.4 million tons, making it the smallest crop since 2011. According to an analysis by Novato wine broker Turrentine Brokerage, the drop from 2018 was the equivalent of more than eighty million gallons of wine down the drain.

The fire and its enormous smoke plumes released so many toxins that the ashy air across the state burned people's eyes, and the skies turned a brownish-orange hue from the Bay Area to Los Angeles's Westside, prompting school closures as far away as Santa Monica and Malibu. But far from holding the company accountable as he had pledged, Newsom had already spearheaded a legislative bankruptcy deal that allowed the utility to continue operating, then signed those new protections into law. Working out of Newsom's gubernatorial office, a group of aides and attorneys crafted a law establishing a $21 billion insurance protection fund for PG&E. It was part of the company's reorganization plan that allowed it to continue operating. The plan, which came in the form of Assembly Bill 1054, protects utility companies from bankruptcy by helping pay for wildfire damages that exceed $1 billion of insurance coverage.

Under the plan, PG&E and other utilities would pay for eligible insurance claims on a rolling basis by pulling from a fire trust fund. All state utilities were required to make an initial contribution to that fund of $4.8 billion in 2019 and were then required to contribute $300,000 annually for the next decade. Before AB 1054, the utilities could recover all costs of such fires from their customers.[15]

The legislation was created to encourage utility companies "to invest in safety and improve safety culture to limit wildfire risks and reduce costs." In return, all utility companies in the state received financial protection. Before the passage of AB 1054, the burden was on utility companies to prove they acted responsibly. After passage of AB 1054, as long as the state provides a safety certification, utility companies are presumed to have acted responsibly. Newsom claims that no other governor in California history has done more to hold PG&E accountable and force the company to make fundamental changes. But that's not saying much, as this chapter will later demonstrate. In response to criticism, the governor's office released this statement:

> Governor Newsom has used every tool at his disposal—passing strict new safety requirements, tying PG&E executives' compensation to the utility's safety record, creating new protections for PG&E customers, demanding a public utilities commission investigation into the company, forcing PG&E's investors to pay billions for safety improvements, and establishing a mechanism to hold PG&E ultimately accountable by authorizing its dissolution and takeover if it fails to adhere to the strict new safety requirements and follow through on its commitment to compensate victims.[16]

Newsom also claimed his and other state officials' actions have resulted in "sweeping governance reforms at PG&E," including a newly constituted board of directors and "billions of additional benefits to ratepayers, victims, and the people of California, ensuring the company emerged from bankruptcy in a position to make massive upgrades necessary to deliver safe, reliable, clean electricity, and to compensate victims swiftly."[17]

After causing so much death and destruction, top-to-bottom reforms were long overdue. But the Newsom-engineered bankruptcy deal allowed PG&E to survive. It gave it new blanketed protections that failed to guarantee full compensation for victims or that ratepayers wouldn't be on the hook for the extensive and pricey new safety measures.

PG&E is a big donor to Democrats and Republicans across the state but has a particularly close relationship with the Newsoms. The company helped fund Newsom's political rise and donated generously to his wife's "gender-justice" film projects, so much so that the company itself is listed in the credits of two of Siebel Newsom's films as an associate producer. It also screened one of those documentaries in the atrium of its corporate San Francisco skyscraper in 2011 when Newsom was lieutenant governor.

Over the past two decades, Newsom and his wife have accepted a combined total of $700,000 in donations from PG&E. During Newsom's gubernatorial campaign alone, PG&E employees had cut $208,400 worth of checks. The PG&E Corporation Foundation also donated $10,000 to the PlumpJack Foundation, a charity named after Gavin Newsom and Billy Getty's wineries and led by Gavin Newsom's sister, Hilary Newsom.

Newsom's trial by wildfire would come less than forty-eight hours after he won his first campaign for governor. On November 19, 2018, California Governor Jerry Brown, with Governor-Elect Gavin Newsom in tow, toured the smoldering remains of the Camp Fire in Paradise with President Donald Trump, whom they both had repeatedly lambasted. It was ten days after the fire first began to rage, and Trump was determining how much federal disaster aid to release. The unlikely trio was appropriately solemn and cordial at a press conference after their tour.

When Trump spoke to the press, he concluded that "we have to do management," referring to improving forest management and maintenance. "A lot of things have been learned. They've been working very hard," he added. "I think you're going to see something very spectacular in the next couple of years."[18]

But Brown begged to differ, blaming the series of blazes on a combination of factors. "If we can really look at the facts, from a very open point of view, there are a lot of elements to be considered," Brown said, without mentioning the growing public anger against PG&E, the likely culprit. "It's not one thing. It's a lot of things. I think if we open our mind, and look at things, we'll get more stuff done." He added: "We'll let science determine this over a longer period of time. Right now, we're collaborating over the most immediate response, and that's very important."[19]

With federal disaster relief funds in the mix that only Trump could release, Brown was doing his best to be diplomatic. Brown had been far more definitive three months earlier, blaming the series of intense wildfires that occurred that summer directly on climate change, which he said has made deadly blazes "part of our ordinary experience."[20] In the fall of 2020, Newsom was singing off the same climate-change song sheet, arguing that several sets of wildfires showed that "this is a climate damn emergency."[21]

While more than two dozen fires raged, Newsom surveyed another fire-ravaged area in Butte County on September 11, 2020, and never even mentioned PG&E. Instead, he vowed to accelerate the state's effort to combat carbon emissions from cars and utilities.

"Mother Nature is physics, biology, and chemistry. She bats last, and she bats 1,000. That's the reality," he said. "The debate is over, around climate change. Just come to the state of California. Observe it with your own eyes."[22]

Just a month later, the Glass Fire would threaten wine country again, including Newsom's own multimillion-dollar PlumpJack Winery. Even though dozens of major fires were burning in the state at the time, officials publicly said they had made it the top priority. Newsom declined to answer questions about the status of his property and whether he or anyone on his winery's behalf lobbied to make saving his property and others nearby a priority. "I have all these things in a blind trust. I don't actively manage these things," he said. "I think it's important to have a firewall there. But in regard to empathy, I have a deep empathy for the people dealing with these things."[23]

Before it was extinguished, the Glass Fire burned over 67,484 acres and destroyed 1,555 structures. Then-Speaker Nancy Pelosi also blamed the wildfires on climate change, even as she advocated for federal "Build Back Better" infrastructure funds for her state, including prescribed burns for overly dense forests. "With more severe droughts and extreme weather and this long fire season, the climate crisis is fueling more fires that are larger, fiercer, and more destructive," she said in December 2021. "In just the last five years, California has seen eight of the ten largest fires on record...three of five of the deadliest."[24]

Shortly after his first inauguration, Newsom took a leading role in PG&E's bankruptcy negotiations, shrugging off conflict-of-interest warnings by good-government groups that deemed Newsom's decision to intervene unseemly because the utility was a big campaign donor. Newsom and his aides met with lawmakers and PG&E officials to hash out a law establishing the $21 billion fund for the massive utility as part of the company's reorganization plan, which allowed it to continue operating. Bankruptcy documents provide clues to Newsom's tight control of the process: PG&E would only support the plan if the terms were "acceptable to the governor's office."[25]

Other Newsom ties to PG&E's bankruptcy came to light after the governor's notorious French Laundry dinner when he violated his own COVID rules by dining maskless with people other than immediate household members. As soon as the French Laundry photos went public, simmering outrage over the Thanksgiving decree and Newsom's "rules for thee, but not for me" exploded in headlines across the country. Amid the media firestorm, Newsom apologized and said he regretted attending the dinner party at a restaurant (sans masks) just a few weeks after advising Californians against doing the same.[26]

The night of the infamous French Laundry dinner, medical executives and lobbyists gathered in honor of Jason Kinney's fiftieth birthday. Kinney is a lobbyist, close friend, and longtime adviser to Newsom who has made his living representing business interests in Sacramento. At the time of the dinner, Kinney and Newsom shared a keen interest in helping PG&E survive its bankruptcy. Kinney is a partner at Axiom Advisors, a top Sacramento lobbying firm with pressing business before the governor. His wide-ranging client list includes Netflix, Marathon Petroleum, Poseidon Water, Acadia Healthcare, and several marijuana companies. Kinney's firm represented a key player in the bankruptcy case—a committee of companies to whom the utility owed millions. This included small companies such as the Davey Tree Expert Company, but also big corporate and union interests like Deutsche Bank, NextEra Energy, and the IBEW 1245 union. Axiom eventually collected at least $400,000 in fees for their lobbying work for the creditors.[27]

After Newsom engineered the bankruptcy deal and it passed the state legislature, the PG&E creditors represented by Axios Advisors were paid in full. Yet when reporters started scrutinizing Kinney's role in the French Laundry dinner, Axiom denied that Kinney had played any role in the PG&E bankruptcy negotiations spearheaded by Newsom's office. Axiom also curiously scrubbed Kinney's bio from its website, removing his previous boast that he had advised Newsom for "nearly 14 years."[28]

The lobbyist at the center of the French Laundry dinner scandal apparently wanted to distance himself (and his corporate clients) from the tsunami of controversy and scorn Newsom was facing. As a veteran political hand, Kinney probably also knew that more media scrutiny of his clients and their ties to the governor would fuel yet more negative press. Newsom's role in PG&E's bankruptcy deal was already under an intense magnifying glass. Critics had slammed his decision to hire a team of New York lawyers to hash it out behind closed doors at a cost of $3 million in taxpayer dollars. (It turned out the firm, O'Melveny and Myers, had previously worked for PG&E for years.)

The Newsom administration also tapped investment bank Guggenheim Securities to assist in drafting the law at an additional $3.7 million in taxpayer expense. The bankruptcy deal instituted a $21 billion wildfire insurance fund available to all of the state's utilities that obtained a safety certification from the CPUC.[29] The bankruptcy court approved PG&E's $59 billion reorganization plan, which involved issuing new debt and equity to help pay $25.5 billion in wildfire-related claims and restitution for victims. But the Chapter 11 action did nothing to immediately prevent more PG&E-sparked fires.

Just six months after a court approved PG&E's bankruptcy in 2020, the utility's continued negligence would spark another deadly fire—this time in picturesque Shasta County. The Zogg Fire, which raced its way through the oak-covered hillsides of Igno Ono in Northern California, took the lives of Feyla McLeod, an eight-year-old girl, and her mother, Alaina. The pair were incinerated in a Ford pickup truck while trying to steer their way out of the inferno's path. Zach McLeod searched for his daughter and wife for two days. They were two of four people who died in the blaze, which burned through 56,388 acres and destroyed 204 buildings. It took a Cal Fire investigation nearly a year before it found that the fire began when a dried-up pine tree fell into a PG&E electric distribution line. A PG&E inspector had deemed the dead tree a fire hazard and designated it for removal, but the work was never done.

On the surface, the bankruptcy plan spearheaded by Newsom appeared to provide expedited restitution to victims whose homes were destroyed and family members killed. PG&E reached a $13.5 billion settlement with an estimated seventy thousand people who suffered losses and damages, and the deal allowed the utility to use equal parts cash and stock to fulfill its restitution requirements. However, most of the victims were never made whole. Their final total claims are expected to exceed $19 billion, but by the end of 2023 they had only received around 60 percent of their losses' value, and the final restitution will be much lower than expected.

"I understand, and I'm very sympathetic to the fact that people had the impression they were going to get 100%, but that was never true," Cathy Yanni, an attorney who serves as trustee of the trust, told the *Wall Street Journal*. "In bankruptcy, no one gets 100%."[30] Fire victims were the only claimants who were partially compensated with shares of company stock. PG&E's lawyers tied those payouts to the company's stock performance, which rebounded slowly after the bankruptcy, leaving many victims in the lurch for several years, unable to rebuild and still living in trailers on their burned-out properties. At the end of 2023, PG&E said it was making the final payments to victims of the fires it caused from 2015 to 2018.

But it can never truly compensate for the damage it's done to all residents across the state. The utility's reckless actions have sent ripple effects across the insurance and construction industries that are leading to far higher prices for all California consumers—even those whose property is nowhere near the fires.

In late 2022, several California insurers started pausing and drastically limiting the number of new home insurance applications they would accept.[31] Then in 2023, State Farm, the state's largest insurer, said it would stop selling new home insurance policies in California. And in January 2024, it raised customers' auto and home insurance rates by 20 percent, citing wildfire risks and soaring construction costs.[32] The increases are expected to affect five million Californians and were approved by the Department of Insurance, another agency riddled with allegations of corruption. California Insurance Commissioner Ricardo Lara faced legal action from Consumer Watchdog, which accused the commissioner of a pay-to-play scheme involving illegal campaign donations from an insurance company and Lara's order for an administrative law judge to make decisions benefitting the insurance company.

PG&E's repeated patterns of negligence and destruction wouldn't be so vile if the state's politicians simply called out the company and kept it from doling out bonuses to executives and hiking customer rates at the same time it is realizing large profits. Despite Newsom's pledge to hold PG&E accountable, the governor has repeatedly and pointedly tried to avoid reporters' questions about his role in the bankruptcy deal and why wildfire victims were not made whole.[33] But in the fall of 2023, with prices at the pump still far higher than in the rest of the country, Newsom seized on a spike in gas prices to portray petroleum suppliers as price gouging. Newsom and State Attorney General Rob Bonta sued oil companies, including BP and ExxonMobil, and their trade group, the American Petroleum Institute, over what the governor deemed a long-standing pattern of deceiving the public over risks associated with fossil fuels.

The suit, filed in San Francisco Superior Court, claimed big oil had been misleading the public for decades about its dirty energy, that its "lies" had contributed to global warming, extreme weather, wildfires, superstorms, extreme heat, drought, and flooding. Not surprisingly, Newsom also blamed oil companies for contributing to climate change while failing to hold PG&E accountable for wildfires that spewed record amounts of carbon and other toxic smoke into the air. Data shows that PG&E wildfires themselves are to blame for reversing years of progress in reducing carbon emissions in California and many other western states over the last two decades. As stated before, the CPUC has long been criticized for its close ties to industry. Initially, in 2015, the commission found that PG&E was responsible for a series of safety violations and slapped it with a $200 million fine.[34] But then, after public scrutiny started to wane in 2020, the CPUC waived the utility's obligation to pay.[35]

According to the Constitution of California, the CPUC is designed to operate independently from the governor's office. Still, several direct witnesses say the opposite is true—that Newsom maintained command and control of the utility watchdog, especially when it came to the PG&E bankruptcy. Governor Jerry Brown appointed close family friends who were former utility executives to the agency, but the CPUC's former executive director, Alice Stebbins, said that in reality the commission maintained far more independence from the governor's office under Brown than under Newsom. After serving less than two years, Stebbins was fired over allegations that she improperly hired several agency officials. She subsequently filed a whistleblower lawsuit claiming that the CPUC illegally retaliated against her for trying to investigate why $200 million was missing from CPUC books. The unaccounted-for $200 million was intended to underwrite programs for the state's blind, deaf, and poor. After a trial lasting several weeks, a jury rejected all of Stebbins' claims and upheld her dismissal.

Any shred of independence the agency maintained vanished after Newsom took office, Stebbins asserted. Newsom installed a new president, Marybel Batjer, to lead the five-member agency. Batjer previously served as a lobbyist for Caesars Entertainment Corporation in the lead-up to its merger with Eldorado, the largest in casino history. Batjer had no experience in the energy sector and was known as a friend to business who had previously advised GOP Governors Schwarzenegger (California) and Kenny Guinn (Nevada). In fact, during Schwarzenegger's time in office,

Batjer served as the administration's liaison to the Department of Corporations, which regulates financial services in the state and oversees lending operations. While serving in this government position, Batjer was named to the board of directors of the Nevada-based Bank Holdings, the parent company of Nevada Security Bank.[36] The bank bought an Orange County, California, financial institution, CNA Trust of Costa Mesa, and owns a loan production office in Northern California. Consumer Watchdog called on her to step down out of a conflict of interest, but Schwarzenegger and Batjer ignored this request.[37]

Before Newsom appointed Batjer, the commission was run by Michael Picker, who served in the post from December 2014 to 2019 and hand-picked Stebbins as his No. 2, giving her the hefty job of reforming the CPUC. Picker stepped down in 2019, retiring after almost five years on the job. Stebbins argues Picker was pushed out for trying to maintain a firewall between its actions against PG&E and other utilities and the governor's office.

"The CPUC was a party to the bankruptcy, and when you're a party to the bankruptcy, you need independence," Stebbins explained in an interview. "[Picker] and the general counsel of the CPUC were basically telling folks in the governor's office that, 'Look, we need independence—we can't do what you're telling us to do.'"[38]

The CPUC says it's "committed to transparency" on its website. Yet in 2021, when ABC10, a local Sacramento affiliate, asked for messages and emails between the CPUC and Newsom's office related to its PG&E bankruptcy bailout, the CPUC voted against providing them. ABC10 sued to receive records from both the CPUC and Newsom regarding PG&E's communications with both offices, and the news station is still locked in a legal battle to get those documents. In March 2024, the station won a partial victory when a Sacramento Superior Court judge ruled that the governor's office had to turn over meetings between Ann Patterson, Newsom's cabinet secretary, and the utility after the TV station uncovered that Patterson had spoken at PG&E's Investor Day in May 2023. Patterson appeared at the shareholder event and referred to PG&E as a "partner" in her remarks, a week after the CPUC approved a $150 million settlement for the utility's role in the Zogg fire, which killed four people and burned through 56,000 acres. PG&E was facing criminal and civil penalties in the suit accusing it of failing to remove a dead tree that led to the fire.

The CPUC laid the groundwork for the settlement, which included dismissing the criminal case, back in 2021 when PG&E managed to obtain an official state safety certificate even after being charged with additional crimes for its role in the 2020 Zogg Fire. Stebbins says she didn't want to sign the safety certification and believed she was forced to do so.[39]

"The bottom line is I was told to sign it," Stebbins told ABC10. "You will sign this. Period." "That safety certificate was probably one of the toughest things I've ever had to sign," Stebbins told us. "We had just gone through the [fire in] Paradise...everyone knew about the hook. Everyone knew that it was terrible and that it was a preventable fire."[40]

"The toughest part for me was maybe six months after the Paradise Fire, there was a [PG&E] shareholder meeting led by the new executive director, Patty Poppe," Stebbins recalled. "In the meeting, she talked about all these things—about fire safety, and she showed pictures of the fire—she was trying to get everyone's attention." Yet when Poppe opened the call for questions, the first person on the line asked when they were getting their dividend checks, according to Stebbins.[41]

"That's what [the shareholders] care about—money. PG&E is about money over safety," Stebbins said.[42] Poppe made $50 million for leading the reviled utility through bankruptcy and public relations disasters.[43] Her compensation came from $41.2 million in stock awards, as well as a bonus of $6.6 million and an annual salary of $1.3 million. The financial windfall came as PG&E was hiking rates on its customers, partly to pay for the damage caused by the wildfires.

"I trusted my governor. I trusted my commissioners. And that was a mistake," Stebbins told ABC10.[44] The near-automatic way PG&E obtained safety certificates set off alarm bells from consumer and safety advocates, including the CPUC's own Public Advocates Office. "For the extensive benefits that a company gets from having a safety certificate, it should come with the accountability," Nat Skinner, the head of safety for the Public Advocates Office, told ABC10. "[The safety certificate] makes it harder to hold the utility accountable. If this had been in place during the 2017, 2018, and 2019 fires, PG&E shareholders would have been on the hook for about $4 billion, not for the tens of billions that they've ultimately ended up paying out.[45]

The PG&E bankruptcy legislation did create a Wildfire Safety Advisory Board of third-party experts, but despite this effort to create a degree of independence, conflicts of interest have arisen. The safety board includes John Mader, an electrical distribution engineer for PG&E since 1998. The governor chooses several members, along with the senate and assembly.

In the wake of the bankruptcy micromanaged by Newsom, customers are paying far more for less reliable service. In 2019, PG&E and other utilities across California knew they could no longer guarantee the safety of their electric grid during high winds, so they instituted a policy of massive power shutoffs. The preemptive outages, some during record-setting heat, have come under deep criticism by those who argue they threaten lives and local businesses and shift the responsibility away from the utilities. PG&E says its customers should expect these types of preemptive service interruptions for another decade, casting them in a series of television and digital advertisements as steps "to keep you safe."[46] And all this continues while Californians pay the highest utility rates in the contiguous United States, outside of New England, and by far the highest of any western state, even though most areas of California enjoy some of the mildest weather in the nation.

Some of these charges come from rate increases PG&E and other utilities have passed on to consumers to cover the billions of dollars in wildfire losses and liability. The *San Jose Mercury News* in January 2024 said rate hikes are rising about eight times faster than the annualized increase in Bay Area consumer prices and were set to push utility bills to a "grim milestone": an average of $308 a month for a combined electricity and gas bill for the first time.[47]

Democratic leaders in the state for years failed to hold PG&E and other utilities accountable as they spread vast sums of money in campaign contributions, lobbying, and other political-pay-to-play schemes around the state. Before Newsom spearheaded PG&E's bankruptcy, consumer groups had long slammed former Governor Brown and his appointees for failing to adequately regulate the public utilities to prevent the downed power wires and exploding transformers from igniting the blazes. For several years when Brown was in office, his sister Kathleen sat on the board of directors of Sempra, the parent company of Southern California Edison and San Diego Gas and Electric. She made more than $1 million in cash and stock.[48] Brown also kept Michael Peevey, a former Southern California Edison executive and longtime family friend, as the head of the CPUC.

Peevey, whose wife Carol Liu was a Democratic state senator at the time, eventually stepped aside in 2014 after a scandal erupted regarding his allegedly inappropriate close relationship with PG&E. According to the LA Times, at one point Peevey asked the firm to donate at least $1 million to a campaign to defeat a 2010 oil firm-backed ballot measure that would have undermined the state's anti-global warming program.

Peevey retired amid the controversy, but not before several damning emails became public, showing how PG&E executives socialized and casually discussed company projects with the officials that were supposed to be regulating them. In one, Brian Cherry, PG&E's then vice president of regulatory relations, describes how he, Peevey, and another PG&E executive "polished off two bottles of good Pinot" while talking work matters at Mr. Peevey's Sonoma County coast vacation home. During the dinner, Peevey gave public relations advice and solicited the $1 million donation described above. Mr. Cherry and two other PG&E executives were fired shortly after their emails became public.[49]

Years earlier, in 2014, many CPUC employees themselves expressed outrage over a judge-shopping scandal involving PG&E.[50] During a public meeting that filled the commission's auditorium in San Francisco, staffers voiced frustration with Peevey and other officials who promised to help PG&E get the administrative law judge it wanted to hear a rate case that could have cost customers $1 billion. To the applause of others, one employee even called Peevey "something like an untouchable mob boss," able to float above any scandal.[51] Peevey's chief of staff had just resigned with three PG&E executives over what the commission called "inappropriate" back-channel communications used to pick the judge in the rate case. One of the fired utility executives told Peevey's aide in an email that the judge initially assigned would pose a "major problem" and that the utility had been "screwed royally" by a prospective replacement judge.[52]

Peevey aide Carol Brown, who responded that she was "working on" changing the judge, resigned as the president's chief of staff but remained with the agency as an administrative law judge.[53] Peevey tried to make the scandal disappear by agreeing to recuse himself from hearing arguments regarding a proposed $1.4 billion penalty against PG&E for the San Bruno explosion. A staff meeting was restricted to agency employees, but the *Chronicle* obtained a tape of the hour-long session. Much of the criticism was aimed at Peevey, whose nearly twelve-year tenure atop the agency was marred by the National Transportation Safety Board's finding that the utility commission had been overly lax in regulating PG&E before the San Bruno disaster.[54]

"He never seems to be affected by it," one commission staffer remarked. "He can just walk through." One employee threatened "a mass staff rebellion" should Governor Brown reappoint Peevey to another six-year term. "Are we just going to throw a couple of people under the bus or are we going to look at the real causes in our culture that create this kind of corruptness and basically sleazy environment?" another staff member asked.[55]

The company was fined $1 million after the scandal became public, a sanction that critics said was a slap on the wrist for a company with annual revenues of $17 billion. During his time in office, Brown was aided in his lax handling of PG&E by several other state officials, including Kamala Harris. Consumer groups for years have faulted Harris's hands-off approach to PG&E while attorney general and her failure to prosecute the utility or hold the CPUC accountable. "She was absent, she was AWOL, she didn't file any charges whatsoever," Jamie Court, the president of Consumer Watchdog, told us while Harris was Biden's running mate in 2020. "She was the first line, and she should have stepped in, and she didn't because of political concerns."[56]

While Harris was still attorney general (she left in 2017 after winning a US Senate seat), Consumer Watchdog was so incensed about her decision not to prosecute two high-profile utility cases that it issued a one-page paper on what it deemed "public utility corruption and Kamala Harris's failure to act for the public."[57] Harris's campaign declined to respond to the criticism when contacted. But Court wasn't the only one calling out Harris. Several California newspapers and other media outlets raised similar complaints while Harris was attorney general and in the years afterward.

There are two investigations Court and other critics cite when they blast Harris for failing to prosecute the CPUC and PG&E. The first involves the San Bruno gas line explosion, which killed eight people, injured sixty-six, and destroyed thirty-eight homes. Harris opened a criminal probe into the blast but never prosecuted the case. The US Attorney's Office eventually took it up and brought criminal charges. In 2016, a federal jury found PG&E guilty of six felony charges—five counts of violating pipeline safety standards and one count of obstructing the investigation into the San Bruno explosion. As described earlier in this chapter, the investigation turned up evidence that Peevey was so aligned with PG&E that he allegedly helped his former employer shop for sympathetic judges.

In explaining her decision not to prosecute the San Bruno case, Harris said that her office had become part of a joint task force with federal investigators at the time. Court counters that it was state Democratic politics and a major conflict of interest within Jerry Brown's administration that kept her from pursuing the case. "Clearly there were prosecutable issues with Mike Peevey and San Onofre, an PG&E, and she let it all go...and it was not good for the public interest," Court argues. "It's all public record, and it was all documented. It's about the political class and not wanting to make trouble for the other members of the class, and I find that appalling when the crimes rise to the level of the facts that we saw." (Court was referring to the San Onofre Nuclear Generating Station, a nuclear plant perched on an oceanside cliff in San Clemente, Calif. that operated from 1968 to early

2012. Harris investigated the CPUC and Southern California Edison deal to have ratepayers pay billions of dollars for its closure and environmental clean-up but quietly and mysteriously dropped the case, as we detail later in the chapter.)

The alleged judge-shopping led the *San Jose Mercury News* to opine that "Peevey's relationship with PG&E, the utility she was charged with regulating, should have gotten him fired in the wake of the 2010 San Bruno explosion. But Gov. Brown inexplicably kept him on the job."[58] And Brown continued defending the CPUC even when the agency was plagued with allegations of back-channel deals and favoritism between the regulators and the utilities they were supposed to keep in line. In 2013, Peevey held an undisclosed meeting—this time with a Southern California Edison executive at a luxury hotel in Warsaw, Poland. The CPUC was in the middle of negotiating how to handle the costs of closing the San Onofre nuclear power plant in San Diego County when reports surfaced alleging that Peevey had gotten involved inappropriately.

The CPUC and Southern California Edison had claimed a settlement that left consumers with a $3.3 billion bill for San Onofre's closure when Southern California Edison and San Diego Gas and Electric would foot only $1.4 billion. Ratepayer advocates wanted to make sure it was negotiated properly. At first, Harris appeared to be investigating that case aggressively: the attorney general's office issued a search warrant for Peevey's home. That search uncovered handwritten notes showing Peevey had held a secret meeting with an Edison executive in Warsaw after the nuclear power plant sprang a radioactive leak and had to be closed. Eventually a deal was cut that left ratepayers footing a big portion of the bill. Documents uncovered during the investigation also showed that Peevey tried to get Southern California Edison and San Diego Gas and Utility to give $25 million to a pet project at the University of California, Los Angeles, a move Democratic State Senator Jerry Hill, who represents San Bruno, called a quid pro quo arrangement.

Harris's investigative team argued in court filings that they could have charged Peevey and the utility companies with conspiracy to obstruct justice—a felony—for the secret meeting in Warsaw. But several news outlets, including KPBS, reported that during her Senate run, Harris let the three-year statute of limitations run out on the secret Poland meeting and never pursued prosecution.

The attorney general's office argued that the statute of limitations actually hadn't passed in the San Onofre case—that the journalists were getting that part of the story wrong. "This is a comprehensive investigation, and the law does not foreclose our pursuit of charges if charges are appropriate and justified," the spokesperson told a KPBS reporter in 2016.[59] A source familiar with the investigation told us that the statute of limitations in the case had not run out when Harris left the attorney general's office. The source also argued that the legal time limits can be renewed if a new piece of evidence is discovered, but did not know if the investigation had gone dormant. "I will say candidly that the investigation took a long time because the CPUC continued to push back and push back on document requests," the source told me. "Sometimes these investigations when folks are in a noncooperative mode take some time."[60]

San Diego consumer lawyer Mike Aguirre, a Democrat who served as city attorney from 2004 to 2008 and was representing ratepayer interests in the San Onofre case, has repeatedly blasted Harris for failing to bring criminal charges in that case. In early 2016, Aguirre accused Harris of stalling the San Onofre probe until her US Senate campaign wrapped up because it could hurt powerful fellow Democrats. "For her to let the statute go is malpractice," Aguirre told the *San Diego Reader* in April 2016.[61] Aguirre specifically questioned a decision by the attorney general's office not to act on a search warrant of the offices of Southern California Edison's parent company and the CPUC. Instead of allowing investigators to search those offices, they served the search warrants to Edison and the CPUC and asked them to turn over all documents and communications related to the San Onofre settlement. "You don't drop it off at the front door and say, 'Hey, gee, send me your records,'" Aguirre, a former federal prosecutor, told KPBS.

"That's the whole point of a search warrant… You go in, and you execute the search warrant, and you seize the records because you're concerned they're going to disappear."[62]

While Edison turned over some records to the attorney general's office, the CPUC withheld many on the grounds that they didn't have enough resources to produce them, while also claiming that some were privileged. The privilege claim, they argued, covered some emails about San Onofre exchanged with Brown's office. Harris never challenged the CPUC's privilege claim, another bone of contention for critics who argue as a representative of the state demanding documents from a state agency she would have easily prevailed. In November 2018, federal judges dismissed the case Aguirre brought over the costs passed on to consumers for the San Onofre shutdown. But they forced Southern California Edison to pay the $5.4 million bill to his firm for its legal work. Aguirre had previously won a deal with the utilities that lowered customers' bill for the plant's closing from $3.3 billion to $775 million.[63]

Early in her own 2020 presidential campaign, Harris sponsored a bill seemingly designed to inoculate her from critics who could question her controversial decisions not to bring charges in the two utility cases. As the Democratic presidential primary kicked into gear, Harris introduced a measure that would ban utilities under bankruptcy, like PG&E, from paying bonuses to executives. Titled the Accountability for Utility Executives Act, Harris touted the bill amid growing frustration with the company and its role in sparking the wildfires. In doing so, she also mentioned a media report that PG&E wined and dined employees days before planned power outages and while the company was planning to pay $11 million in performance bonuses to its executives.[64] It attracted no cosponsors and didn't gain traction in the GOP-controlled upper chamber. And by then, another fire season was underway in the West.[65]

CHAPTER EIGHT

Green Warriors, Blackouts, and Brownouts

T HE ROLLING, SUN-DAPPLED HILLS of Napa Valley produce some of the most cherished and expensive wines in the world. While only an hour drive from San Francisco's downtown squalor, it feels a world away, a pastoral escape for California's elite who can afford its abundance of Michelin-rated restaurants, spas, and boutique inns, which have sprung up throughout the valley over the last thirty years. Despite its understated high-end ambience, California's wine country is also ground zero for one of the fiercest environmental wars in the country, pitting vintners against eco-warriors in a battle over the heart of America's winemaking Eden and some of its most sought-after soil.

For years, the two sides waged quiet zoning battles with vineyard and resort owners eventually, literally, gaining ground—taking over more and more land once strictly set aside for open space and agriculture. Entrenched and determined eco-zealots, in league with woke local bureaucrats, have escalated their tactics by intimidating officials into blocking wine-tourism resort projects over questionable and sometimes bogus environmental complaints. Vineyards have complained of being hobbled by "gross regulatory overreach" and excessive red tape, and some wineries have been penalized for such heinous crimes as planting trees, making jam, and holding tastings on their property in violation of the agricultural zoning laws that restrict profiting from food sales or other products besides wine. Caymus Vineyard was even fined $1 million for bottling too much wine on site.[1]

Most Napa Valley wineries are barred from hosting weddings on their grounds due to an obscure 1989 law. Only a handful of wineries can do so: those grandfathered in before the law went into effect. In nearby Sonoma County you can host a wedding, but in 2024 environmentalist extremists got a measure on the ballot that would impose a ban on operating large farms, the first such prohibition in the nation. If passed, the law would require several organic dairy farms that have been owned and operated in the area for generations to scale back drastically or shut down entirely within three years.[2]

The bohemian eco-crusaders label the large farms "factory farming" and claim that some subject animals to cruel conditions and pollute local waters with runoff. The dairy farmers counter that their cows have more pasture for grazing and far better living conditions than most other dairies across nation. If the "factory farming" bill passes, the Agribusiness Institute at Cal State Chico projects a $121 million loss for local businesses such as animal feed providers and veterinarians, and a $38 billion reduction in consumer spending from job losses. It could also force the removal of 2.9 million farm animals from the county. The total economic loss would amount to nearly half a billion dollars.[3]

At one modest property, Hoopes Vineyard in Napa County, guests can taste wine under a string of lights next to a pen of rescue goats and squawking chickens. A small store sells greeting cards and hand sanitizer. In 2022, local extremists sued Hoopes, accusing the owner of creating a "public nuisance" by offering the wine tastings, as well as yoga classes, and citing her for not having a permit for her 120-square foot chicken coop.[4] The winery had offered tastings dating back to 1990s when it was first established, but the Hoopes purchased it in 2017 and were thus not grandfathered in. The family has run up half a million in legal fees so far.

Grape growers, the lifeblood of Napa's multibillion industry, have tried to push back, filing a raft of lawsuits against the county. Things have become nasty and divisive, especially for the smaller vineyards. Wine-growers point out that Napa wineries are known for their innovative green technologies—with many winning worldwide acclaim for their environmental stewardship—but their commitment isn't good enough for the region's hardcore green warriors.

In late 2023, a new legal battle erupted into public view. The FBI subpoenaed Napa County, demanding records of dozens of high-profile vintners and their wineries, including a former coowner of the Dallas Cowboys and an ex-US ambassador to Austria. The agency also pressed the Farm Bureau, a powerful voice for the local wine industry, to turn over documents to the US Department of Justice. A month later, locals discovered the dead body of Farm Bureau CEO Ryan Klobas next to his car in the hillsides.[5]

Police said the forty-five-year-old suffered from a self-inflicted gunshot wound, but others believe there's more to the story. Klobas had reported that his briefcase full of documents had been stolen just days before federal authorities subpoenaed the organization for information about its political action committee. He also said the apparent theft had occurred weeks earlier, on December 1, the night of the Farm Bureau's Christmas party.[6] Seven of the vintners the FBI subpoenaed had donated to the Farm Bureau's PAC, the Fund to Protect Napa Valley Agriculture. Chuck Wagner, Caymus's owner, has said he is "mad as hell" that his name appeared among the FBI subpoenas because he's unaware of anything he has done wrong other than his alleged violation for producing too much wine. Others, including Robin Baggett, the former general counsel for the Golden State Warriors and owner of Omega Winery, has brushed off the probe as a "political witch hunt" meant to further intimidate successful vineyard owners.[7]

These aggressive "eco-mob" tactics come as no surprise for anyone familiar with California's history of environmental terrorism, which famously includes attempts by protesters in the 1980s and '90s to prevent timber harvests by blocking roads and setting up camps in tree canopies. Militant hippies chained themselves to trees in old-growth forests to save endangered spotted owls from loggers. Environmentalists were successful in protecting 6.9 million acres of old forest.[8] Between 1989 and 1995, timber cutting on federal land fell by roughly 90 percent, according to the Oregon

Forest Research Institute, and at least thirty-two thousand logging industry employees lost their jobs.[9]

Fast-forward to today and even die-hard climate change advocates say the denser forests have led to more destructive wildfires. In 2021, Nancy Pelosi signed on to a bipartisan infrastructure bill that required prescribed burns for "overcrowded" forests.[10]

With so much forestland now under tight protection, you might think the spotted owl would be thriving. But researchers say the populations have continued to plummet, in some places by as much as 80 percent. The new culprit is something environmentalists could never have predicted or controlled: competition from the barred owl, a species that moved in from the east. The US Fish and Wildlife Service now proposes killing up to four hundred thousand of the barred owls over the next thirty years, creating an ethical conundrum of whether one species should be proactively killed to save another.[11]

The irony of this colossal effort to protect a species, only to have Mother Nature interfere, has been a consistent theme over the last century in California. Environmentalists hell-bent on saving every species down to the state's flower-loving fly have fashioned a hodgepodge of conflicting and contradictory laws that often cause more harm to the environment. The state's green agenda has grown so extreme that even its beloved trees and rare animal species are mere collateral damage in the all-out war on fossil fuels.

California's tree-hugging crusaders are now openly at war over plans for a sprawling solar farm in the Mojave Desert that poses a threat to iconic desert trees and the official state reptile. As state policymakers race to achieve Governor Newsom's goal of net zero carbon pollution by 2045, there's far more solar infrastructure that needs to be built. State regulators have already approved Newsom's ban on the sale of gas-powered vehicles by 2035 in an effort to reduce carbon emissions.[12] The Aratina Solar Center project will encompass 2,300 undeveloped acres and will require cutting down as many as 4,700 Joshua trees—some of which have stood in the desert for more than a hundred years.

The trees made world famous by the Irish rock band U2 now enjoy some state protection (Newsom signed the Joshua Tree Conservation Act in 2023), but not *these* Joshua trees. That's because when the Kern County Board of Supervisors unanimously approved the project in October 2021, the trees were not protected. Some environmentalists argue the project drives a bulldozer through the 2023 law that aimed to protect the trees. "Let's destroy the environment to save the environment. That seems to be the mentality" a high school teacher told the *Los Angeles Times* in May 2024. "It's hard to comprehend."[13] Project owner Avantus claims the solar energy produced and stored by Aratina will have the carbon emissions reduction effect equivalent to planting fourteen million trees.[14]

While some environmentalists can swallow the loss of a few thousand Joshua trees, others can't stomach the threat to the desert tortoise, the official reptile of the Golden State, whose population has already been cut in half over the past two decades. The federal government lists the Mojave desert tortoise, as well as the desert tortoise whose habitat overlaps with the Mojave species, "threatened" under the Endangered Species Act.[15] The Mojave ground squirrel is another threatened species whose habitat lies squarely in the path of the solar project. State wildlife officials reportedly ordered the company to relocate any desert tortoises or ground squirrels that construction crews encounter, but there doesn't appear to be anyone monitoring these so-called requirements. As usual, this project demonstrates how poorer residents bear the brunt of the sacrifices California asks of its residents in pursuit of clean energy. California environmental lawyer Jennifer Hernandez wrote an entire book, *Green Jim Crow*, on how California's climate policies often undermine progressive civil rights and racial equity goals.[16]

Residents in the project area have poverty rates twice that of the state average. Dangerous toxins have been discovered in the soil that construction could release into the air, causing valley fever, a dangerous lung infection. Private equity firm KKR, the desert solar project's primary owner, says it will ultimately power 180,000 homes—but not in Kern County. Most of the power is slated for use in wealthier communities hundreds of miles away in Northern California.

One inked contract will send power to Silicon Valley Clean Energy and Central Coast Community Energy, two nonprofit green-energy suppliers. Of course, Newsom never mentions these trade-offs, or wind energy's deadly impact on birds and reports of harm to whales and other ocean life, when attacking big oil and making sweeping statements about the success of renewable energy and his green agenda.[17]

"California is doing what no state has done when it comes to protecting the environment, our state, and our kids' future," he declared in 2022.[18]

For all of Newsom's bragging about the state's trailblazing clean energy and environmental achievements, there are plenty of dirty open secrets. Despite years of many municipalities placing strict limits on residential water use because of an ongoing drought crisis, after California experienced record-breaking rainfall in 2023 and 2024, 80 percent of the water was lost to runoff because there's inadequate infrastructure to capture it.[19] For decades, California has been bandying about a solution to collect and more fairly distribute water throughout the state, but the solutions are costly, and many environmentalists oppose them. The Delta Conveyance Project, a proposed forty-five-mile tunnel, would cost $20 billion, according to a new report from the California Department of Water Resources.[20] Newsom calls the project, which has been under discussion in various iterations since the 1960s, his "number one climate resilience program."[21]

The project would build a tunnel to carry water from the Sacramento River to either the southern end of the Sacramento-San Joaquin Delta or to Livermore's Bethany Reservoir. The project purports to bolster the State Water Project, which provides water to 27 million residents and 750,000 agricultural acres. Its architects say the tunnel would better protect the area from the effects of major earthquakes while also mitigating the effects of climate change, such as rising sea levels and drought. Construction wouldn't start until 2029 and would finish in 2044, at the earliest. If it already existed, it could have funneled enough water to supply 9.5 million people for all of 2023, according to state officials. They put the project's cost benefits at $38 billion—or $2.20 for every dollar spent on it.[22]

Environmentalists, locals, Indian tribes, and fishermen aren't sold, however. First, it mostly benefits Southern Californians. Secondly, the same state water regulators say the Sacramento-San Joaquin Delta is in the middle of an "ecosystem collapse" caused by "reduced and modified flows, loss of habitat, invasive species, and water pollution."[23] Threatened and endangered fish species, including winter-run Chinook salmon, Delta smelt, and steelhead trout, are all in jeopardy—and environmentalists worry building a tunnel would only exacerbate the threat.

"This project gets more expensive every single time a new version is proposed, and this type of project has never been brought to completion under budget," Peter Gleick, cofounder of the Pacific Institute, an environmental think tank, warned. "Water conservation and efficiency improvements are far cheaper than the Delta project."[24]

Local and state politicians want to force consumers to buy electric cars to meet long-term climate change goals but aren't doing anything to quell the main source of California's carbon emissions: Los Angeles's sprawling smog-and-traffic-plagued freeways.[25] The city's meager subway system is crime riddled and lacks basic shelters at most stops. Even if the city could reduce the crime and homeless squalor in the stations, the metro takes nearly three times as long to reach one's destination than driving.

While Los Angeles drivers suffer daily in snarled traffic, a bigger boondoggle transportation project has sucked up tens of billions in state money with nothing to show for it. The high-speed electric train service between San Francisco and Los Angeles, derisively dubbed the "train to nowhere," needs $100 billion to become reality—and another $7 billion just to complete the first segment of track. That's roughly $100 billion over budget and four years and counting past the original projected 2020 completion date.[26]

A more sordid tale is the struggle to keep the state's lights on. In the middle of a late summer heat wave in 2020, with most California residents still stuck in their homes because of COVID restrictions and restaurants struggling to reopen in the face of social distancing rules, the state was hit with the most severe power shortages it had experienced in two decades.

Without warning, hundreds of thousands of Californians abruptly lost power in a blackout due to blistering temperatures and a strained electric grid.

"We failed to predict and plan, and that's simply unacceptable," Newsom said in a press briefing after the rolling blackouts of mid-August 2022.[27] He held an emergency meeting that weekend with top energy regulators and signed an executive order to temporarily lift restrictions on power generation and pollution during peak hours. He and other state officials spent the rest of the summer pleading with residents to lower their thermostats. The governor was frantically trying to avoid repeating history, keenly aware that the rolling blackouts in 2003 were partly to blame for former Governor Gray Davis's successful recall, which led to the election of Republican Governor Arnold Schwarzenegger.

Despite Newsom's constant touting of his green agenda, he wasn't really coming clean on the whole story behind the energy crisis. More than half a century of environmentalist opposition to oil pipeline construction, nuclear plants, and coal-producing plants had wreaked havoc on California's energy supply. For years, the state's energy production hasn't met its energy needs, meaning customers get hit with the extra transportation costs. Newsom has blamed climate change and hotter summer months for forcing him to issue dire warnings to all state residents to conserve energy for weeks at a time. But triple-digit temperatures aren't new in California. What's new over the last two decades is the way California generates electricity with unreliable solar and wind power, both of which expanded rapidly thanks to government subsidies along with the state's renewable mandates.

Moreover, heavy carbon taxes have made it harder for gas and nuclear generators to make money. Many have shut down, only further exacerbating the issue of insufficient power. As a result, California has the highest gas and utility prices in the nation, which state regulators, appointed by Newsom, have allowed to continue climbing upward. "When we destroy our refining capacity before we develop the ability to do something else, we're putting ourselves in extremely high prices and chronic scarcity," Ed Ring, director of water and energy policy at the California Policy Center, explained in an interview. "It's all scarcity driven."[28]

California's summer electric-generation capacity increased by about 10,700 megawatts between 2010 and 2020—potentially enough to power eight to ten million homes. The problem is that gas-fired capacity during this time declined by 4,390 megawatts and nuclear by 2,150. Solar and wind surged 17,000 megawatts, but these sources can't be commanded to run when people need them. Thus, California relies on imports from other states in the evenings. During heat waves that span the Southwest, California must resort to emergency measures to reduce electricity demand. This includes asking users to turn up their thermostats and providing incentives for industrial businesses to power down. In 2022, a desalination plant in Carlsbad cut water production by about 20 percent to free up power for homes—the opposite of what the state needed during that year's drought.

Despite the Democrat-controlled legislature's goal of deriving 100 percent of its electricity from carbon-free sources by 2024, the state still relies on foreign imported oil, as well as imports of dirty, coal-fueled electricity from Utah and New Mexico, with nearly half of its electricity production coming from natural gas. Newsom campaigned on shutting down Aliso Canyon, a gas-storage facility in north Los Angeles that was the origin of the largest methane leak in US history. But five years later, with energy costs soaring and Newsom worried about more rolling blackouts, his administration okayed a plan for the plant to produce even more gas to avoid power shortages. He's also approved extensions of gas and nuclear power plants scheduled for closure. But even those measures haven't been able to keep energy costs in check.

Gas and utility prices for California consumers have skyrocketed in recent years, becoming a double whammy for anyone with a car or an electricity bill. They pack a particularly hard punch for California's middle class and working poor. In early 2024, the average price of gas sat above $5.30 per gallon—by far the highest in the country, nearly two dollars more than the national average. Meanwhile, early that year, Newsom-appointed regulators gave Pacific Gas and Electric (PG&E), a utility company serving the northern third of the state with 5.6 million customers, the go-ahead to hike power rates in January to the tune of twenty-eight to forty-two dollars per month.[29] Additional increases took effect in March and April of 2024. Along with the state's other two major providers, Southern California Edison and San Diego Gas and Electric, the power trio has nearly doubled electricity rates over the last decade.[30]

These massive increases are pushing lower-income residents to the brink of homelessness or to joining the exodus of residents leaving the state. With roughly 25 percent of California households unable to pay their utility bills, they face what Columbia University's Diana Hernández calls the "heat or eat dilemma; today's unpaid energy bill is tomorrow's eviction notice."[31] Low-income customers in PG&E service territory are facing a crisis of affordability, says Matt Freedman, a lawyer with the utility-customer advocacy group TURN. Freedman estimates that 180,000 customers disconnected for nonpayment in 2023, and about a third of PG&E low-income customers were late in paying their bills even before the latest rate hikes on consumers. In an interview, Freedman said the most recent rate hike was particularly galling because it was done via "consent agenda," which doesn't require any public debate, and which was implemented "right after PG&E released record shareholder earnings."[32]

One of the problems is entirely self-made. For decades, the state's left-wing politicians and environmentalists have pushed the adoption of rooftop solar with numerous tax incentives for going green. But now those solar customers are paying less money to maintain the grid, spreading the cost to other lower-income utility customers in the form of higher rates. The net energy metering program, which pays solar customers for their electricity generation, is pushing $6.5 billion onto other customers' rates, the California Public Utilities Commission's (CPUC's) Public Advocates Office estimated in early 2024.[33] The program's annual cost to customers without solar panels has nearly doubled since 2021. There are also programs to help low-income customers who can't pay. The funds that go to these customers are made up for by increasing rates on the non-solar-paying population.

The massive financial hit to utilities for their role in causing catastrophic wildfires across the state also contributes to higher consumer bills—even though the utilities have admitted their failure to safely maintain their equipment and cut vegetation. Now the utilities are passing on the costs of burying power lines to customers when consumer advocates argue there are other and cheaper fire-mitigation methods available. PG&E rates are skyrocketing because there are no caps on utility spending and capital investments trigger shareholder profits. The utility authorized $4.7 billion in capital investments from 2020 to 2022 but spent $14 billion, with most of that passed down to customers, according to Freedman.[34]

"A judge told [PG&E] to do 60 percent overhead [fix] and 40 percent [burying wires] underground, but then state regulators at the California Public Utility commissioner overruled him and approved the inverse—majority underground—and that's all profit," Freedman said. "That's driving their decision."[35]

Newsom, who says he's protecting consumers when it comes to attacking oil companies for high gas prices, has little qualms about the state's powerful utilities hiking rates on consumers. And he's done nothing about the ongoing revolving door between the energy industry and the commission created to oversee them. PG&E spreads so much fundraising and lobbying dollars to politicians around the state that it usually gets its way outside the courtroom, despite pleading guilty in 2020 to eighty-four counts of involuntary manslaughter for its role in causing the massive 2018 Camp Fire in Northern California.[36] "It's a bad look for elected officials to accept campaign contributions from a convicted felon, but that's just our position, it's never carried the day," Freedman said.[37]

As detailed in Chapter 7, Newsom and his wife raked in over $700,000 in PG&E donations to charity and campaign cash before they stopped accepting the donations after his election to governor in 2018 amid a public backlash against the utility's role in causing several deadly wildfires. In early 2024, the CPUC sided with the utilities they were supposed to oversee and agreed to stick customers with a new monthly flat fee based on income in exchange for a reduction in the overall prices of electricity. The rate cut will vary between 8 percent and 18 percent, depending on the utility, season, and time of day. The new flat-fee charge will be twenty-four dollars for most customers regardless of how much power they use, but lower-income households—many that already qualify for discounted rates—will have fees of six or twelve dollars. Some environmentalists argue this scenario will serve as a disincentive to conserve energy, something Californians have been urging people to do for years. And those owning solar panels will still get hit with the fee even when their solar generation pays for all their homes' electricity needs.

Solar customers and the industry as a whole already took a major hit in 2023 when the CPUC slashed the value of electricity generated by residential rooftop solar panels by 75 percent, making it harder for residents to recover the expensive costs of installing the systems. The change crushed solar sales and forced the industry to lay off thousands of workers.[38]

Over the last decade, California's solar market experienced double-digit growth, fueled by the state's campaign for cleaner, renewable energy. But the surge has outpaced the grid's storage capabilities, creating a rift among progressives over its effectiveness. Most residential solar systems produce excess power with no way to capture it for later use. For example, only 14 percent of residents who installed panels in 2022 doled out the roughly $30,000 for batteries to store extra power, leaving utilities to rely mostly on fossil-fuel-burning plants to make up the production difference.[39] California also requires all new homes to include rooftop solar-power systems, but not batteries. California passed a mandate that all new single and multifamily homes must be constructed with solar to help it reach its goal of sourcing 50 percent of its electricity from renewables by 2030. But the new law has divided some environmentalists from the progressive's approach. They argue that because rooftop solar workers aren't unionized, the residential solar largely benefits wealthier residents and solar companies, while the more cost-effective way to supercharge clean-energy production is to build large-scale private solar farms and projects that prop up the grid.

From time to time, the heavy-handed environmental mandates have generated negative publicity—even with most media outlets across the state biased toward promoting officials' extreme green agenda. In late spring of 2023, José Andrés wanted to open a high-end Eastern Mediterranean restaurant in Palo Alto. But the city warned the world-famous chef that his restaurant wouldn't be able to connect to a gas line already constructed to serve the site because its council had recently changed its rules banning natural gas in new construction. These new regulations put Andrés's restaurant in a bind. Gas cooktops are necessary to "achieve [Andrés's] signature, complex flavors," lawyers for the mall housing the restaurant told the city. Palo Alto finally relented, but gas bans have passed in some seventy California cities, including Los Angeles.

But what about foodies who desperately want to attain the same effect in their own kitchens? They were out of luck until a Ninth Circuit Court ruling came to their rescue. The court, known for its liberal record, forced Berkeley to reverse its ban on natural gas in new buildings, prompting other cities to suspend their own efforts to institute all-electric buildings.

Nuclear power, which California once led the nation in innovating, could help alleviate the state's power crunch. However, safety advocates and environmentalists have stymied scaling it up for decades. California's "no nukes" culture led to massive demonstrations against the opening of the state's second—and to date, last—plant in the mid-1980s. The state had two nuclear power plants, Diablo Canyon and San Onofre—with the ability to generate 4390 Mwe (a single Mwe is one million watts of electric capacity) and designed to withstand major earthquakes—until 2013, when San Onofre was shuttered, taking 2150 MWe offline. Although Diablo Canyon was slated to begin decommissioning in 2024, Newsom took a 180-degree turn and approved extending its operation to 2030 amid efforts to reach the state's strict carbon-reduction mandates. Nuclear power is carbon neutral after all. To that end, the US Department of Energy awarded the plant, which provides roughly 9 percent of the state's electricity, a $1.1 billion credit in 2022 as part of Biden's Build Back Better infrastructure bill.

"Amid intensifying climate impacts in the West and across the country, California is focused on meeting our bold climate and clean energy goals while tackling the challenges of extreme weather that puts lives at risk and strains our grid," Newsom stated at the time. "This investment creates a path forward for…Diablo Canyon Power Plant to support reliability statewide and provide an onramp for more clean energy projects to come online."[40]

Despite the acknowledgment that nuclear power enables the state to avoid burning fossil fuels, Sacramento has made no moves to repeal its 1976 law prohibiting new construction. And an environmental group filed suit in April to block Diablo Canyon's stay of execution.

California Democrats' green agenda doesn't come cheap. Transitioning to 90 percent clean electricity by 2035 and 100 percent by 2045 requires California utilities to build more clean energy faster, which carries a price tag of $370 billion.[41] Democrats have found one ready source for its green transportation agenda in hiking gas taxes on consumers, relying on a bait-and-switch strategy to sell it to voters. Back in 2018, they wanted to raise gas taxes, which were already the second highest in the nation. When Republican counterparts tried to fight it, they scared voters into backing the taxes with a multi-million-dollar campaign of television ads and freeway billboards—paid for by state funds. The messaging warned that a failure to raise taxes would result in deadly pothole-ridden streets.

Years later, California's gas taxes are the nation's highest, and the promised road repairs are far behind schedule and way over budget. Much of the tax revenues filter into bottomless political money pits. In 2019, the California Department of Transportation inspector general determined that the department had misspent millions, causing it to disallow more than $13 million in state and local expenditures. Proposition 69, which passed in 2018, was supposed to end the practice of siphoning off tax dollars by putting transportation funds in a so-called lockbox where politicians couldn't touch them for anything but transportation costs. But since voters approved the gas tax in 2018, Newsom deftly intercepted the road-repair money, rationalizing it as a way "to help reverse the trend of increased fuel consumption and reduce greenhouse gas emissions associated with the transportation sector."[42]

A more recent California Department of Transportation (Caltrans) audit showed just how irresponsible the department is with other people's money. Though not a bank, it had been in the habit of handing out salary advances to employees, and then failing to collect on them, wasting as much as $1.5 million. The inspector general said the "forfeiture balance might have risen from $1.5 million to nearly $3 million if our investigation had not prompted it to take action."[43] Further holding back progress are the steep costs involved in road construction and repair. According to a recent Reason Foundation's highway report, California spends $186,549 per lane-mile on its roads, nearly twice the US average of $94,870.[44]

The radical green agenda of Newsom and other Democrats not only squeezes California consumers, but it also benefits Chinese companies. Los Angeles County, for instance, used gas-tax funds to purchase electric buses from a Chinese company at a cost of $1.7 million each. Even though these buses broke down because they could not handle steep inclines, the county inanely spent an additional $65 million to purchase more of the same buses. (In contrast, a clean US-manufactured natural-gas bus costs $300,000.) The buses are built by Build Your Dreams (BYD), a US subsidiary of a Chinese company backed by billionaire Warren Buffett, whose president contributed $40,000 to Newsom's campaign. BYD also was the source for one of Newsom's controversial no-bid COVID contracts.

During the first months of the COVID pandemic, as states scrambled to secure protective equipment, BYD, a massive Chinese manufacturing corporation and automaker, proactively contacted California officials and boasted that it could churn out N95 masks at its Chinese manufacturing sites. A 2019 report by the Alliance for American Manufacturing warned that BYD is simply "an arm" of the Chinese Communist Party, having received billions of dollars in grants and subsidies from the Chinese government, while working "hand-in-hand" with its military and US-sanctioned Huawei "to penetrate the US market."[45] Despite these red flags, Newsom readily accepted BYD's offer, providing a $990 million no-bid deal. For weeks, Newsom refused to release the contract to the press or the Democrat-controlled state legislature.[46]

In May 2021, BYD was forced to return $250 Million to the state for failing to meet a certification deadline for masks. But California never blacklisted the company. After BYD increased its delivery times, Newsom extended the contract in July 2021 for another $315 million. Two years later, during Newsom's audacious weeklong taxpayer-funded trip to China, the governor came under fire for visiting BYD electronic vehicle headquarters in Shenzhen and driving around in a $160,000 Chinese hybrid EV while posing and grinning for the state-run Chinese media. Members of Congress mocked the trip on social media, with Representative Jay Obernolte, a California Republican, pointing out that the Newsom administration had attempted to restrict sales of hybrid vehicles like the one he showcased in China.[47]

"I find it ironic that Governor Newsom is using his time in China to promote the Chinese produced BYD hybrid when his own administration is attempting to restrict sales of hybrid vehicles like the one he drove," Obernolte said.[48]

Former Representative Michelle Steel, another California Republican whose parents fled communist North Korea and raised her in Japan, didn't mince words. "It is a slap in the face to Californians to see Governor Newsom promote the CCP's [Chinese Communist Party's] electric cars built off the backs of slave labor," she said, referring to the millions of Uyghurs and other imprisoned minority populations China depends on for much of its forced labor.[49]

Representative Chris Smith, who cochairs the Congressional-Executive Commission on China, often rails against American consumers' failure to make the connection between EVs and China's deplorable record of benefiting from child and slave labor. "If you want an EV, you better check under the hood and find out what the source of [the batteries] was," Smith told reporters outside of the US Capitol in March 2024. Smith has held several hearings about cobalt mining in Africa, which uses child slave labor involving thirty-five thousand children a year, many of whom are getting sick and dying from their exposure to the mining chemicals.[50]

This gross misspending, waste, and diversion of gas-tax revenues into projects having nothing to do with roads or highways has become part of "the California way." Although the last gas-tax hike took effect with the promise that the money would go toward repairing crumbling roads and bridges, about 30 percent of the additional revenue has been designated for other transportation priorities, including public transit, bike lanes, and walking paths. And the law does not include a single reform to address the well-documented waste at the California Department of Transportation. The California state auditor has repeatedly cited Caltrans for a lack of cost control, which inevitably leads to waste, fraud, and abuse. The Reason Foundation's latest report ranked California's highways forty-seventh in the nation in overall cost-effectiveness and condition.[51] It took the state only a matter of months after the last gas-tax increase to move motor-fuel tax revenues to the California Department of Food and Agriculture, the state Department of Parks and Recreation, the general fund, and local law enforcement.[52]

How does California's seventy-eight-cent gas tax compare with the states to which Californians are fleeing in droves? Here's the 2024 data from the Tax Foundation: Texas, twenty cents per gallon; Florida, thirty-eight cents per gallon; and Nevada, twenty-four cents per gallon. (These three states have no income tax, and their roads are better).[53] Illinois, at sixty-six cents per gallon, has the second-highest gas tax in the country.[54]

California gasoline is already more expensive because the state requires a special, more costly blend. And recent legislative efforts to prevent even higher gas prices may have the opposite effect, some industry watchers warn. The intention of 2023's Gas Price Gouging and Transparency Law was to prevent oil refineries from profiteering during shortages. At least one analyst, Andy Lipow of Lipow Oil Associates, said instead it "may lead some gasoline importers to halt doing business in the state and that could exacerbate the supply situation at exactly the same time supplies from outside the state are needed."[55]

Additionally, a key Bay Area refinery is dumping gasoline production to churn out renewable diesel. "Throw in regularly scheduled maintenance that will occur at two critical refineries in May and the normal penchant for speculative buying in global markets in the second quarter, and you have wholesale prices that have gone ballistic," said Tom Kloza, global head of energy analysis at the Oil Price Information Service.[56]

Despite sky-high gas prices, steep gas taxes, and horrible traffic congestion—not to mention the greenhouse gas emissions the congestion causes—California's green warriors aren't making much noise about abandoning single-passenger travel in favor of public transportation. Perhaps that's because California's track record in that area is dismal, as mentioned above. Now policymakers want to take that abysmal record and hike costs for freight rail. The California Air Resources Board proposes banning older locomotives that don't use zero-emissions technology, but zero-emissions train technology doesn't even exist yet.[57]

"And what's going to happen is it's going to dramatically raise the cost of shipping anywhere in California, and that's going to have a ripple effect across the country," Ed Ring of the California Policy Center told the *Daily Caller* in 2024. "This is another example of California's environmentalist regulations raising the cost of living."[58]

Adding to Californians' energy costs are infrastructure upgrades required by unprecedented demand, not the least of which will go toward helping the state meet its goal of having all new light-duty vehicles be electric by 2035. The CPUC's Public Advocates Office estimates that making the upgrades to meet that goal will cost about $26 billion.[59]

Time and time again, California officials have prioritized fighting climate change regardless of the impact on consumer prices, choice—even scientific progress.

In September 2023, California Attorney General launched a war against the oil and gas industry in concert with Newsom's ongoing attacks on oil companies for so-called price-gouging. The governor had no proof that the industry was hiking prices on customers but went ahead with the accusations anyway, blaming the high state prices on producers, not the state's taxes and regulations. In October 2024, Newsom signed a bill forcing refineries to maintain minimum storage levels or face million-dollar-a-day penalties.[60]

Shortly after Newsom signed it, Phillips 66 announced plans to shut its large Los Angeles-area oil refinery because of "market dynamics" in the state.[61] The U.S. Energy Information Agency later cited the law and the refinery closure as evidence of "ongoing challenges to the state's fuel market."[62]

Meanwhile, Bonta continued to target oil and gas companies in a landmark civil suit, modeled on the successful multi-state litigation against tobacco companies in the 1990s.[63] He went forward with the suit despite readily acknowledging it would drive gas prices even higher.[64] On top of the price hikes Bonta's lawfare will likely spur, analysts predict an additional 65 cents per gallon after the California Air Resources Board approved new regulations in the fall of 2024.[65]

The costly regulations, lawsuits and refinery exits will only further disrupt West Coast gasoline supply, sending a rippling effect to neighboring states.

The swing states of Arizona and Nevada recently sent bipartisan letters from their governors warning Newsom that the new mandates on refineries he signed into law would create shortages and drive up prices in their states because 80% of their gasoline comes from California refineries. But the Newsom-appointed California Air Resources Board approved them anyway.[66]

While Newsom and Bonta are thumbing their noses at consumers' pain at the pump, the governor and those he's appointed to state boards and agencies are using green policy to exact political revenge on Elon Musk.

As Musk was boosting Trump on the 2024 campaign trail, the California Coastal Commission, which is charged with protecting the state's shoreline from development, rejected Musk's SpaceX bid, supported by the U.S. Air Force, to increase rocket launches off the coast.

Commissioners weren't shy about the political motivations behind the decision, openly citing Musk's support for Trump.[67]

"We're dealing with a company, the head of which has aggressively injected himself into the presidential race, and he's managed a company in a way...that I find very disturbing," agency Chair Caryl Hart said during a fall 2024 meeting. Hart is the wife of Mickey Hart, the longtime drummer for the Grateful Dead, the iconic band, which sprung from the 1960s counterculture hippie movement.[68]

Newsom doubled down on the political retribution, pledging in November 2024 to prevent Musk's Tesla from receiving any new state tax credits if Trump ends the federal tax credit for EV-purchases.[69]

California's petty green politics and self-inflicted energy wounds—unrealistic carbon-reduction mandates, rolling blackouts, sky-high utility rates gas-tax hikes, and incomplete transportation boondoggles—are merely a glimpse of what we will see if progressives are allowed to continue in their crusade to impose their green agenda on all Americans.

CHAPTER NINE

Profiteering Pandemic

IT WAS A CRISP fall night when a dozen friends, political colleagues, and business associates sat down for a three-star Michelin dinner inside the warm glow of a private dining room at an understated farmhouse in Napa Valley. Reservations are mythically difficult to obtain at the French Laundry and often require several months on the waiting list. Just to book dinner requires a nonrefundable deposit of $350 a person for a ten-course tasting meal. The final bill depends on the selection from the wine list featuring the world's "most famous producers, hard-to-get cult wines and some little-known gems," as the elite eatery's website states.[1] When the luxurious restaurant first reopened indoor dining during the COVID pandemic, owner and chef Thomas Keller capitalized on the high demand, sharply inflating dinner-seating fees to $850 a person.[2] Yet on this particular evening, the political price the elite group paid was far higher—at least in the short term.

It was November 6, 2020, and those gathering maskless in a private room facing the courtyard included California Governor Gavin Newsom, his wife, and several top state medical executives and lobbyists. Among them was Jason Kinney, a close friend and longtime adviser to Newsom who also made his living representing business interests in Sacramento. The photos taken on the scene captured a "careless, Gatsby-esque vibe," the *New York Times* opined in an editorial headlined "Gavin Newsom, What Were You Thinking?"[3] The final bill for Newsom's party is still shrouded in some secrecy. Willie Brown, San Francisco's former mayor and Newsom's political patron, wrote that he heard the wine tab alone that night was $12,000.[4]

California was the first state to impose far-reaching lockdowns and restrictions because of the coronavirus, and the last to lift them more than a year later. In late March, Newsom ordered all forty million residents to stay home and mandated some of the strictest requirements anywhere in the country. The governor first imposed mask mandates in public settings in June 2020 and didn't lift them until March 1, 2022. California residents were inundated with Newsom's slow-the-spread lectures about wearing masks in public and even in between bites while dining out with family members or roommates.[5]

"Going out to eat with members of your household this weekend? Don't forget to keep your mask on in between bites," the California's governor's official Twitter page instructed.[6] "Do your part to keep those around you healthy. #SlowtheSpread." The pedantic hectoring came in the form of official statements, televised service announcements, and covid19.ca.gov tweets and other social media posts, imploring those who dared to dine out in still struggling reopened restaurants to "minimize the number of times you take your mask off." Some of the ads came complete with how-to graphics showing proper face-covering practices.[7] When residents did venture out, large digital signs on the near-empty interstates confronted motorists with grave warnings: "Avoid gatherings. Stay home. Save Lives."

In the first months of the pandemic, surfers and paddleboarders alone in the ocean but flouting beach closures were arrested in Los Angeles County by police patrolling the shore by boat. They were fined thousands of dollars. Police in Encinitas, California, ticketed twenty-two people who were found "watching the sunset" and having picnics near the beach for breaching the state's stay-at-home order. The violations carried fines up to $1,000 or six months in jail, or both.[8] Just a few months later, Anthony Fauci, then serving as the White House's ubiquitous chief medical advisor and arbiter of all things COVID, and the San Francisco County Health Department would begin encouraging socially distanced outdoor exercise as one of the best ways to combat contracting the virus.

In a particularly farcical moment of the pandemic experience in California, city-run beaches opened before state-run coastal areas did. Residents flooded onto the city-run beaches, which were so overrun that state-mandated social distancing became impossible. Meanwhile, state-run beaches just yards away remained empty. Taking it to an even more extraordinary level of absurdity, during the summer of 2020 parking lots for many beaches remained closed to enforce social distancing, but cities allowed Black Lives Matter supporters to hold crowded protests there. Newsom ordered churches and other houses of worship to stop holding in-person services in numerous counties considered at widespread risk for coronavirus transition. Some churches were fined hundreds of thousands of dollars for breaking the rules.[9]

Eventually, a California appeals court ruled that outlawing church gatherings violated religious freedom rights. That judgment followed a Supreme Court decision nearly a year earlier that determined that California officials, including Newsom, unlawfully discriminated against houses of worship by imposing stricter rules than they did for other public gathering places. "Since the arrival of COVID-19, California has openly imposed more stringent regulations on religious institutions than on many businesses," Justice Neil Gorsuch wrote in that ruling. "When a state so obviously targets religion for differential treatment, our job becomes that much clearer."[10]

The state's four largest school districts first shuttered schools on March 13, 2020. Newsom, whose own elementary-age children went to a reopened private school, tried to push a February 2021 school reopening plan. But teachers' unions flexed their muscles and pushed back, and the governor failed to order schools to reopen as other states did. California had the fewest students attending in-person instruction as of June 2021.[11]

Just days after the French Laundry bombshell story broke, amid the backlash over Newsom's and his pals' maskless dining hypocrisy, Newsom stayed the course with his harsh government mandate, declaring a month-long curfew starting the week before Thanksgiving. The mandate outlawed the celebration of Thanksgiving with anyone but immediate family members from the same household and shut down all nonessential work and gatherings from 10 p.m. to 5 a.m. It applied to all fifty-four of the state's fifty-eight counties in the purple tier (the most restrictive color swath in the state's reopening plan) where COVID was spreading rapidly. Photos capturing Newsom's night at the French Laundry went public just two days before he issued the Thanksgiving decree.

Simmering public anger over his strict approach to COVID quickly boiled over. Several social media memes captured the public pushback to the edict—with one using a clip from the holiday Claymation movie *Santa Claus Is Comin' to Town* parodying Newsom's sweeping COVID crackdown and comparing him to the character of the oppressive German villain Burgermeister Meisterburger, who cancels Christmas and outlaws toys in that 1970 classic. While amusing, the memes failed to capture the level of contempt many Californians felt for the series of harsh decrees, especially after Newsom's uneven treatment of different types of industry sectors. The governor prioritized lockdown carve-outs for Hollywood over relief for restaurants, churches, and schools.

Kinney, who was at the center of the scandal as the birthday boy that night, was well known around the state capitol for his close ties to Newsom—even serving as a ghost writer for his speeches and an unofficial fixer when the governor found himself in tough spots. Newsom and Kinney first got to know each other back in the early 2000s when Newsom was serving as a San Francisco supervisor and Kinney was working as a senior communications advisor and chief speechwriter for then-Democratic Governor Gray Davis, who was recalled in part because of his failure to prevent rolling energy blackouts. Before becoming a lobbyist, Kinney served as a consultant with the California Democratic Party for much of the previous decade.

Kinney also became a convenient conduit between Newsom and influential party leaders. He would go on to run Newsom's 2016 campaign to legalize marijuana while Newsom was lieutenant governor and serve on the transition team after he was elected governor. He then joined Axiom in 2019, after Newsom took his oath of office. In that post, he lobbied the governor's office for several business clients while still serving as a close, unpaid adviser to his longtime friend. The birthday dinner wasn't the first time Kinney's work had faced serious scrutiny. In 2013, the California Fair Political Practices Commission fined Kinney $12,000 for violating California laws requiring him to disclose a year's worth of lobbying activity on behalf of a developer after he had discussed that client's policy concerns with lawmakers.[12]

After Kinney's 2016 role as an official mouthpiece for Proposition 64, the 2016 Newsom-championed ballot initiative to legalize cannabis use, the top cannabis companies then turned around and hired his firm. Critics said it seemed like Kinney was cashing in on his political insider status and close ties to Newsom. He wasn't the only one. Former Attorney General Bill Lockyer, whose four-decade career included serving as the leader of the state senate, spent eight years regulating the marijuana industry and fighting Washington on the issue of legal marijuana, then cofounded a licensed pot distributor after Prop. 64 passed. *Capitol Weekly* described Kinney as "a sort of majordomo" for Newsom, jumping in during crises when the governor needed "strategic policy and political recommendations."[13] During COVID and afterward, Newsom would face scrutiny for carveouts benefitting some of Kinney's top clients, including Netflix, as this chapter will later discuss. The "French Laundry Supper Club crew," as the *Sacramento Bee* described Newsom's tight-knit relationships with lobbyists, lifted the veil on Newsom's work on behalf of Kinney's clients and other special interests—so much so that the governor was forced to appoint a chief ethics advisor to monitor his relationships with them and impose a ban on lobbying by his campaign and political consultants.[14]

The international backlash over Newsom's double standards for himself and his elite circle of friends that fateful French Laundry night would eventually fuel an expensive but ultimately futile recall of the governor and damage his personal credibility—even among many lifelong Democrats. A *Politico* article quoted state political analyst David McCuan suggesting that Newsom had undermined his presidential ambitions and revealed a "fatal personality flaw" in attempting to use strict pandemic policies to build "sizzle" and a national profile on the cable political talk show circuit.[15]

Then-GOP state Representative Kevin Kiley, who unsuccessfully sued Newsom over his abuse of his COVID executive authority and who now represents one of the most conservative congressional districts in California, predicted Harris's ascension ahead of Newsom when Biden selected her to be his running mate in 2020. "Now that Kamala Harris has elbowed Gavin Newsom out of running for president any time soon, perhaps he can give his full attention to the parochial matter of governing California," Kiley tweeted.[16]

Gil Duran, Jerry Brown's former spokesman, also saw the writing on the wall. "Coronavirus failures—and Kamala's rise—thwart Governor Newsom's presidential dreams," Duran concluded. "Once Newsom accepts that he will never be president, he'll be able to govern California...instead of attempting to triangulate his way to 1600 Pennsylvania Ave," Duran wrote.[17]

The tony maskless dinner with well-heeled lobbyist buddies was Newsom's most visible misstep during the pandemic, but his record of failing to protect the state's most vulnerable and those he forced out of work with strict lockdowns is far worse. New York Governor Andrew Cuomo was hyper-scrutinized for his handling of COVID, especially when it came to nursing home deaths. The same could not be said for Newsom, although he too was vulnerable on the issue. In the fall of 2021, Cuomo succumbed to a ballooning sexual harassment scandal in an astonishing reversal of fortune. Just months earlier, he was holding court, competing with President Trump for national television audiences locked down in their homes, with his near-daily detailed and candid press conferences about his handling of the COVID crisis in the hardest-hit state. There was talk of a Senate or presidential run. He even appeared via video at the 2020 Democratic National Convention, delivering an endorsement of Biden that was a weird mix of New Yorker braggadocio and COVID victory speech.

But that was before the state attorney general launched an investigation into multiple sexual harassment allegations against Cuomo and other charges involving Cuomo's misuse of power to hide the true extent of New

York state nursing home deaths during the pandemic. Cuomo was facing impeachment so decided to resign instead. Appalling nursing home death tolls were hardly limited to New York. In fact, California's nursing home deaths exceeded New York's by roughly four hundred (though the Golden State has nearly twice the population of New York.) The five states with the highest number of COVID-related deaths in nursing homes are Pennsylvania with 10,616; Texas with 9,466; California with 9,431; New York with 9,038; and Ohio with 8,541, as of January 2022, according to *Becker's Hospital Review.*[18]

Roughly one in eight Californians who died of COVID lived in an assisted living facility. Like Cuomo's administration, the Newsom administration did not require accurate reporting on COVID-19-positive patients and deaths in nursing homes to the state Division of Occupational Safety and Health, known as Cal/OSHA, in the first year of the pandemic.[19] A *Sacramento Bee* investigation found that the California Department of Public Health was regularly updating a list of COVID-19 infections and deaths at nursing homes, but only about half of the facilities bothered to report those deaths to Cal/OSHA.[20] As many as sixty-four nursing homes were failing to report the deaths, making its spread impossible to fully track in the workplaces where it was the deadliest. The state's final numbers for nursing-home-related COVID deaths are still disputed, though you wouldn't know it from the state's media coverage. In contrast to New York City's media saturation, California has far fewer media outlets than Manhattan and tends to pull its punches when covering Newsom and other leading Democrats.

Some brave Democrats launched blistering attacks on Newsom's pandemic record of managing nursing homes during COVID. Then-Assemblymember Jim Wood, a Democrat who chaired the Health Committee, slammed the president of the state nursing home association for saying California was the shining star in the nation when it came to preventing coronavirus outbreaks at nursing homes.[21] "Where is the proactive, patient-centered, public safety approach here?" he said during a committee hearing in early October 2021. "Because I don't feel it right now. And yet here we are. Here we sit. We have to wait for news articles. We have to wait for people to die."[22]

Wood was blunter in an interview two months later. "The number of Covid infections and deaths that happened in skilled nursing homes in California is truly appalling," he said. "I expect better from us."[23] Wood and others were particularly incensed over news that the state allowed Shlomo Rechnitz, California's largest nursing home owner, to operate many facilities even as their license applications were left in pending status or outright denied.[24] State rules require nursing home operators to be licensed by the California Department of Public Health, but the agency allowed Rechnitz's facilities to ignore those rules and operate while license applications were "pending." A *CalMatters* investigation uncovered evidence of a state licensing process that is "opaque, confusing and rife with inconsistencies."[25]

"I'm just a little speechless when it comes to this ownership nightmare in California and how it's gotten to this point," Molly Davies, the Los Angeles County long-term care ombudsman told *CalMatters*. Davies's office advocates for residents of nursing homes and other adult care facilities. "Really there's an issue of the process having no integrity," she added. Some homes still listed the previous owners of the nursing homes as the official license holders.[26]

According to CalMatters, one such home was Northpointe, a ninety-nine-bed nursing home that was fined more than $900,000 in 2018 (later reduced to $537,000 plus interest) for subpar patient care.[27] A state inspection report found that residents experienced painful bedsores, and staff said they had trouble distributing needed medications to all the patients.

The families of 14 deceased COVID victims sued another facility, Windsor Redding Care. The complaint listed 142 violations substantiated by investigators including neglect, abuse, staffing and infection control issues between January 2018 and June 2021. In November 2020, the federal government fined the facility $152,000 as a result of the inspections.

Democratic Assemblymember Al Muratsuchi of Los Angeles cited the lawsuit against the facility, noting that it "clearly provides Exhibit A of the broken state licensing system for nursing homes." Commenting on its failure to obtain a license, he observed, "The fact that this facility had its license application denied and yet they continued to operate during this pandemic, which unfortunately led to an alleged 24 deaths from COVID, highlights the urgent need for the state to fix its broken licensing system."[28] But in June 2024, the Court of Appeals in California affirmed a trial court decision finding that the facilities arbitration agreement didn't apply to the family members even though they had signed on behalf of their deceased relatives.[29]

The nursing home criticism quickly faded once Newsom pledged to make radical changes to the way Sacramento was overseeing the $5.45 billion in state funds doled out to roughly 1,200 skilled nursing homes across the state. And there were other competing California COVID scandals making even bigger local headlines because of the sheer magnitude of their impact.

Even though it received little press coverage outside of California, Newsom presided over the biggest financial scandal in state history. The federal government's infusion of unemployment insurance cash during the pandemic was meant to help tens of millions of people forced from their jobs stay afloat. But in California, the antiquated distribution system was flooded and fell apart. Scammers orchestrated an unprecedented level of fraud while California workers, many whose industries were devastated by COVID lockdowns and restrictions, struggled to survive.

A single mother who lost two jobs and was living in her car with her son was forced to wait five months before receiving payments.[30]

A security guard worried whether fellow workers seeking unemployment would wind up in the homeless camps he once patrolled.

An office manager filed for food stamps and MediCal to survive while fighting a yearslong legal battle to get funds.[31]

Shan Balogh, a twenty-eight-year-old out of work traveling salesmen made thirty-eight phone calls to California's jammed Unemployment Development Department in three months trying to inquire about the $11,700 the agency owed him. Three days after making seventeen calls in one day, his mother was awakened by a 4 a.m. phone call. Shane had committed suicide.[32]

Newsom's COVID lockdown policies decimated the restaurant, sports, and some parts of the entertainment industries, with millions of Californians getting layoff notices within a matter of months. By September 2020, more than forty thousand small business had closed, and more than five million unemployed workers were forced out of work.[33] Faced with the second-highest unemployment rate in the country, Bank of America, the unemployment debit card contractor for the California Employment Development Department (EDD), warned the agency that it might not have enough plastic to print the millions of cards that the agency needed. Across the country, most states were struggling to avoid a modern-day Great Depression by working with the federal government to expedite payments to laid-off workers as quickly as possible.

Nowhere, however, was the failure as colossal as California. The EDD paid out $188 billion in unemployment benefits since the first pandemic shutdowns, with $31 billion of that sum paid to fraudsters. Along the way, nearly a million of out-of-work Californians, who prior to COVID hit lived paycheck to paycheck, were wrongly denied benefits and forced to spar with the state's unemployment agency to get their promised payments. Some who struggled to feed their families became angry and suicidal.[34]

The stories of people struggling to get through on the EDD's jammed call lines are legendary. Out-of-work residents were put on hold for more than four hours, only to get through to a receptionist and have their calls answered by a recording that said, "Thank you for calling. EDD is now closed."[35] Another legitimately unemployed worker, who struggled to get the agency to verify his identity, reported calling EDD five hundred times in a week. In the summer of 2021, agency lines were so inundated by residents desperate for their unemployment payments, companies that autodialed EDD sprung up, with services beginning at $15 to $300. Even then, some customers reported that their calls kept getting cut off.

Nearly four years later, more than 120,000 people were still fighting layers of bureaucracy to try to get their payments even as they were struggling to make ends meet with postpandemic inflation sending gas and food prices soaring.[36] "I really feel like I'm a hostage," an office manager, who asked to be identified only as Carole M. and has been awaiting an appeal hearing since November 2022 told *CalMatters* the following year. "I had no money, and I kept saying: 'How long is this going to take?'"[37] Thousands of businesses went belly up, yet Newsom's wineries, restaurants, and hotels quickly received federal Paycheck Protection Program loans and continued to flourish. At least nine companies partially owned by Newsom received more than $3 million in these loans, according to the Small Business Administration and an ABC7 analysis of the records.[38]

Nearly a million deserving California workers couldn't obtain the EDD benefits they deserved, while fraudsters were raking in tens of billions. The funds lost include $400 million to roughly thirty-five thousand prisoners, including several big-name death-row inmates, according to a state audit and a Sacramento district attorney's investigation.[39] Some criminals even filed claims on behalf of famous inmates like Scott Peterson, who in 2004 was convicted of murdering his wife, Laci Peterson, while she was eight months pregnant, and Cary Stayner, who murdered four women near Yosemite Park in 1999. One person was able to scam more than $21,000 using the name of the now-late Senator Dianne Feinstein.

In 2022, when the EDD tried to claw back some of the lost funds, it mistakenly seized money from many identity-theft victims, not the real criminals. The victims included a Stanford University employee who had her wages garnished after the EDD seized her tax refund.[40] Folks who suffered from the identity theft were blindsided and bewildered by the aggressive government action and outraged that the EDD gave billions to crooks and then mistakenly confiscated money from lawfully abiding residents to pay it back. The state auditor's report found that some fraud could have been avoided if administrators had followed reforms recommended a decade earlier.[41] Unlike at least thirty-five other states, California lacks the technology to cross-check its state prisoner rolls against unemployment claims. The state had implemented a fraud-detection system but reportedly shut it off in 2016 when the federal grant paying for the $2 million per year program ran out.

Despite the massive fraud scandal at the state's Labor and Workforce Development Agency, President Biden nominated Julie Su, the woman who ran the broken unemployment insurance distribution program, to be the Department of Labor's deputy secretary.[42] When Labor Secretary Marty Walsh left the agency in February 2023, Biden then promoted Su to take over.[43] Her nomination, however, stalled amid vocal Republican opposition, citing the $31 billion EDD fraud that occurred under her watch, though Biden continued to allow her to run the department as an acting secretary

Both Republicans and some Democrats also took issue with Su over her support for California's controversial AB5, known as the gig worker bill. The law, which Newsom signed into effect, essentially outlaws all forms of contract work, including Uber and Lyft services, as well as freelance journalism and most other independent contracting. (Uber, Lyft, and courier services such as DoorDash subsequently won exemptions from the law in November 2020.)[44] The outcome was predictable: many businesses and nonprofit enterprises that relied on independent contractors stopped using those workers—both because workers who had built self-sufficient careers did not want to trade the freedom of freelance work for the false benefits of employment, and because many companies couldn't afford to convert them to full-time employees.

After the law's passage, countless self-employed Californians suddenly lost work opportunities and faced steeply declining incomes. Making matters worse, AB5 took effect in January 2020, mere weeks before Newsom locked down the state in response to COVID-19. When Californians most needed the freedom and flexibility that independent contracting provides, they were frozen out of the labor market. The AB5 fallout figured prominently in Su's Senate confirmation hearings. Su promised not to bring a similar gig worker law to the federal level.

Just as critics warned, the Department of Labor in January 2024 under Su's control as the unconfirmed acting secretary issued its own gig worker rule that would force companies to treat some workers as employees rather than as less-expensive independent contractors. Big app-based platforms such as Uber, Lyft, and DoorDash said they believed the new rule wouldn't force them to reclassify their gig drivers, but business groups slammed the rule for creating uncertainty for employers.[45] As of this writing, there are at least five pending lawsuits filed by business groups, a trucking company, and freelance writers challenging the new rule. The California state legislature has passed more than one hundred exemptions to the rule in the wake of a bipartisan backlash.

While Newsom was grappling with fallout over the state's gig worker law in the middle of a largely self-created COVID unemployment crisis, his efforts to help businesses were purely performative.

After Tom Steyer, a hedge fund billionaire turned environmentalist and far-left activist who lobbied in favor of ending the state's cash bail system, dropped his campaign for the Democratic presidential nomination in February 2020, he had time on his hands.[46] In April, Newsom tapped Steyer to lead a new state COVID Task Force on Jobs and Business Recovery. Under pressure to rescue the state's economy, which was still in a free fall, Newsom set high expectations. "We want to make this meaningful," he said at the press conference announcing it. "This is not something where in six months, I'm looking forward to giving you a draft or putting out a long, thick report."[47]

Yet, after seven months passed, the sole accomplishment of Steyer's commission was a very thin report, a twenty-seven-page document titled *Recovery for All* that included a series of aspirational recommendations.[48] Then on November 20, the task force was summarily disbanded. Its report, *Politico* pointed out, included "no specific new initiatives to protect California businesses in the pandemic," and it "was not immediately clear why Newsom was shutting down his task force just as California [was] enter[ing] a new round of business closures."[49]

But Newsom was instrumental in helping some industries—those he and his wife had close personal ties to and those who had donated richly to his campaign coffers and her documentary filmmaking charity. While Newsom was mismanaging unemployment and COVID relief payments and keeping most businesses that couldn't move to remote work closed, he issued an exemption for the television and movie industries, deeming them "critical infrastructure," which allowed them to continue filming and operating during the pandemic.[50] Plenty of studios took advantage of the carveout, including Netflix, which started filming a new season of *The Kominsky Method*, a comedy starring Michael Douglas.

The Netflix connection figures into Newsom's infamous French Laundry incident, which helped fuel the unsuccessful 2021 recall campaign against him. Jason Kinney, whose birthday the group was celebrating at the French Laundry that night, also lobbies for Netflix, one of the businesses that had pressed for Hollywood exemptions from lockdowns. In fact, Netflix nearly tripled spending on lobbying in California during the first year of the pandemic, jumping to an average of $70,725 a quarter. Paramount Pictures, meanwhile, spent at least $85,000 that year to influence "essential business" rules that California agencies produced.

Fast-forward to the final weeks of the recall campaign against Newsom in 2021. Paramount Pictures provided $40,000 to the antirecall campaign's coffers. That check followed a $3 million infusion from Netflix CEO Reed Hastings in late May, the most from any single donor.

Yet three years later, when those decisions hadn't aged well and amid speculation Newsom could replace Biden on the Democratic presidential ticket, Newsom tried to dodge responsibility for keeping the film industry open for business while locking down churches, bars, and gyms.

Newsom's unlikely antagonist was left-leaning Chuck Todd, then the anchor of *Meet the Press*, who confronted Newsom about his heavy-handed approach after Newsom agreed to debate Florida Governor Ron DeSantis. (DeSantis imposed some COVID lockdowns and harsh rules in the beginning of the pandemic but didn't require any businesses to shut down and eventually lifted all pandemic-related restrictions in September of 2020.)

"You found a way to allow the motion picture industry and the movie industry to get back to work, but you didn't allow people to grieve together at funerals or at churches," Todd remarked in his unexpectedly tough interrogation of Newsom. "This is the anger between the populace and the elites: here you prioritize this industry, but you were tougher on those that just wanted to go worship."[51]

In a futile effort to explain the lockdown disparity, Newsom first claimed that "there's a lot of humility" before completely dodging responsibility: "We didn't know what we didn't know," he sputtered. "And it was hardly 'I'—it was 'we' collectively. I think all of us, in terms of our collective wisdom, we've evolved."[52]

While Newsom protected the entertainment industry, every other sector of the economy lagged when the state and the country lifted the lockdowns. In 2021, California was among the states that bounced back most slowly from COVID, with unemployment stuck at 8.3 percent for several months, the second-highest unemployment rate in the nation, next to Hawaii.

As outlined in the previous chapter, Newsom provided a $990 million no-bid mask-manufacturing deal to the Chinese company Build Your Dreams (BYD) and was later embarrassed when the EV car manufacturer was forced to return a quarter-billion dollars for failing to meet a deadline. Newsom was hardly chastened by the negative press that generated. Declaring a "state of emergency" because of the pandemic, he brazenly granted no-bid contracts worth hundreds of millions to health service providers and other corporations, some of which donated to charities at his "behest."

Because of the obvious ethical issues involved, several states prohibit such directed donations. In California, they are officially labeled "behested payments" and fully sanctioned, even encouraged. In 2020 alone, corporate interests, including Facebook, Google, and Blue Shield of California, donated $227 million to charities at Newsom's "behest," a huge spike compared to just $12.1 million in 2019, his first year in office. In contrast, former Governor Jerry Brown successfully requested just $37 million in behested payments during his entire eight years in office. TikTok, the social media platform many US lawmakers want to ban for its connections to the Chinese Communist Party, donated $300,000 at Newsom's behest in one of the first months of the pandemic to a nonprofit promoting the governor's strict pandemic lockdowns and COVID masking mandates. Of course, tech companies like TikTok had perhaps the most to financially gain from keeping people at home, remote, isolated, and glued to their devices.

During the pandemic, Newsom doled out eight thousand no-bid

contracts in 2020 alone worth a combined $11.9 billion, far more exclusive, noncompetitive deals than any previous California governor had ever awarded. Yet the return on that investment is still unclear in many cases.

For example, Newsom awarded a $1.7 billion no-bid contract to [Valencia Branch Laboratory] to process COVID tests for the state. Less than a year later, the lab had processed only 1 to 8 percent of all California's tests. Whistleblowers came forward to disclose fraud, waste, and dozens of other problems, including those related to safety and disinfection procedures. The state decided to terminate the contract. In total, at least a half-dozen corporate recipients of no-bid contracts, including Blue Shield and United-Health, had made or went on to make substantial contributions to Newsom's reelection campaigns.

Other decisions Newsom made during the pandemic would come back to haunt him years later. In the middle of COVID, during the chaos and upheaval of the pandemic and when most of the legislature was working remotely, Newsom quietly decided to make a dramatic change to financial regulations throughout the state.[53] In a September 2020 press release, Newsom took direct credit for the changes, though they came in the form of two assembly bills he readily signed into law that month. "In an effort to strengthen consumer financial protections in California, Governor Gavin Newsom proposed an initiative to modernize and revamp the current Department of Business Oversight, including an increase in staff and authority, to enhance its regulatory scope and become a national model for consumer protections," the release, put out by the revamped Department of Financial Protection and Innovation (DFPI), declared.[54]

The new DFPI added new financial mandates and staff, including a "consumer outreach team engaging vulnerable populations," and "an Office of Financial Technology Innovation that will engage with new industries and consumer advocates to encourage consumer friendly innovation and job creation in California." The governor then placed the agency under the control of a commissioner he appointed and directed it "to bring administrative and civil actions, and to prosecute those civil actions before state and federal courts," and "to hold hearings and issue publications, results of inquiries and research, and reports that may aid in effectuating the purposes of this law."[55] The new directives and empowered commissioner gave the governor greater control and retaliatory power over banks that failed to comply with his woke goals of "encouraging" green innovation or "engaging" with certain DEI communities, as columnist Susan Shelley described it in an Orange County Register column.[56] In fact, California banks could have faced administrative penalties from the department if they failed to meet these new obligations.

Conversely, the new laws also gave some banks the ability to cozy up to key politicians by funding their pet "innovation" projects that may or may not have been rejected by more hard-nosed banks or venture capital firms as risky investments. Thus, Newsom and the state legislature ushered in a venture capital boom in green-energy investments aimed at combating climate change.

In March 2023, the chickens came home to roost when the Silicon Valley Bank (SVB) collapse threatened these "clean-energy" start-ups. It was the second-largest bank collapse in US history and the first since the predatory-lending-spawned 2008 financial crisis. The bank had "relationships with more than 1,500 companies working on technologies aimed at curbing global warming," the New York Times reported.[57] Immediately after the DFPI's expanded regulatory powers became effective on January 1, 2021, Newsom asked SVB to donate to the California Partners Project, the "child well-being and gender equity" charity run by his wife, Jennifer Siebel Newsom. It was just days later when the first $25,000 payment from the bank came through. That year, SVB channeled a total of $100,000 to Siebel Newsom's nonprofit. John China, the former president of SVB Capital, the venture capital and credit investing arm of the bank, is a founding member of the California Partners Project's board of directors.[58]

Two years later, when SVB's explosive collapse spread panic in the banking industry, Newsom lobbied for the federal government's rescue package for the beleaguered financial institution, now on the verge of collapse. In the governor's frantic attempt to save the institution, he glaringly failed to disclose several of his business and personal accounts held by the bank, including that of his three wineries, as well as the deep ties between its executives and his wife's charity. Newsom's status as an SVB customer wasn't hidden or even subtle. Three wineries he partially owns, CADE, Odette, and PlumpJack, were listed as clients of SVB on the bank's website at the time of its implosion.

Newsom also maintained accounts at SVB, according to reports citing a longtime former employee of Newsom who handled his finances.[59] Still, the governor didn't bother disclosing these close ties to SVB even while furiously lobbying the federal government for help stabilizing the failing bank. "Over the last 48 hours, I have been in touch with the highest levels of leadership at the White House and Treasury," he said in a statement just days after the bank's failure.[60]

The California government also went out of its way to assist SVB in the middle of its March 2023 tailspin. The DFPI, in an order taking possession of the bank, declared that despite its $1.8 billion in losses, SVB was "in sound financial condition prior to March 9." Three days later, the US Treasury, Federal Reserve, and Federal Deposit Insurance Corporation announced it was removing the $250,000 FDIC limit on insurance of bank deposits. The determination assured that Newsom and all other depositors who held millions of uninsured dollars in SVB would get all of their money back.

President Joe Biden, worried SVB's collapse would have a domino effect in the banking sector, hailed the solution as one that "protects American workers and small businesses, and keeps our financial system safe."[61] The government's move to protect the bank's high-end clientele of tech investors, venture capitalists, and even wineries sparked a fierce debate over the morality of the intervention. "There is definitely a class element," economist Dean Baker of the Center for Economic and Policy Research told the *Intercept*. "Look at how easily we can toss tens of millions of dollars at people who couldn't figure out how limits on FDIC deposit insurance work, but the idea of giving $10k in debt relief to a student who might have used bad judgment in taking out a loan when they were 18, gets so many people upset about moral hazard and individual responsibility."[62]

But none other than Larry Summers, former Treasury secretary and an ex-president of Harvard University, admonished those who questioned the bailout, arguing that action was needed lest the SVB collapse and that of Signature Bank, which failed shortly after SVB, start a run on other banks across the country. "This is not the time for moral hazard lectures or for lesson administering or for alarm about the political consequences of 'bailouts,'" he tweeted. "Confidence is most important now. Afterwards there is much to review regarding risk management, regulation, accounting for capital conventions, and what all this means for stress testing."[63]

The federal regulators' decision to step in and bail out the bank saved thousands of small clean-energy and other "innovative" tech startups that would have failed without it. But it also helped bigger companies that would have been forced to take a loss but would have easily survived, firms such as Sequoia Capital, the world's most prominent venture capital firm, which got covered for $1 billion it had with SVB. It also bailed out Kanzhun Ltd., the Beijing-based tech company, which received at least $900 million in bailout funds.[64] Kanzhun was one of several Chinese companies that did business with SVB.

Still, the Feds can't just wave their magic wand without repercussions. There is no free lunch in the financial industry. Somebody always pays the price.

While Hollywood and green-energy projects thrived during COVID, low-wage workers in service industries suffered the most while school closures and virtual learning hit black and Latino students the hardest. In Sacramento County, test scores among the economically disadvantaged during the 2020–2021 school year for nonnative English speakers went down to 32.18 percent compared to 37.08 percent during the 2018–2019 school year, according to California's 2022 Smarter Balanced assessment. For math, 20.35 met or exceeded the standard during the 2021–2022 school year, down from 26.8 in 2018–2019.[65]

"Children who tend to demonstrate higher performance have more resources outside of school. When it comes to standardized test scores, we can predict student test scores fairly accurately just by looking at the source of resources that they have at home," said Jacob Hibel, codirector of the Center for Poverty and Inequality Research at UC Davis.[66] In the fall of 2022, Newsom put out a press release hailing his efforts to make up for COVID learning loss, claiming California outperformed other states in minimizing learning loss. He argued the results showed the importance of the state's $23.8 billion investment to support students returning to the classroom, with 89 percent of schools offering summer programs with mental health and tutoring services.[67]

"According to the National Assessment of Educational Progress (NAEP) results in reading and math for 4th and 8th graders nationwide, California's NAEP reading scores remained relatively steady while most other states and the national average showed declines, and math scores didn't decline as much as most other states or the national average," the governor's office said in the press release.

The governor never mentions that California public schools are among the lowest performers in the nation—so overall, their post-COVID testing declines may have been minimal because they were far lower to begin with. *U.S. News and World Report* ranks California thirty-eighth out of fifty for pre-K through twelfth grade public education.[68] The extended school closures and virtual-only learning across the state took a heavy emotional toll. A study in the medical journal *Injury Epidemiology* published in March 2023 found that overall, suicides for adults declined during 2020 and 2021, but youth suicides increased, especially when schools were fully closed and offering virtual learning only. The study, based on publicly available data from the California Department of Public Health, found that young people aged ten to nineteen experienced twenty-one more suicides across the state compared to prepandemic levels.[69]

One school district in North San Diego County showed just how far teachers' unions would go to battle parents over reopening classrooms: it hired private investigators to try to dig up dirt and follow conservative board members around town, and when that didn't work, spent more union funds to try to recall those they couldn't intimidate off the boards.

The school board for the San Dieguito Union High School District, a high-performing area with thirteen thousand students and six hundred teachers, had scheduled school reopenings for January 2021 but reversed course when the union sued in December to block that action. School board Trustee Michael Allman, who was elected to the board in the fall of 2020, was the lone dissenting vote. Allman's outspoken opposition won strong support from local parents organizing on a Facebook forum, a coalition that quickly grew to more than two thousand supporters. Other board members, including President Maureen "Mo" Muir, had also started pushing back against COVID school closures.

The San Dieguito Faculty Association (SDFA), the local affiliate of the California Teachers Association (CTA), launched a recall campaign against Allman just five months into his four-year term. The union accused Allman, a former energy company executive, of violating the district's code of conduct, charges he denies and that he believes arose from a public war of words over schools' pandemic policies taking place on social media sites. The SDFA then gave itself permission to spend up to $60,000 hiring a private firm to gather the five thousand signatures needed to recall Allman. At least $14,500 of that came directly from the CTA. Yet even with the private help, the union eventually gave up and the recall failed to qualify.

Allman had fought back, spending nearly all his free time going door to door defending himself. He said he heard from supporters that recall signature gatherers were falsely accusing him of being under criminal investigation, among other "outlandish lies," so he sent a cease-and-desist letter to SDFA President Duncan Brown. "It's hard to beat the unions. I prevailed because I have the support of parents who are speaking up like never before," Allman said in an interview. "Put yourself in my shoes. Teachers are spreading lies about me in the community, so I went door-to-door with parents to say, 'Hey, I'm a good guy, and I support parents.'"[70] He says he had a roughly 50 percent conversion rate of area residents who said they had already signed the recall petition. (State rules allow for the rescinding of signatures.) But the SDFA, again with significant CTA help, successfully forced a special election for another seat on the school board, which was held by Ty Hume, the only black member of the all-white panel. Hume, a businessman and openly declared independent, had been appointed after a union-backed trustee resigned earlier that year. Hume's appointment gave non-union-aligned members a three-to-two majority on the board.

The SDFA took issue with Hume's appointment, arguing that voters should have had a say in his election. His opponents produced the necessary signatures to rescind the appointment and call a special election, which cost the district up to $500,000 to hold. The school district was operating in the red at the time, using money from its general reserves to try to balance its budget. "I'm someone who has no allegiance—only to the students and their families—and [the union] is bringing people down from all over the state to go door to door to collect signatures against me," Hume told us.[71] But the gambit worked: Hume was defeated by union-backed candidate Julie Bronstein, who out-fundraised him with donations from the SDFA and another public employee union, as well as the local Democratic congressman, Scott Peters.

In a more bizarre twist, the same union hired a private investigator to follow Mo Muir home to see whether she was in fact living in the district she represented, as required by law. The private eye determined that the board president was renting out her home, which was up for sale, leading the local teachers' union president to file a complaint with the district attorney. But Muir explained that she was spending time at the home of her elderly mother-in-law in Lake Tahoe during the height of the pandemic lockdowns. She sold her home but rented another within the district boundaries. The district attorney didn't take any action, but Muir announced that she would not seek reelection that fall after an eruption of GOP infighting cost her the county GOP party's endorsement.

The union targeted the only black man ever elected to the school board even though Encinitas, one of the cities the board serves, just months prior had created a new social equity committee and tapped Marlon Taylor, president of the nonprofit Encinitas4Equality and the first black trustee of the Encinitas Union School District, as one of its eight members. Hume's supporters have argued that it's outrageous that the city of Encinitas celebrated a like-minded community volunteer while next door the teachers' union worked to remove the only other black school board trustee in the area because the union wasn't involved in his selection and they expected him to challenge their positions.

"The irony is thick and deep," said Ginny Merrifield, executive director of the Parents Association of North County, which pushed for expanded school reopening amid COVID pandemic closures. "The real motivation is to control the district policy, the upcoming June contract negotiations, and the school reopening process. We should be focused on the students, but this was never really about the students and that's what's sad about it."[72] Hume, a Bronx native whose father was a teamster and whose mother was a public school teacher, tried to defend himself by asserting that he wasn't not a member of either political party and considered himself an independent. But that type of free thinking is not what the unions wanted and expected from the school board.

It's no coincidence that the union homed in on this particular school district. The affluent seaside communities of North County San Diego, home to some of the state's best schools, had been at the vanguard of the reopening push since late 2020.

Frustrated by the union resistance to expanding in-classroom learning for high school students, parents in the area formed the Parents Association of North County to achieve that goal. Throughout the fall of 2020, as parents pushed for reopening schools, the union threw up roadblock after roadblock. In the fall of 2020, the superintendent and union ignored a school board vote requiring teachers to provide remote instruction from their classrooms to prepare for the reopening process.[73]

On Christmas Eve 2020, the local union, the SDFA, with legal assistance from the CTA, issued a cease-and-desist order blocking the district from reopening after winter break as planned. In February, the district applied to the state for a waiver to return to in-person learning, but the SDFA and its allies organized an email campaign to block it even though it had already been approved by the San Diego health authorities. In early 2021, the Parent Association of North County sued the state to overturn pandemic-related rules limiting the number of days of in-person learning, or completely blocking some schools from reopening at all.

Amid the legal wrangling, some of the parents in the case expressed deep concerns that their children either attempted suicide or expressed suicidal thoughts after learning their schools were continuing solely with distance learning. There were at least three suicides of students at high schools in the school district that occurred during the pandemic lockdowns, although it's difficult to know all the relevant factors that contributed. Parents in the case cited a spike in teen mental health cases nationwide, arguing that their children were suffering both socially and in their educational pursuits amid the isolation and loneliness brought on by school closures and lackluster remote learning options.

In March of 2021, San Diego Superior Court Judge Cynthia Freeland ruled in the association's favor, prohibiting the state from enforcing its restrictions that she agreed were "arbitrary," interfered with local school districts' reopening plans for in-person instruction, and denied children's "fundamental California right to basic educational equality."[74] The judge's decision applied to the entire state, sending a clear message to the statewide CTA and the Newsom administration that their guidelines weren't mandates and they must allow school districts to reopen more rapidly. That move and others rankled the North County union, which had a history of working with the district's trustees to approve union positions, set teacher and superintendent salaries, and control the district's finances. Merrifield, of the Parents Association of North County, said the unions were particularly aggressive because they worried that the board would set a precedent.

"This district in particular is a canary in the mine for everybody," she said. "What happens here is an example of what happens in other places around the state. We're small but we're definitely on the radar."[75] Merrifield said her organization is incredibly supportive of most teachers, whom she credits for working hard to adapt to remote learning techniques throughout the pandemic. But she argued the online learning and social isolation had been incredibly harmful to the social and emotional well-being of students. Parents felt like they had no control and were locked out of the discussion and the process. "The unions had all the controls, and the parents had none," she said. "That trust that existed was betrayed. Families, especially families of color, were disproportionately impacted by the learning loss and the loss of access to special [in-person] programs. So, the harm was significant."[76]

Conclusion

WHEN DONALD TRUMP CLINCHED the 2024 election late on Tuesday night Nov. 6, California's liberal elite plunged into a public meltdown. Jimmy Kimmel fought back tears on his late-night show, Christina Applegate said she was "reeling and sobbing," and Barbra Streisand, who'd previously threatened to move to England if Trump won, wrote on X.com that there were "no words left."[1] Rapper Cardi B posted a video rant that said, "This is why some of y'all states be getting hurricanes," before deleting it, an apparent reference to states that went red.[2]

Within two days, activist-driven protests ignited in Los Angeles, denouncing Trump's plans to deport illegal immigrants.[3] One group marched around Los Angeles City Hall, waving "abolish ICE" signs and demanding immediate action to officially designate Los Angeles a sanctuary city.[4] (It's worth noting that California law already shields illegal immigrants from federal enforcement.) To make matters worse for progressives across the state, Trump flipped 10 counties in California red, and Proposition 36, a tough-on-crime proposition many Democrats opposed, won in a landslide.[5] In Los Angeles, voters finally sent far-left District Attorney George Gascon packing after two previously failed recall attempts.[6]

But at least in one corner of the state, two cunning politicians were seizing the day while others wallowed.

Newsom's political star power had dimmed as Kamala Harris, his homegrown rival and occasional ally, ascended to the top of the Democratic

Party after she and other party leaders shoved Biden aside in the aftermath of his disastrous June debate performance. Before her anointing, speculation had swirled around Newsom, who had pushed the limits of plausible spin by repeatedly defending Biden's cognitive abilities—until the debate made it obvious the president no longer had control of his faculties.[7] After Harris's decisive defeat, Newsom's stock is on the rise again. The San Francisco Chronicle noted that although Trump's victory represents a debilitating loss for Democrats, it carries a "silver lining" for Newsom, who "is now positioned to become the leader of the Democratic resistance."[8]

Forty-eight hours later, Newsom and his hand-picked state Attorney General Rob Bonta eagerly took up the mantel, casting themselves as defenders against Trump and protectors of California's brand of progressive values that the rest of the nation had just roundly rejected.[9] With Harris now out of his way, Newsom seized on the moment to kick-start his 2028 White House run. His intention was clear: the race for future control of the Democratic Party would start in California.

Their grandstanding wasn't subtle—both men were clearly positioning themselves for higher office. Newsom appears to have his sights on the 2028 presidency, while Bonta has an edge in the 2026 governor's race as Newsom's chosen successor.[10]

Newsom appointed Bonta in 2021 when President Biden tapped Xavier Becerra, California's former Attorney General, as his Health and Human Services secretary. The governor was familiar with Bonta from his years as a deputy San Francisco city attorney, which overlapped with Newsom's time as mayor and Harris' tenure as district attorney.[11] The governor has used his bully pulpit to call special legislative sessions and push liberal measures in the Democratic super-majority-controlled Assembly and state Senate while Bonta files lawsuits and civil rights investigations against their political adversaries.[12] In September 2023, Bonta launched a war against the oil and gas industry synchronized with Newsom's ongoing attacks on oil companies for so-called price-gouging.[13]

Just days after the 2024 election, Newsom and Bonta threatened to direct their lawfare against Trump, vowing to protect what they declared as the state's top priorities of climate change, abortion rights, and shielding illegal immigrants from deportation.[14] "The freedoms we hold dear in California are under attack—and we won't sit idle," Newsom said in a statement. "California has faced this challenge before, and we know how to respond. We are prepared to fight in the courts, and we will do everything necessary to ensure Californians have the support and resources they need to thrive."[15]

It's familiar ground for Newsom, who played the role of Trump's foil during his last two years as president. During Trump's first term, California sued the federal government over his past rules and regulatory actions more than 123 times, every 12 days on average, costing taxpayers more than $41 million in billable legal hours, according to Cal Matters.[16]

For all its effort, the state scored some significant victories: preserving the state's clean air mandates, the Deferred Action of Childhood Arrivals, or DACA, that benefits illegal immigrants who came to the United States as children, and the Affordable Care Act.[17] California also sued over the first Trump administration's blocking abortion providers from receiving federal family planning dollars. The Biden administration later overturned Trump's rule.[18]

Now Newsom is using the same playbook, hoping it will boost his presidential chances, even though this time the political landscape has shifted significantly to the right.

Newsom's statements about protecting "California values" may seem absurd to those who have recently experienced California's freewheeling dystopian decline—those forced to sidestep feces and overdosed corpses on the way to work; to those beaten, carjacked, or robbed in its streets, censored by its media, crushed by its bureaucracy, fleeced by its politicians, cheated by its charlatans, or mocked by its celebrities and leaders.

Yet the truth remains that nowhere will you find a more vast and diverse set of human and natural resources conducive to human flourishing.

During the 2023 debate between Florida Governor Ron DeSantis and

California Governor Gavin Newsom, DeSantis got under Newsom's skin when he said that "California has more natural advantages than any other state in the country. You almost have to try to mess up California."[19]

But mess it up they have.

Trump piled on while capturing the state's current dichotomies. Standing on the cliffs of his Rancho Palos Verdes golf course with the glittering Pacific behind him, the Republican nominee denounced California as a "hellscape" that Kamala Harris and her allies would unleash on the nation if given the chance.

"We cannot allow comrade Kamala Harris and the communist left to do to America what they did to California. California is a mess," Trump said.[20]

If only DeSantis and Trump were exaggerating. California is now a one-party state ruled by entrenched political dynasties whose behavior undercuts their lofty promises to aid the less fortunate. When the state's so-called "progressive vision" is derailed by political scandals and most voters shrug off personal scandals and entrenched corruption, it's a sign that either a malaise has set in, or the disillusioned have simply packed up and left.

When you zoom out far enough, California starts to look less like an innovative, boundary-pushing Democratic state concerned with the upward mobility of its citizens, and more like a large feudal kingdom "dominated by a small class of exceedingly wealthy and well-connected people, resembling the nobility of the Middle Ages," as Joel Kotkin, *The Coming of Neo-Feudalism: A Warning to the Global Middle Class*, has put it.[21] *Wired* magazine's Antonio García Martínez described Silicon Valley as "feudalism with better marketing," but the phrase can readily be applied to the state as a whole.[22] Decades ago, a cabal of wealthy elites began to rule California by seizing control of governmental and corporate levers to push progressive policies aiming for *equity* and *diversity*. The curious thing is, these radical strategies backfired and actually led to more *inequity* across the state, and its widely touted *diversity* turned out to be strictly demographic.

Ideologies, technologies, and tools have been updated, but the feudalistic contradictions and extreme outcomes remain. As opportunity dwindles for citizens trying to eke out an existence in the Golden State, the once vibrant California Dream is rapidly vanishing.

As of this writing, California once again has the nation's highest level of poverty, 18.9 percent between 2022 and 2023.[23] California's notoriously high costs for housing, utilities, insurance, and gas strike a devastating blow to working-class families, often driving them into poverty or homelessness. When considering those living at or near poverty, the Public Policy Institute, a California think tank, says that number expands to 31.1 percent of the population.[24] Individuals and companies are now fleeing the state in record numbers, and who can blame them? The dreamy paradise once described as a real-life land of milk and honey is now dotted with briar patches and drying up fast, with no signs of rejuvenation in sight.

This book is both an effort to fix California and a cautionary tale. America's future is inextricably yoked to California because of both the state's sheer size and the enormous influence of its political figures, who remain dead set on controlling the White House for decades to come.

As of this writing, California Governor Gavin Newsom spent the 2024 campaign unsuccessfully minimizing his failures in California in an attempt to elevate his profile for a future White House run, while Vice President Kamala Harris endured a drubbing, with Donald Trump soundly defeating her in the 2024 Presidential election. After Democratic leaders shoved Biden aside, Harris party and media elites magically anointed her as their chosen one. During the Biden administration, the Health and Human Services and the Department of Labor secretaries, along with a host of other DC officials, hailed from California. All brought their liberal values and questionable political practices to bear on national policy.

In the summer of 2024, after Biden's primetime implosion during the June 27 debate against Trump, Newsom still thought he had a shot at leapfrogging over Harris to seize the Democratic presidential nomination. Pushing back against Republicans ridiculing the state of his state, Newsom issued a sanitized press release listicle, "The 10 Ways California Leads the Nation."[25] The list ranges from the vague category "Belonging and Unity," to "Climate Action," to the preposterous "Transportation," with Newsom hailing the state's high-speed rail project connecting Los Angeles and San Francisco for just having cleared its final regulatory hurdle.[26] The statement was a farcical departure from reality. The project, which voters approved in 2008, is $100 billion short.[27] The *New York Times* has labeled the "tortured" undertaking "a multi-billion nightmare," questioning whether it will ever be finished.[28]

As we've chronicled throughout *Fool's Gold*, California is leading the nation in all the wrong ways, tarnishing its once golden reputation: the state has the highest poverty rate, highest retail crime, highest number of homeless, highest housing costs, highest gas prices, highest illiteracy rates, record illegal immigration, worst unemployment, worst business climates, and worst wage stagnation. (Worker wages have gone up less than in any other state.)

Despite Newsom's claims that the state has a high rate of "inclusion and belonging," when it comes to inequality, as measured by the Gini Coefficient, a leading measure of income and wealth distribution, California is routinely among the top few states.[29]

Over just the last few years, California has exported its progressive policies to other parts of the country and to the federal level, even while the state's citizens have watched these same progressive social experiments fail them at home.

Immigration

Democrats' broad support for a porous border or no border at all began in California. The widespread embrace of an open border gave birth to sanctuary city and state policies, preventing local law enforcement from handing felons of violent crime over to federal immigration authorities for deportation. The Biden-Harris campaign embraced a free-flowing border, and at least ten to twelve million illegal immigrants have entered the country under their watch, providing ready voters for the Democratic Party, whose leaders gave them a safe haven, regardless of criminal histories or threats to national security. At the writing of this book, the San Diego border sector had the most illegal crossings of any sector in the country. If California Democrats or colleagues they've managed to influence gain power at the federal level, illegal immigration will only accelerate across the nation.

Healthcare and Homebuyer Subsidies for Illegal Immigrants

In early 2024, while running a more than $49 billion deficit, Newsom moved forward with a plan to have California become the first state to provide health insurance for illegal immigrants. The move added roughly seven hundred thousand immigrants between the ages of twenty-six and forty-nine to those already on the state's Medicaid rolls, which includes those already eligible: the young and those over the age of fifty. Newsom said he was moving forward despite deep deficits because it shows "California's commitment to health care as a human right."[30]

The state legislature late in the summer of 2024 approved a bill that would make undocumented immigrants eligible for up to $150,000 in state-supported home loans with zero interest rates. Following California's lead, the Biden administration in May of 2024 announced a new regulation enabling at least a hundred thousand illegal immigrants brought to the United States as children to enroll in the Affordable Care Act.[31] It fell short of Biden's initial proposal to allow those individuals to sign up for Medicaid, but don't expect the debate to end there. During her failed campaign, Harris wanted to give lower-income and first-time home buyers $25,000 to use as a downpayment.[32] It's not a stretch to think she, Newsom, and other like-minded progressives would support this added benefit for illegal immigrants struggling to buy a home in this country if they regain control of the White House or Congress.

Strict Carbon Limits on Fuel Emissions and EV Standards

In 2021, California declared war on natural gas and imposed standards that would have required auto dealers to sell a certain share of battery-powered cars in 2025 or face stiff fines. And in 2022, the state ratcheted up the rules, requiring 35 percent of new passenger cars, trucks, and SUVs sold in the state to be electric or hydrogen by 2025, and 100 percent of them by 2035. Sixteen states and the District of Columbia followed suit and signed on to California's 2021 standards.[33] Virginia, which is now run by GOP Governor Glenn Youngkin, backed out of those standards in June of 2024. In March of 2024, Biden's Environmental Protection Agency imposed the most ambitious new standards to cut carbon emissions from passenger vehicles even though EV sales had begun to slow. In September 2023, California Attorney General Rob Bonta launched a war against the oil and gas industry synchronized with Newsom's ongoing attacks on oil companies for so-called price-gouging.[34] Bonta targeted the oil and gas companies in a landmark civil suit, modeled on the successful multi-state litigation against tobacco companies in the 1990s. He did so even though he knew it would drive prices even higher.[35] On top of any price increase Bonta's lawsuit could spur, analysts say drivers statewide could see gas prices spike as much as 65 cents per gallon after the California Air Resources Board approved new regulations. The board conveniently put off voting on them until Nov. 8, 2024, three days after the election when voters were distracted.[36] The swing states of Arizona and Nevada recently sent bipartisan letters from their governors warning Newsom that the new mandates on refineries he signed into law would create shortages and drive up prices in their states because 80% of their gasoline comes from California refineries.[37]

Crime

California Democrats may have hit pause on its long history of soft-on-crime policies after even the most liberal of city voters ousted Chesa Boudin, their far-left radical district attorney whose tenure was marked by spiking crime, drug overdoses, and deaths in the city by the bay. And the 2024 election, Los Angeles voters followed suit by ditching District Attorney George Gascon after two failed recalls and by passing Proposition 36, which overturns a decade of more lenient laws, including those reducing charges from felonies to misdemeanors as long as the value of the amount stolen falls under $950. But don't think for a minute they've abandoned it altogether. In 2018, California became the first state to completely eliminate cashless bail for suspects awaiting trial.[38] Voters overturned the important reform in 2020 after a referendum campaign led by the bail bond industry. The state now has a patchwork of bail rules set in motion by court policies and lawsuits, though the state Supreme Court ruled in 2021 that bail must be "affordable" for those facing charges. Since then, other states have moved to change their cash-bail system, including Illinois, Indiana, Kentucky, Nebraska, New Jersey, New Mexico, and New York.

Gig Worker Rules

Just months before the pandemic, California approved AB5, a labor-backed ballot initiative mandating better wages and health benefits for independent contractors such as rideshare workers, delivery workers, and writers, but the law had the unintended but predictable consequence of causing layoffs of these freelancers and independent contractors when their employers couldn't afford to provide the added benefits. The timing was horrendous, coming as it did at the beginning of the pandemic when workers needed all the flexibility they could get. The outrage over the layoffs led to several carveouts for rideshare companies and other apps to deliver food, buy groceries, and transport customers. California Labor Secretary Julie Su headed the state agency when the law was passed, then got a promotion to the federal level when Biden named her as his Department of Labor deputy, and she promised not to impose similar restrictions on gig workers as California's at the federal level. In February 2024, however, Su announced plans to nationalize the notorious gig worker law. The Trump administration is expected to repeal it, but the law could be reinstated once again if Democrats return to power in Washington.

Increasing the Minimum Wage

In the fall of 2023, Newsom signed a bill mandating a twenty-dollar-an-hour minimum wage for fast-food workers. It went into effect in April and also created a fast-food regulatory council, which has the ability to raise fast-food workers' minimum wage each year. After the new law went into effect, California restaurants cut 9,500 jobs between September 2023 and January 2024, according to the Hoover Institution.[39] The Shake Shack burger chain announced it would close six California locations, including five in Los Angeles. Rob Lynch, the company's CEO, said that he didn't want the company to cater "only to the highest-income burger eaters" but to be a staple for middle-class families. "That's harder to do when the government artificially raises labor costs," he said.[40]

Rubio's California Grill, popular across the state for its fish tacos, shut down 48 of its 130 locations in May, with a spokesperson for Rubio's telling the *New York Post* that the "closings were brought on by the rising costs of doing business" in California.[41] One month later, the company filed for bankruptcy. Other fast-food restaurants, including McDonald's and In-N-Out Burger, simply raised prices and decreased employees' hours while implementing more automation. California lawmakers voted to increase the minimum wage to fifteen dollars per hour in 2016, and phased in the increase over several years while tying boosts in pay to the rate of inflation. Biden followed suit in 2021, using his executive powers to raise the hourly minimum wage for federal contractors to fifteen in one of his earliest actions in office. In the private market, employers often compensate for high wage requirements by laying off workers and reducing or eliminating benefits. But in the federal government, the mandated higher wages are simply passed along to taxpayers in higher contracting costs for the same services.

Parental Notification Laws

In July, California became the first state to prohibit school districts from requiring staff to notify parents of any gender transitions their children are making in public schools, the Associated Press reported. Before Newsom and state Democrats took up the legislation, the rules were already in place as guidance issued by the state Department of Education but didn't carry the full weight of the law. Six other states have policies their school districts say support transgender students, and advocates for the California law hope it can serve as a model for regulations established in response to the surge in bills across the country designed to prevent schools from keeping secrets about their children's gender transitions from parents.

These are just a few of the ways California is exporting its values and failures to other states and the nation. When Newsom heralds California as a model for the nation, the rest of the country shouldn't be deceived about this recipe for failure. Taking the playbook national will mean more homelessness, more poverty, more crime, more illegal immigration, more inequality, and a higher cost of living for everyone.

To fix California, or at least prevent the exporting of its maladies to the rest of the country, it's good to know how California got there. That's what we set out to do in *Fool's Gold*—to show which forces, and which individuals, are responsible for turning the Golden State into a shadow of its former self, diminishing its value and allure for all but the wealthiest elite.

It's not only past time to fix California, it's time to stop the contagion from spreading.

ACKNOWLEDGMENTS

I COULD NOT HAVE COMPLETED this book without the understanding and dedication of my husband, Paul Hennebury, and the sweet support of my daughter, Hailey. I'm also grateful beyond words to my mother, Peggy Crabtree, who noticed and fostered my writing from a young age. Paul and Peggy provided immeasurable support, looking after Hailey during weekends and school breaks when the book was all-consuming. My sister, Kathryn Brant, one of my biggest cheerleaders, offered encouraging words along the way, often flagging outrageous news stories for further investigation.

Heart-filled thanks also goes out to my dear friends Nicole Duran and Ruth Baurle, who selflessly provided extensive research at critical times, and my close neighborhood friends, including Ruth's husband Eric Baurle, and every member of the Young family. Longtime California residents suffering alongside me through the state's leftward march, the group of dear friends served as tipsters, a mini-focus group, and part-time therapists.

Having Jedd McFatter as a co-author is a gift. Jedd is one of the most talented document divers I've known, who also happens to have a heart of gold. For that connection, I thank my agent, Jonathan Bronitsky, who had the foresight to pair us together. I'm also grateful for the leadership, editing, and guidance of legendary investigative journalist Peter Schweitzer and his team at the Government Accountability Institute, where Jedd serves as research director.

Alex Pappas, my editor at Hachette, provided thoughtful feedback and suggestions and exhibited great patience when my daily political coverage for RealClearPolitics, where I work full-time as a national political correspondent, blew up over the summer in the aftermath of the assassination attempts against now President-elect Donald Trump. Also worthy of recognition: Carl Cannon, RealClearPolitics' Washington bureau chief, a true wordsmith and the most gracious boss I've had in my 30-year journalism career, as well as Cathi Warren and Anne Welty, our devoted copywriters, and the entire RCP team. Carl, a fellow native Californian and avowed political Independent, gave me the green light to take on the book despite a busy election year ahead and sent along relevant news articles and tidbits.

This past year was the busiest but most gratifying of my life. I'm so grateful to you all for helping me stay on track and persevere through deadline after deadline amid the most unusual, tumultuous, and dramatic presidential elections of our time.

—Susan Crabtree

* * *

I want to thank Peter Schweizer and the Government Accountability Institute (GAI) for giving me the courage, the freedom, and the skills to dive down rabbit holes and take my investigations as far as they can go. I'm grateful to Peter for his wisdom as an author and investigator and look forward to many more years working alongside him to expose government corruption and cronyism.

A special heartfelt thanks goes to Seamus Bruner, longtime GAI colleague and great friend, for all his guidance and support in each phase of writing this book. I couldn't have done it without you.

My coauthor, Susan Crabtree, is an exceptional journalist and a gracious collaborator. Her insight as a longtime resident of California was invaluable when writing this book.

At GAI, I'm blessed to work with some of the very best researchers and editors in the country. In particular, I want to thank Peter J. Boyer for all of his helpful edits, and Price Sukhia for his research assistance in the early stages of the book. I also want to thank Sam Schaefer, Joe Duffus, Steve Stewart, and all the members of my research team who wish to remain anonymous.

I'm grateful to my agent, Jonathan Bronitsky, for pairing me up with a great author to write this book, and I want to thank Alex Pappas, my editor at Hachette, for his guidance and patience throughout the process.

Most of all, I'm grateful to my family, especially my three children—Leora, Analise, and James. Without your love, support, and understanding, this book would never have been completed.

—Jedd McFatter

ENDNOTES

INTRODUCTION

1. https://www.ocregister.com/2024/11/09/newsom-uses-a-stunt-to-position-himself-as-a-leader-of-the-anti-trump-resistance/; https://www.nytimes.com/2024/11/13/us/politics/democratic-governors-trump.html.
2. https://www.sfchronicle.com/opinion/editorials/article/downtown-san-francisco-17852552.php.
3. https://www.hoover.org/research/san-francisco-falls-abyss.
4. https://news.stanford.edu/stories/2022/09/wildfire-smoke-unraveling-decades-air-quality-gains.
5. https://www.usnews.com/news/best-states/california.
6. https://www.usnews.com/news/best-states/rankings/opportunity.
7. Kevin Starr, *California: A History* (New York: Modern Library Chronicles, 2005); https://news.stanford.edu/stories/2022/09/wildfire-smoke-unraveling-decades-air-quality-gains.

CHAPTER ONE: THE FAILED PROGRESSIVE VISION

1. https://www.wunderground.com/history/daily/us/ca/san-bruno/KSFO/date/2023-11-10.
2. https://www.wsj.com/articles/san-francisco-cleans-up-for-xi-why-not-for-thee-242c67e3?mod=hp_opin_pos_5; https://www.nationalreview.com/the-morning-jolt/san-francisco-finally-cleans-up-its-drug-markets-and-encampments-for-xi-jinpings-arrival/; https://sfstandard.com/2023/11/14/city-clears-homeless-encampments-apec/.
3. https://www.hoover.org/research/despite-california-spending-24-billion-it-2019-homelessness-increased-what-happened.
4. https://twitter.com/globaltimesnews/status/1724261103482605780; https://abc7news.com/apec-2023-san-francisco-summit-events-during/14042057/; https://www.breitbart.com/politics/2023/11/15/watch-chinese-flags-line-san-francisco-streets-for-xi-jinping/; https://www.sfgate.com/food/article/chinatown-night-market-apec-18478279.php; https://sfstandard.com/2023/11/06/san-francisco-apec-chinatown-art-block-party/; https://www.youtube.com/watch?app=desktop&v=TUccOTirv58.
5. https://www.chinadaily.com.cn/a/202311/17/WS65570f4da31090682a5eec6f.html; https://sjvsun.com/california/newsom-faces-criticism-over-s-f-clean-up-for-xi

-jinping-visit/; https://cbsaustin.com/news/nation-world/san-francisco-cleans-up
-before-biden-xi-meeting-businesses-close-stores-target-walgreens-old-navy-illegal
-street-vendors-fentanyl-drug-spread-china-communist-party-governor-gavin-newsom
-california-apec-conference.

6. https://abc7news.com/san-francisco-budget-announcement-defund-sfpd-the-police
    -london-breed-press-conference/6345069/; Peter Mancina, "The Birth of a Sanctuary-
    City: A History of Governmental Sanctuary in San Francisco," in *Sanctuary Practices in
    International Perspectives: Migration, Citizenship and Social Movements*, ed. Randy Lippert
    and Sean Rehaag (Abingdon, UK: Routledge, 2014), 205–218; https://nypost.com
    /2021/12/15/behind-london-breeds-defund-the-police-turnaround-in-san-francisco/.

7. Social/racial/economic justice: https://www.gov.ca.gov/wp-content/uploads/2024/06
    /2024-SOTS-Letter.pdf; "climate justice": https://www.gov.ca.gov/2022/11/16/california
    -releases-worlds-first-plan-to-achieve-net-zero-carbon-pollution/; "restorative justice":
    https://a18.asmdc.org/news/20231013-ab-1104-rehabilitation-and-reentry-prep
    -incarcerated-people.

8. https://www.city-journal.org/article/compassionate-enforcement.

9. https://www.sfchronicle.com/bayarea/matier-ross/article/Gavin-Newsom-draws
    -line-on-SF-street-behavior-13286274.php.

10. https://www.sfchronicle.com/bayarea/matier-ross/article/Gavin-Newsom-draws
    -line-on-SF-street-behavior-13286274.php.

11. https://www.aol.com/news/heinous-psychopathic-murder-details-emerge
    -120000500.html.

12. https://fox40.com/news/local-news/sacramento-county/prosecutors
    -say-suspect-in-killing-of-sacramento-woman-should-have-been-in-jail/.

13. https://www.kcra.com/article/gunman-who-killed-3-daughters-in-sacramento
    -county-church-was-in-us-illegally/39330254; https://www.abc10.com/article/news/crime
    /david-mora-rojas-arden-arcade-church-shooting/103-ed7a79fb-5d23-446d
    -8ff8-b999fa0c6720.

14. https://abc30.com/selma-police-officer-gonzalo-carrasco-jr-killed-in-line-of-duty
    -fresno/12765989/.

15. https://abc30.com/nathaniel-dixon-gonzalo-cassrasco-junior-selma-police-offer
    -killed-murder-charges/12866619/; https://abc30.com/selma-police-officer-gonzalo
    -carrasco-jr-killed-in-line-of-duty-fresno/12765989/.

16. https://www.yourcentralvalley.com/news/selma-police-shooting/the-criminal
    -history-of-suspected-selma-cop-killer-nathaniel-dixon/.

17. https://www.yourcentralvalley.com/news/selma-police-shooting/the-criminal
    -history-of-suspected-selma-cop-killer-nathaniel-dixon/.

18. https://www.cbsnews.com/sacramento/news/cbs13-getting-answers-for-the-da/.

19. https://www.ppic.org/blog/testimony-retail-theft-in-california/#:~:text=By%20
    contrast%2C%20commercial%20burglary%20has,shoplifting%20from%202014%20
    to%202022.

20. https://www.cdcr.ca.gov/research/wp-content/uploads/sites/174/2024/01/Fall
    -2023-Population-Projections-Publication.pdf; https://www.cdcr.ca.gov/research/wp
    -content/uploads/sites/174/2024/01/Fall-2023-Population-Projections
    -Publication.pdf.

21. https://www.gov.ca.gov/2024/08/27/governor-newsom-announces-new-milestone
    -in-transformation-of-san-quentin-rehabilitation-center/.

22. https://calmatters.org/newsletters/whatmatters/2021/11/california-crime
-robberies-police/; https://fortune.com/2023/08/28/nordstrom-closes-san-francisco
-store-downtown-market-street-remote-work/; https://finance.yahoo.com/news
/why-starbucks-whole-foods-and-others-are-closing-stores-in-downtown-san
-francisco-205713063.html; https://finance.yahoo.com/news/why-starbucks-whole-foods
-and-others-are-closing-stores-in-downtown-san-francisco-205713063.html.

23. https://reformcalifornia.org/news/heres-a-list-of-companies-fleeing-san-francisco-and-why.

24. https://www.sfchronicle.com/sf/article/drugs-crime-nancy-pelosi-federal-building
-18292237.php.

25. https://www.inc.com/bill-murphy-jr/after-76-years-in-n-out-burger-just-made
-a-heartbreaking-announcement.html.

26. https://www.courts.ca.gov/documents/Prop47FAQs.pdf.

27. https://georgegascon.org/campaign-news/george-gascon-takes-oath-of-office-and-institutes
-sweeping-reforms-to-transform-the-largest-criminal-justice-jurisdiction-in-america/.

28. https://redstate.com/eric-neff/2024/07/02/unsealed-affidavit-in-criminal-case
-against-george-gascons-ethics-deputy-reveals-depths-of-corruption-n2176030; https://
s3.documentcloud.org/documents/24777645/diana-teran-warrant-affidavit.pdf;
https://www.latimes.com/california/story/2024-06-26/video-shows-controversial
-azusa-arrest-of-gascon-aide; https://theavtimes.com/2022/01/06/gascon-aide-sues-pd
-over-drunk-in-public-arrest/.

29. https://www.foxla.com/news/diana-teran-top-aide-los-angeles-da-gascon-arraigned;
https://dainca.org/2024/06/25/new-details-on-gascons-ethics-czar-charged-with
-stealing-deputy-data/.

30. https://redstate.com/eric-neff/2024/07/02/unsealed-affidavit-in-criminal-case
-against-george-gascons-ethics-deputy-reveals-depths-of-corruption-n2176030.

31. https://www.sfchronicle.com/politics/article/london-breed-prop-47-18653803.php;
https://www.axios.com/local/san-diego/2024/06/20/mayor-todd-gloria-prop-47
-reform-ballot-measure-crime; https://www.cbsnews.com/sacramento/news/leaked-email
-governor-refused-to-negotiate-with-das/; https://www.latimes.com/california/story/2024
-07-03/newsom-pulls-anti-crime-ballot-measure-california-democrats-chaotic
-response-to-prop-47-reform; https://www.latimes.com/california/story/2024-07-03
/newsom-pulls-anti-crime-ballot-measure-california-democrats-chaotic-response
-to-prop-47-reform; https://www.politico.com/news/2024/08/16/newsom-condemns
-prosecutors-ballot-measure-00174478.

32. https://www.cbsnews.com/sacramento/news/leaked-email-governor-refused
-to-negotiate-with-das/; https://www.cbsnews.com/sacramento/news/california-retail-theft
-reform-initiative-political-rift/.

33. https://www.politico.com/news/2024/07/03/newsom-and-democratic-leaders
-drop-their-crime-ballot-measure-00166409.

34. https://www.governing.com/policy/california-passes-10-bills-to-crack-down-on
-retail-theft.

35. https://www.latimes.com/politics/story/2024-election-live-results-california
-congress-assembly-senate-props and for Gascon/Hochman outcome; https://www.latimes
.com/politics/story/2024-election-live-results-district-attorney-la-county-gascon-
hochman.

36. https://www.ocregister.com/2020/03/14/its-time-we-get-fair-nonpartisan-ballot
-measure-descriptions/.

37. https://www.foxnews.com/us/third-strike-trans-rape-suspect-prompts-rebellion-against-ca-law-after-attack-womens-prison.

38. https://www.huffpost.com/entry/gavin-newsom-marijuana-dnc_n_579a280ee4b01180b5320d2c?section=.

39. https://www.huffpost.com/entry/gavin-newsom-marijuana-dnc_n_579a280ee4b01180b5320d2c?section=.

40. https://www.youtube.com/watch?v=ORWUPA-OwCQ; https://www.ocregister.com/2020/03/14/its-time-we-get-fair-nonpartisan-ballot-measure-descriptions/; https://www.nytimes.com/2024/08/30/us/california-shoplifting-trump-harris.html; https://data-openjustice.doj.ca.gov/sites/default/files/2023-06/Crime%20In%20CA%202022f.pdf.

41. https://www.theguardian.com/us-news/2023/oct/07/california-governor-vetoes-bill-to-decriminalize-natural-psychedelic-drugs; https://www.politico.com/news/2022/08/23/newsom-safe-injection-sites-california-00053349.

42. https://www.sfchronicle.com/projects/2023/san-francisco-drug-trade-honduras/.

43. https://www.sfchronicle.com/projects/2023/san-francisco-drug-trade-honduras/.

44. https://www.sfchronicle.com/projects/2023/san-francisco-drug-trade-honduras/.

45. https://www.washingtonexaminer.com/opinion/editorials/2580911/china-exposes-californias-moral-corruption/.

46. Peter Schweizer, *Blood Money: The Story of Life, Death, and Profit Inside America's Blood Industry* (New York: Simon & Schuster, 2001), 23–25.

47. 2022: 111,029; 2023: 107,543; 2024: on pace.
    https://www.cdc.gov/nchs/pressroom/nchs_press_releases/2024/20240515.htm#:~:text=The%20new%20data%20show%20overdose,psychostimulants%20(like%20methamphetamine)%20increased; https://nida.nih.gov/research-topics/trends-statistics/overdose-death-rates; https://www.sfexaminer.com/news/health/2024-sf-drug-overdose-deaths-nearly-match-record-2023-pace/article_1f9690bc-e162-11ee-9a0f-238d6307303c.html.

48. https://www.gov.ca.gov/2024/02/27/california-seizes-record-62000-pounds-of-fentanyl/.

49. https://www.theguardian.com/us-news/2024/feb/22/los-angeles-unhoused-deaths-increase-housing-crisis-fentanyl-overdoses.

50. https://www.sfchronicle.com/health/article/drugs-fentanyl-meth-speedball-18499833.php.

51. https://www.kqed.org/news/11839409/5-reasons-its-so-expensive-to-build-housing-in-california.

52. https://www.huduser.gov/portal/sites/default/files/pdf/2023-AHAR-Part-1.pdf.

53. https://www.breitbart.com/politics/2023/12/21/report-california-sees-surge-in-number-of-homeless-women/.

54. https://www.huduser.gov/portal/sites/default/files/pdf/2023-AHAR-Part-1.pdf.

55. https://www.huduser.gov/portal/sites/default/files/pdf/2023-AHAR-Part-1.pdf.

56. https://www.huduser.gov/portal/sites/default/files/pdf/2023-AHAR-Part-1.pdf.

57. https://calmatters.org/commentary/2024/05/homelessness-california-politician-blame-shift/.

58. https://www.vcstar.com/story/news/2019/08/28/newsom-drops-plan-california-homeless-czar/2142244001/.

59. https://www.facebook.com/MRTEmpowerCommunity/videos/governor-gavin-newsom-endorses-mark-ridley-thomas-for-city-council/252256852871286/.

60. https://www.gov.ca.gov/2019/05/21/in-oakland-governor-gavin-newsom-announces-the-formation-of-the-homeless-and-supportive-housing-advisory-task-force/.

61. https://www.courthousenews.com/wp-content/uploads/2023/08/USA-v-Ridley-Thomas-GOVT-SENT-MEMO.pdf.

62. https://calmatters.org/commentary/2024/04/newsom-criticizes-homelessness-cities-counties/.

63. https://www.latimes.com/homeless-housing/story/2024-09-17/non-profit-helped-conceive-californias-homeless-housing-program-then-left-string-of-failed-projects.

64. https://prd.cdn.sos.ca.gov/Lobbying_Directory.pdf.

65. https://www.sacramentoadvocates.com/panorea-avdis.

66. https://smdp.com/2024/03/01/california-spends-billions-on-homelessness-yet-the-crisis-keeps-getting-worse/; https://bcsh.ca.gov/calich/documents/homelessness_assessment.pdf.

67. https://sfstandard.com/2024/10/15/homelessness-sprawling-nonprofits-crankstart-foundation.

68. https://calmatters.org/housing/2023/02/california-homelessness-spending-report/.

69. https://www.realtor.com/news/trends/things-that-affect-your-property-value/; https://ibo.nyc.ny.us/iboreports/close-to-home-does-proximity-to-a-homeless-shelter-affect-residential-property-values-in-manhattan-2019.html.

70. https://www.facebook.com/KUSINews/videos/446528399571248/.

71. https://www.disabilityrightsca.org/latest-news/disability-rights-california-opposes-proposition-1.

72. https://fortune.com/2024/03/21/gavin-newsom-homeless-vote-proposition-1-millionaires-tax/.

73. https://www.gov.ca.gov/2024/07/25/governor-newsom-orders-state-agencies-to-address-encampments-in-their-communities-with-urgency-and-dignity/.

74. https://www.dailymail.co.uk/news/article-12750963/Chinas-Xi-Jinping-Hongqi-dwarfed-Joe-Biden-Beast-cadillac.html; https://sfstandard.com/2023/11/14/china-xi-jinping-san-francisco-protests/.

75. https://www.newsweek.com/xi-jinping-china-paid-supporters-san-francisco-apec-1844295; https://www.newsweek.com/china-ccp-san-francisco-police-department-assault-xi-jinping-joe-biden-apec-1846143.

76. http://us.china-embassy.gov.cn/eng/zgyw/202311/t20231127_11187772.htm; https://www.breitbart.com/politics/2024/03/02/exclusive-peter-schweizer-fentanyl-a-chinese-operation-much-more-than-it-is-a-mexican-drug-cartel-operation/.

77. https://www.sfgate.com/politics/article/newsom-says-sf-cleaned-up-apec-18488808.php.

78. https://www.sfgate.com/politics/article/newsom-says-sf-cleaned-up-apec-18488808.php.

79. https://www.dailymail.co.uk/news/article-12882819/Rapper-Chino-Yang-San-Francisco-Mayor-London-Breed-Diss-Track.html.

80. https://www.dailymail.co.uk/news/article-12834105/Poopie-dance-homeless-swarm-San-Francisco-Chinese-President-Xi.html.

81. https://nypost.com/2023/11/10/news/san-francisco-clears-drug-addicts-and-homeless-out-of-downtown-ahead-of-biden-and-xi-jinping-summit/.

82. https://oversight.house.gov/wp-content/uploads/2024/10/CCP-Report-10.24.24.pdf.

CHAPTER TWO: GROWING UP GETTY

1. https://www.sfgate.com/bayarea/article/heads-above-the-rest-bruce-wolfe-on-the
   -method-2611301.php; https://www.sfgate.com/art/article/Supporters-working-to-get
   -Gavin-Newsom-bust-in-6290507.php.
2. https://sfist.com/2016/12/22/91k_bronze_gavin_newsom_bust_headed/.
3. https://sfgov.org/arts/sites/default/files/SFACbustltr.pdf.
4. For those unfamiliar with the uniquely Californian concept of "behested payments,"
   this means that while serving as lieutenant governor, Newsom made specific solicita-
   tions to these organizations to donate funds for the project.
5. https://kiosk.sfartscommission.org/objects-1/info?query=Portfolios%20%3D%20
   %22451%22%20and%20Disp_Maker_1%20%3D%20%22Bruce%20Wolfe%22%20
   and%20Disp_Obj_Type%20%3D%20%22Sculpture%22%20and%20Disp_Obj
   _Type%20%3D%20%22Sculpture%22&sort=0.
6. https://sites.tufts.edu/reinventingpeace/2013/07/08/democracy-dictatorship-and-statues/.
7. https://www.latimes.com/california/story/2021-12-18/gavin-newsom-childhood
   -struggle-to-read-shaped-his-life-and-career; https://www.legacy.com/us/obituaries
   /sfgate/name/william-newsom-obituary?id=1956226; https://www.texaspolicy.com
   /california-gov-gavin-newsom-the-groomed-from-birth-leftist-who-expects
   -to-be-president/; https://www.devex.com/organizations/tci-international-22445; https://
   www.city-journal.org/article/native-son.
8. https://spitfirelist.com/news/ex-nazi%E2%80%99s-brilliant-u-s-career-strangled
   -in-a-web-of-lies/.
9. https://www.city-journal.org/article/native-son; https://www.newyorker.com/magazine
   /2018/11/05/gavin-newsom-the-next-head-of-the-california-resistance.
10. https://www.newyorker.com/magazine/2018/11/05/gavin-newsom-the-next-head
    -of-the-california-resistance.
11. https://www.newyorker.com/magazine/2018/11/05/gavin-newsom-the-next-head
    -of-the-california-resistance.
12. https://www.newyorker.com/magazine/2018/11/05/gavin-newsom-the-next-head
    -of-the-california-resistance.
13. https://www.newyorker.com/magazine/2018/11/05/gavin-newsom-the-next-head
    -of-the-california-resistance.
14. https://www.city-journal.org/article/native-son; https://politicalgraveyard.com/parties
    /D/1948/CA.html; https://publishing.cdlib.org/ucpressebooks/view?docId=ft0m3nb
    07q;chunk.id=d0e1437;doc.view=print.
15. https://www.city-journal.org/article/native-son; https://publishing.cdlib.org/ucpresse
    books/view?docId=ft0m3nb07q;chunk.id=d0e1437;doc.view=print; https://www.truman
    library.gov/photograph-records/96-7; https://www.latimes.com/la-op-rarick15-2008
    jun15-story.html.
16. https://projects.sfchronicle.com/2019/jerry-brown-timeline/; https://www.pbs.org/wnet
    /americanmasters/jerry-brown-a-progressive-in-pinstripes-menswear-fashion
    -history/29138/; https://www.kpbs.org/news/midday-edition/2018/09/12/story-brown
    -family-story-california; https://calmatters.org/commentary/2019/01/gavin-newsoms
    -keeping-it-all-in-the-family/.
17. https://calmatters.org/commentary/2019/01/gavin-newsoms-keeping-it-all-in-the-family/;
    https://www.city-journal.org/article/governor-mchottie-takes-charge-in-california;

https://www.latimes.com/politics/la-pol-ca-road-map-jerry-brown-gavin-newsom
-connection-20190106-story.html; https://www.placer.ca.gov/DocumentCenter/View
/58588/PowerPoint-Item-02A.

18. https://calmatters.org/commentary/2019/01/gavin-newsoms-keeping-it-all-in-the
-family/; https://www.businessinsider.com/nancy-pelosi-2013-3#pelosi-met-her-husband
-paul-at-georgetown-university-she-was-a-mother-of-five-by-1969-when-the-family
-moved-to-san-francisco-paul-worked-as-a-banker-while-nancy-raised-their
-children-and-started-a-democratic-party-club-at-her-home-3; https://www.sfgate.com
/bayarea/article/Belinda-Barbara-Newsom-dies-at-73-3183702.php; https://www.sfgate
.com/opinion/article/A-New-City-Supervisor-2856655.php.

19. https://www.newsmax.com/insidecover/new-green-loan-obama/2011/09/30
/id/412909/; https://www.sfgate.com/bayarea/article/Belinda-Barbara-Newsom-dies-at
-73-3183702.php;https://www.sfgate.com/politics/article/NEWSOM-S-PORTFOLIO
-Mayoral-hopeful-has-parlayed-2632672.php.

20. https://www.businessinsider.com/nancy-pelosi-2013-3#after-raising-18-million
-for-democrats-through-her-leadership-pac-in-2002-pelosi-got-the-top-job-when
-dick-gephardt-stepped-down-as-minority-leader-she-was-the-first-woman-to-ever
-lead-a-party-in-congress-16.

21. https://www.latimes.com/politics/la-pol-ca-road-map-jerry-brown-gavin-newsom
-connection-20190106-story.html.

22. https://www.sfexaminer.com/news/a-san-francisco-politics-origin-story-the-burton
-machine/article_2102f872-81a0-5c72-90fd-6bc3cb62d118.html.

23. James Reginato, *Growing Up Getty: The Story of America's Most Unconventional Dynasty*
(New York: Gallery Books, 2022); https://www.newsweek.com/surprising-newsom
-pelosi-harris-ties-getty-oil-dynasty-1717810; https://www.city-journal.org/article/native
-son; https://www.townandcountrymag.com/society/money-and-power/a40157248/ann
-getty-house-interiors-growing-up-getty-book-excerpt/.

24. Reginato, *Growing Up Getty*.

25. Reginato, *Growing Up Getty*; https://www.businessinsider.com/ivy-getty-heiress-getty
-oil-fortune-net-worth-2023-3#jean-paul-getty-the-son-of-oil-millionaire-george-f
-getty-made-his-first-million-in-the-oil-trading-business-by-24-by-the-time-of-his
-death-he-was-widely-considered-to-be-one-of-the-richest-men-in-the-world-2; https://
www.nytimes.com/1984/04/22/business/oil-heir-gordon-p-getty-steering-a-new
-generation-out-of-oil.html.

26. Reginato, *Growing Up Getty*; https://www.nytimes.com/1984/04/22/business/oil-heir
-gordon-p-getty-steering-a-new-generation-out-of-oil.html; https://www.telegraph.co.uk
/luxury/jewellery/sabine-getty-lockdown-life-getty-familys-2700-acre-countryside/;
https://www.dailymail.co.uk/news/article-1354353/John-Paul-Getty-III-dies-54
-paralysed-30-years.html; https://www.architecturaldigest.com/story/the-getty-family
-homes-inside-the-american-dynastys-real-estate-portfolio; https://www.tatler.com/gallery
/dynasties-the-gettys; https://www.news24.com/news24/getty-billionaire-dies-20030417;
https://www.forbes.com/sites/afontevecchia/2014/07/11/the-tragedy-of-the-gettys
-billions-affairs-severed-ears-drug-overdoses-and-oil/?sh=1f677cc12353.

27. Reginato, *Growing Up Getty*; https://www.latimes.com/projects/la-pol-ca-gavin-newsom
-san-francisco-money/.

28. Reginato, *Growing Up Getty*; https://www.thedailybeast.com/when-j-paul-getty-refused
-to-pay-his-grandsons-ransom; https://www.latimes.com/local/obituaries/la-me-john

-paul-getty-iii-20110208-story.html; https://www.latimes.com/archives/la-xpm-2003
-apr-18-me-getty18-story.html.

29. Reginato, *Growing Up Getty*; https://www.latimes.com/projects/la-pol-ca-gavin-newsom
-san-francisco-money/; https://www.texaspolicy.com/california-gov-gavin-newsom
-the-groomed-from-birth-leftist-who-expects-to-be-president/.

30. https://archive.org/details/rg-80.18.07-san-jose-mercury-article-november-20-1981
/mode/2up; Reginato, *Growing Up Getty*; https://www.texaspolicy.com/california-gov
-gavin-newsom-the-groomed-from-birth-leftist-who-expects-to-be-president/.

31. https://www.texaspolicy.com/california-gov-gavin-newsom-the-groomed-from-birth
-leftist-who-expects-to-be-president/.

32. https://archive.org/details/rg-80.18.07-san-jose-mercury-article-november-20-1981
/page/n1/mode/2up?q=suave.

33. https://spitfirelist.com/for-the-record/ftr-673-nancy-pelosi-bormann-democrat/;
Reginato, *Growing Up Getty*.

34. https://spitfirelist.com/news/ex-nazi%E2%80%99s-brilliant-u-s-career-strangled
-in-a-web-of-lies/; https://www.legacy.com/us/obituaries/sfgate/name/william-newsom
-obituary?id=1956226; https://www.texaspolicy.com/california-gov-gavin-newsom-the
-groomed-from-birth-leftist-who-expects-to-be-president/; https://www.devex.com
/organizations/tci-international-22445; https://www.city-journal.org/article/native-son.

35. https://www.latimes.com/politics/la-pol-ca-gavin-newsom-business-20181028-story
.html; Reginato, *Growing Up Getty*; https://www.courts.ca.gov/documents/Newsom_Jr
_William_A_6048.pdf; https://www.sacbee.com/news/politics-government/capitol
-alert/article164240567.html.

36. https://www.sacbee.com/news/politics-government/capitol-alert/article164240567
.html.

37. https://www.sfchronicle.com/bayarea/article/Judge-William-Newson-gavin-father
-dad-dies-13461955.php.

38. https://www.forbes.com/profile/gordon-getty/; https://www.nytimes.com/1983/12/11
/business/the-tangled-fight-for-getty-oil.html; https://www.newyorker.com/magazine
/2023/01/23/the-getty-familys-trust-issues; https://www.latimes.com/projects/la-pol-ca
-gavin-newsom-san-francisco-money/; https://www.sacbee.com/news/politics-government
/capitol-alert/article164240567.html.

39. Reginato, *Growing Up Getty*; https://www.sacbee.com/news/politics-government/capitol
-alert/article164240567.html.

40. https://abc7news.com/william-newsom-judge-alfred-iii-gavin/4888962/; https://www
.sacbee.com/news/politics-government/capitol-alert/article164240567.html.

41. https://www.sacbee.com/news/politics-government/capitol-alert/article164240567
.html; https://www.latimes.com/politics/la-pol-ca-john-burton-california-democratic
-party-chairman-20170112-story.html; https://www.sfexaminer.com/news/a-san
-francisco-politics-origin-story-the-burton-machine/article_2102f872-81a0-5c72
-90fd-6bc3cb62d118.html.

42. https://www.sfexaminer.com/news/a-san-francisco-politics-origin-story-the
-burton-machine/article_2102f872-81a0-5c72-90fd-6bc3cb62d118.html; https://www
.nytimes.com/1983/04/11/obituaries/rep-phillip-burton-democratic-liberal
-dies-on-visit-to-california.html; https://www.govinfo.gov/content/pkg/CHRG-103hhrg
84707/pdf/CHRG-103hhrg84707.pdf; https://centerforpolitics.org/crystalball/articles
/how-nancy-pelosi-got-to-congress/.

43. https://www.sacbee.com/news/politics-government/capitol-alert/article164240567
.html.
44. https://www.latimes.com/projects/la-pol-ca-gavin-newsom-san-francisco-money/.
45. https://www.sfgate.com/politics/article/NEWSOM-S-PORTFOLIO-Mayoral-hopeful
-has-parlayed-2632672.php; https://spectator.org/how-newsom-became-governor-a
-spoils-system-and-a-billionaire-pseudo-father/; https://www.dailymail.co.uk/news
/article-3369810/Heir-Getty-family-fortune-files-money-art-estate-son-died
-ulcers-methamphetamine-overdose.html; https://people.com/human-interest/john
-gilbert-getty-cause-of-death/.
46. https://www.wbur.org/onlyagame/2019/10/18/california-governor-gavin-newsom
-lebron-james-fair-pay-to-play-act.
47. https://www.wbur.org/onlyagame/2019/10/18/california-governor-gavin-newsom
-lebron-james-fair-pay-to-play-act.
48. https://www.wbur.org/onlyagame/2019/10/18/california-governor-gavin-newsom
-lebron-james-fair-pay-to-play-act.
49. https://calmatters.org/politics/2024/04/gavin-newsom-baseball-college/.
50. https://magazine.lmu.edu/articles/californias-catholic-browns/.
51. https://calmatters.org/politics/2024/04/gavin-newsom-baseball-college/.
52. https://calmatters.org/politics/2024/04/gavin-newsom-baseball-college/.
53. https://www.wbur.org/onlyagame/2019/10/18/california-governor-gavin-newsom
-lebron-james-fair-pay-to-play-act.
54. https://www.sacbee.com/news/politics-government/capitol-alert/article7965822.html.
55. https://www.sacbee.com/news/politics-government/capitol-alert/article7965822
.html; https://www.latimes.com/entertainment-arts/tv/story/2023-09-15/jerry-brown
-the-disrupter-american-masters-pbs-review.
56. https://www.sfgate.com/politics/article/NEWSOM-S-PORTFOLIO-Mayoral-hopeful
-has-parlayed-2632672.php; https://www.sfgate.com/style/article/balboa-cafe-celebrates
-a-century-4765752.php.
57. https://plumpjackwinery.com/our-story/; https://www.forbes.com/sites/johnmariani
/2019/05/31/gordon-getty-makes-his-plumpjack-wines-with-as-much-passion
-as-he-does-his-own-music/?sh=2d1a74436c5f; https://www.napawineproject.com
/plumpjack-winery/; https://www.britannica.com/topic/Sir-John-Falstaff.
58. https://calmatters.org/commentary/2019/01/gavin-newsoms-keeping-it-all-in-the
-family/; https://plumpjackwinery.com/our-story/.
59. https://www.latimes.com/politics/la-pol-ca-gavin-newsom-business-20181028-story
.html; https://www.sfgate.com/bayarea/matier-ross/article/Society-Pals-Falling-Out
-Affects-Newsom-Getty-3316206.php; https://www.plumpjack.com/team; https://
www.guidestar.org/profile/46-3078706; https://projects.propublica.org/nonprofits
/organizations/463078706.
60. https://www.sfgate.com/politics/article/NEWSOM-S-PORTFOLIO-Mayoral-hopeful
-has-parlayed-2632672.php;https://www.sfgate.com/bayarea/matier-ross/article
/Society-Pals-Falling-Out-Affects-Newsom-Getty-3316206.php.
61. https://spectator.org/how-newsom-became-governor-a-spoils-system-and-a-billionaire
-pseudo-father/.
62. https://calmatters.org/politics/2019/01/willie-brown-sees-proteges-rise-to-the-top/.
63. https://www.sacbee.com/news/politics-government/capitol-alert/article164240567
.html.

64. https://www.sfgate.com/politics/article/Brown-flip-flops-on-term-limits-He-now-supports-2672945.php.
65. https://calmatters.org/politics/2019/01/willie-brown-sees-proteges-rise-to-the-top/.
66. https://www.sfgate.com/politics/article/New-poll-shows-Gonzalez-out-in-front-He-leads-2526805.php.
67. https://www.sacbee.com/news/politics-government/capitol-alert/article164240567.html.
68. https://www.newsweek.com/history-gavin-nwsom-kimberly-guilfoyle-relationship-1768386.
69. https://www.sfgate.com/entertainment/garchik/article/New-Kennedys-or-not-focus-is-on-city-s-first-3314198.php.
70. https://www.sfgate.com/bayarea/matier-ross/article/Contract-reportedly-out-on-life-of-dog-case-3315925.php.
71. https://www.newsweek.com/history-gavin-nwsom-kimberly-guilfoyle-relationship-1768386.
72. https://www.newsweek.com/history-gavin-nwsom-kimberly-guilfoyle-relationship-1768386.
73. https://abcnews.go.com/US/story?id=2581600&page=1.
74. https://www.sfgate.com/bayarea/matier-ross/article/Newsom-s-latest-affair-of-the-heart-could-turn-2540493.php.
75. https://wng.org/articles/the-long-game-1714509753.
76. https://www.latimes.com/politics/la-pol-ca-gavin-newsom-gay-marriage-20180515-story.html; https://www.sfgate.com/news/article/Judge-strikes-down-ban-on-same-sex-marriage-THE-2722877.php.
77. https://www.sfgate.com/bayarea/matier-ross/article/BEHIND-THE-STORY-Year-of-rumors-before-the-2619993.php.
78. https://www.nytimes.com/2007/02/02/us/02newsom.html.
79. https://www.latimes.com/politics/la-pol-ca-governors-race-gavin-newsom-affair-20180207-story.html.
80. https://www.latimes.com/politics/la-pol-ca-governors-race-gavin-newsom-affair-20180207-story.html.
81. https://www.dailymail.co.uk/news/article-5369055/Ex-San-Fran-mayors-mistress-says-MeToo-doesnt-apply.html; https://apnews.com/general-news-27df6d4da2c3498aa973b7fef44bdced.
82. https://www.latimes.com/entertainment/la-et-weinstein-accusers-list-20171011-htmlstory.html.
83. https://www.sfgate.com/bayarea/matier-ross/article/Putting-a-price-tag-on-fixing-Schwarzenegger-s-2624504.php.
84. https://www.city-journal.org/article/native-son.
85. https://www.sacbee.com/news/politics-government/capitol-alert/article165220752.html;https://web.archive.org/web/20081209000025/http://www.sfgate.com/cgi-bin/article.cgi?f=%2Fn%2Fa%2F2007%2F08%2F10%2Fstate%2Fn000208D48.DTL; https://content.time.com/time/specials/packages/article/0,28804,1834724_1834723_1834714,00.html.
86. https://www.ppic.org/wp-content/uploads/content/pubs/op/OP_998JCOP.pdf.
87. https://www.sfgate.com/magazine/article/Newsom-in-Four-Acts-What-shaped-the-man-who-2736568.php.

88. https://ballotpedia.org/Gavin_Newsom.

89. https://www.dailymail.co.uk/news/article-9242121/Gavin-Newsom-went-Getty
-dynasty-darling-scandal-ridden-governor-facing-recall.html.

90. https://www.foxnews.com/media/gavin-newsom-admits-dining-swanky-french
-laundry-pandemic-dumb-mistake; https://nypost.com/2020/11/19/californias-gavin
-newsom-just-proved-himself-a-hypocrite-and-a-liar/.

91. https://www.wsj.com/articles/gavin-newsom-california-recall-what-to-know-11630411624

92. https://calmatters.org/politics/2022/10/gavin-newsom-campaign-president/.

93. https://www.politico.com/newsletters/california-playbook/2020/12/04/newsom
-issues-regional-stay-at-home-order-ballard-charged-scotus-sends-church-challenge
-back-harris-names-flournoy-chief-maloney-beats-cardenas-for-dccc-wei-named
-legislative-affairs-secretary-491055.

94. https://www.record-bee.com/2023/12/13/internal-documents-reveal-the-story-behind
-californias-unemployment-crash/.

95. https://www.washingtonexaminer.com/news/2438756/gavin-newsom-blames
-progressive-advocates-and-judges-for-californias-homelessness-crisis/.

96. https://www.politico.com/news/2023/12/01/newsom-desanitis-debate-cheating
-00129555.

97. https://www.foxnews.com/politics/desantis-rips-newsom-calif-speech-says-state
-hemorrhaging-population-florida.

98. https://www.latimes.com/entertainment-arts/business/story/2023-12-01/newsom
-desantis-debate-draws-4-7-million-viewers-fox-news; https://www.floridadaily.com
/susan-crabtree-philip-wegmann-opinion-desantis-takes-on-newsom-in-red-vs-blue
-state-debate/.

99. https://www.dailywire.com/news/desantis-rips-newsom-over-california-exodus
-newsom-refuses-to-address; https://www.newsweek.com/ron-desantis-holding-feces-map
-during-gavin-newsom-debate-goes-viral-1848617.

100. https://www.nbcnews.com/politics/2024-election/gavin-newsom-fox-debate
-rcna127563.

CHAPTER THREE: FEEDING THE DRAGON

1. https://web.archive.org/web/20071123223712/http://www.sfgov.org/site/mayor
_index.asp?id=22014; https://www.economist.com/united-states/2021/08/28/the-trials
-of-gavin-newsom.

2. https://www.sfgate.com/politics/article/NEWSOM-S-PORTFOLIO-Mayoral
-hopeful-has-parlayed-2632672.php; https://www.latimes.com/archives/la-xpm-2004
-feb-01-me-sfchinese1-story.html; https://www.foundsf.org/index.php?title=Boom_and
_Bombshell:_New_Economy_Bubble_and_the_Bay_Area.

3. https://www.latimes.com/projects/la-pol-ca-gavin-newsom-san-francisco-money/;
https://www.sfweekly.com/news/bringing-up-baby-gavin/.

4. https://web.archive.org/web/20210126125714/https://www.latimes.com/archives/la
-xpm-2004-feb-01-me-sfchinese1-story.html; https://www.sfweekly.com/news/bringing
-up-baby-gavin/.

5. https://www.sfgate.com/politics/article/SAN-FRANCISCO-Newsom-tells-goals-for
-second-2705918.php.

6. https://www.sfgate.com/politics/article/SAN-FRANCISCO-Newsom-tells-goals-for -second-2705918.php.

7. https://www.latimes.com/projects/la-pol-ca-gavin-newsom-san-francisco-money/; https://www.sfgate.com/politics/article/PROFILE-Julie-Lee-rose-quickly-as -political-2687322.php; https://web.archive.org/web/20210126125714/https://www .latimes.com/archives/la-xpm-2004-feb-01-me-sfchinese1-story.html; https://sfstandard .com/opinion/2024/03/20/willie-brown-gay-rights/; https://www.sfgate.com/politics /article/Newsom-names-transition-team-183-people-2545722.php.

8. http://www.fogcityjournal.com/othervoices/h_brown_archive001.shtml.

9. https://www.sfgate.com/politics/article/A-busy-Newsom-connects-with-China -s-elite-2590264.php; https://www.latimes.com/archives/la-xpm-1995-11-19-tm-4900 -story.html; https://www.sfgate.com/politics/article/SAN-FRANCISCO-Newsom-joins -Feinstein-on-2592929.php.

10. https://www.sfgate.com/politics/article/SAN-FRANCISCO-Newsom-joins -Feinstein-on-2592929.php; https://www.sfgate.com/politics/article/A-busy-Newsom -connects-with-China-s-elite-2590264.php; https://www.bizjournals.com/sanfrancisco /stories/2005/11/14/story1.html.

11. https://www.sfgate.com/politics/article/A-busy-Newsom-connects-with-China -s-elite-2590264.php.

12. https://www.sfgate.com/business/article/Harnessing-the-tiger-in-China-Hong-Kong -2524366.php.

13. https://www.sfgate.com/business/article/Harnessing-the-tiger-in-China-Hong -Kong-2524366.php; https://www.economist.com/business/2004/09/23/the-king-of -guanxi.

14. https://www.economist.com/business/2004/09/23/the-king-of-guanxi; https://www .sfgate.com/business/article/Harnessing-the-tiger-in-China-Hong-Kong-2524366 .php; https://www.scmp.com/article/75088/shui-site-security-run-gangs.

15. https://www.economist.com/business/2004/09/23/the-king-of-guanxi; https://ora.ox .ac.uk/objects/uuid:54dddc90-6618-4f95-a43c-4d2947484761/files/mb49d4c8 ec523211025149161ef3530ce.

16. https://www.nytimes.com/2004/05/18/style/shanghais-new-heaven-on-earth.html; http://www.cnn.com/2007/BUSINESS/04/09/boardroom.lo/.

17. https://www.bizjournals.com/sanfrancisco/news/2018/03/15/how-chinasf-brings -businesses-to-the-bay-area-from.html.

18. https://www.bizjournals.com/sanfrancisco/stories/2008/11/10/daily54.html; http://jeannelawrence.com/wordpress1/2009/01/20/shanghai-social-diary-a-green -tech-summit-and-a-birthday-party/.

19. "Mayor Newsom Announces Opening of ChinaSF Beijing Office: New San Francisco Office in Beijing Is a Welcome Addition to Continued Efforts for Greater Economic Ties Between China and the United States," *States News Service*, October 1, 2010, Gale Academic OneFile Select, accessed November 19, 2024, link.gale.com/apps/doc /A238441502/EAIM?u=anon~81fdc025&sid=sitemap&xid=7a19dba6.

20. https://www.huffpost.com/entry/san-francisco-china_n_1699722.

21. https://www.bloomberg.com/news/articles/2018-03-27/local-u-s-officials-woo-chinese -investment-despite-trump-threat; https://oewd.org/sites/default/files/Documents/Bid %20Opportunities/RFP%20208%20FINAL.pdf; https://meetthefreshmen.marathon strategies.com/meet-the-freshmen/309/kevin-mullin/#_ednref39.

22. https://projectpengyou.org/jobs/beijing-program-manager-publicprivate-partnership/; https://oewd.org/sites/default/files/Documents/Bid%20Opportunities/RFP%20205 _final.pdf.

23. https://www1.hkexnews.hk/listedco/listconews/sehk/2021/0726/2021072601006.pdf.

24. https://web.archive.org/web/20180315173902/http://www.chinasf.org/about-us/.

25. https://www.youtube.com/watch?v=yBu1LwOsrJs.

26. https://bizfileonline.sos.ca.gov/api/report/GetImageByNum/112124038128135113 182105216161060197146232208247; https://opencorporates.com/companies/us_ca /200908510210.

27. https://www.spur.org/publications/spur-report/2010-06-07/organizing-economic -growth.

28. https://www.bizjournals.com/sanfrancisco/news/2018/03/15/how-chinasf-brings -businesses-to-the-bay-area-from.html.

29. https://projects.propublica.org/nonprofits/search?q=%22San+Francisco+Center+for +Economic+Development%22; https://opencorporates.com/companies?q=%22SAN +FRANCISCO+CENTER+FOR+ECONOMIC+DEVELOPMENT%22+&utf8 =%E2%9C%93.

30. https://www.hkgbusiness.com/en/company/San-Francisco-Center-For-Economic -Development-Limited; https://opencorporates.com/companies/hk/1332111.

31. https://www.bizjournals.com/sanfrancisco/news/2018/03/15/how-chinasf-brings -businesses-to-the-bay-area-from.html; https://www.chinadaily.com.cn/a/201803/13 /WS5aa6fb3fa3106e7dcc14128d.html; https://web.archive.org/web/20180112063844 /http://www.chinasf.org/blog/.

32. https://usa.chinadaily.com.cn/epaper/2013-04/15/content_16401881.htm.

33. https://web.archive.org/web/20170823124758/http://chinasf.homestead.com/why -sf.html.

34. https://web.archive.org/web/20110205160835/http://www.sfced.org/about-sfced/press /20111/chinasf-gets-free-office-space-in-shanghai.

35. https://global.chinadaily.com.cn/kindle/2014-11/10/content_18894051.htm; https:// www.openthebooks.com/substack-california-gov-gavin-newsom-reaped-106-million -in-campaign-cash-from-979-state-vendors-who-pocketed-62-billion/.

36. https://web.archive.org/web/20130618112010/http://sfced.org/china-sf/chinasf-services/.

37. Eric Young, "San Francisco Officials Build Business Bridge to China; ChinaSF Lures Backers," *San Francisco Business Times*, October 13, 2008. https://www.bizjournals.com /sanfrancisco/stories/2008/10/13/story13.html.

38. https://www.theatlantic.com/business/archive/2010/10/how-to-drive-us-clean -energy-job-growth-collaborate-with-china/63961/.

39. https://www.ft.com/content/7e14459c-4dbd-11e3-8fa5-00144feabdc0; https://www .chinadaily.com.cn/world/2014-09/18/content_18621992.htm.

40. https://images.forbes.com/lists/2006/10/EP46.html; https://en.prnasia.com/releases /global/Suntech_Chairman_and_CEO_Dr_Zhengrong_Shi_Named_One_of _TIME_s_2007_Heroes_of_the_Environment_-6206.shtml.

41. https://www.washingtonpost.com/business/economy/chinese-solar-panel-maker -flames-out/2013/05/03/9b7f29d6-ac2c-11e2-9493-2ff3bf26c4b4_story.html.

42. https://www.theguardian.com/environment/2008/jan/05/activists.ethicalliving.

43. https://www.washingtonpost.com/business/economy/chinese-solar-panel-maker -flames-out/2013/05/03/9b7f29d6-ac2c-11e2-9493-2ff3bf26c4b4_story.html.

44. George Raine, "SFO Harnesses Solar Power to Supply Terminal 3 Lights," *San Francisco Chronicle*, September 21, 2007; https://www.aviationpros.com/home/news/10385468/sfo-harnesses-solar-power-to-supply-terminal-3-lights.

45. Gavin Newsom, *Mayor Newsom Announces Visit to Sister City Shanghai, China*, YouTube video, https://www.youtube.com/watch?v=Wgjcvtk16Zw.

46. https://www.forbes.com/sites/china/2010/06/21/nows-the-time-to-avoid-dependence-on-china/?sh=4c27913f250f.

47. Elizabeth Browne, "Solar Giant Suntech moving to S.F," *San Francisco Business Times*, October 22, 2007.

48. David R. Baker, "Chinese Solar Firm Basing North American Headquarters in S.F.," *San Francisco Chronicle*, October 23, 2007.

49. Elizabeth Browne, "Solar Giant Suntech moving to S.F," *San Francisco Business Times*, October 22, 2007.

50. https://www.forbes.com/sites/china/2010/06/21/nows-the-time-to-avoid-dependence-on-china/.

51. https://web.archive.org/web/20100823081424/http://www.sfced.org/international/chinasf/chinasf-en/our-advisors.

52. https://web.archive.org/web/20230325220406/https://www.theatlantic.com/business/archive/2010/10/how-to-drive-us-clean-energy-job-growth-collaborate-with-china/63961/.

53. https://www.forbes.com/sites/china/2010/06/21/nows-the-time-to-avoid-dependence-on-china/?sh=4c27913f250f.

54. https://money.cnn.com/2009/02/11/news/international/powell_shi.fortune/index.htm.

55. https://www.reuters.com/article/idUSBRE94I004/.

56. https://www.prnewswire.com/news-releases/suntech-selected-by-cupertino-electric-for-35mw-of-solar-projects-130808053.html; https://businessfacilities.com/feds-ok-359-million-loan-for-az-solar-farm/.

57. https://www.forbes.com/sites/toddwoody/2012/07/30/suntech-fraud/.

58. https://www.usatoday.com/story/money/business/2013/03/20/suntech-bankruptcy/2002429/.

59. https://www.reuters.com/article/idUSBRE94I004/; https://www.icij.org/investigations/offshore/offshore-web-nets-chinese-giant-italian-solar-scandal/; https://www.washingtonpost.com/world/europe/sting-operations-reveal-mafia-involvement-in-renewable-energy/2013/01/22/67388504-5f39-11e2-9dc9-bca76dd777b8_story.html.

60. https://www.yahoo.com/news/suntech-powers-stock-delisted-nyse-220505680.html.

61. https://money.cnn.com/2009/02/11/news/international/powell_shi.fortune/index.htm.

62. https://www.wsj.com/articles/SB10001424052702304428004579354803691977882.

63. https://www.greentechmedia.com/articles/read/solyndra-suing-chinas-suntringli-for-1-5-billion-anti-trust-violation.

64. https://docs.google.com/file/d/0BxLyP98NDSMbdnhqcVpHS3pBQVE/edit?pli=1&resourcekey=0-VYRAVMv6xBUDanmC65Qx6w.

65. https://en.prnasia.com/releases/global/Trina_Solar_to_Locate_North_American_Base_in_San_Francisco_-15404.shtml.

66. https://en.prnasia.com/releases/global/Yingli_Green_Energy_Establishes_Regional_Headquarters_in_New_York_City_and_San_Francisco-21523.shtml.

67. https://grizzlyreports.com/we-believe-renesola-is-a-fraudulent-company-most-projects
-never-existed/.
68. https://grizzlyreports.com/Research/SOL.pdf.
69. https://www.bizjournals.com/sanfrancisco/news/2018/03/15/how-chinasf-brings
-businesses-to-the-bay-area-from.html.
70. https://www.forbes.com/profile/zhang-li/?sh=1576c35b3b38; https://www.justice.gov
/usao-ndca/pr/chinese-national-real-estate-developer-appears-court-face-charges
-bribing-prominent; https://www.facebook.com/117477138301514/posts/pfbid0rbc
NJaUZtfMb446d3s1Y9ETNbERW2CZiJrLuAFkb4CTWAJrmm9SaCXchTDyd-
N2gql/?mibextid=cr9u03.
71. https://www.chinadaily.com.cn/a/201803/13/WS5aa6fb3fa3106e7dcc14128d.html.
72. https://www.facebook.com/share/iRoxbd1ehaoeg6tL/?mibextid=WC7FNe.
73. https://powersearch.sos.ca.gov/advanced.php.
74. https://sf.curbed.com/2020/2/28/21157317/555-fulton-nuru-housing-development
-san-francisco-fbi; https://www.sfcityattorney.org/2020/02/27/city-attorney-issues-14
-more-subpoenas-in-widening-public-corruption-investigation/.
75. https://www.justice.gov/usao-ndca/pr/property-developer-zl-properties-fined-1
-million-after-pleading-guilty-honest-services.
76. https://www.justice.gov/usao-ndca/pr/chinese-national-real-estate-developer
-appears-court-face-charges-bribing-prominent.
77. https://www.justice.gov/usao-ndca/pr/former-san-francisco-public-works-director
-admits-string-briberies-and-corruption.
78. https://www.sfchronicle.com/sf/article/Mohammed-Nuru-will-be-sentenced-today
-17398030.php.
79. https://www.sfchronicle.com/sf/article/Mohammed-Nuru-will-be-sentenced-today
-17398030.php.
80. https://www.sfchronicle.com/bayarea/article/After-backing-Mohammed-Nuru-for
-years-city-15021627.php.
81. https://www.sfgate.com/politics/article/City-workers-We-were-told-to-vote-work-for
-2812182.php.
82. https://www.sfgate.com/politics/article/City-workers-We-were-told-to-vote-work-for
-2812182.php.
83. https://www.sfchronicle.com/bayarea/article/After-backing-Mohammed-Nuru-for
-years-city-15021627.php.
84. https://www.sfgate.com/bayarea/article/SAN-FRANCISCO-Supervisors-plan
-to-aid-S-F-2801347.php.
85. https://www.sfchronicle.com/bayarea/article/After-backing-Mohammed-Nuru-for
-years-city-15021627.php.
86. https://www.justice.gov/usao-ndca/pr/former-san-francisco-public-works-director
-sentenced-seven-years-federal-prison.
87. https://www.justice.gov/usao-ndca/pr/jury-convicts-former-san-francisco-public
-utilities-commission-general-manager-0.
88. Rachel Gordon, "Mayor Urges PUC Staff to Take Risks," *SFGate*, March 26, 2004, https://
www.sfgate.com/politics/article/Mayor-urges-PUC-staff-to-take-risks-2775324.php;
https://www.sfgate.com/bayarea/matier-ross/article/City-yanks-its-repainted-SUV
-from-S-F-official-3324440.php.
89. Gordon, "Mayor Urges PUC Staff to Take Risks."

90. https://sfist.com/2021/11/04/harlan-and-naomi-kellys-house-named-in-fraud-indictment-has-trail-of-suspicious-dbi-permits/.

91. https://www.justice.gov/usao-ndca/pr/jury-convicts-san-francisco-broker-and-investor-victor-makras-fraud-real-estate-loan.

92. https://missionlocal.org/2022/08/victor-makras-convicted-bank-fraud/.

93. https://www.sfgate.com/bayarea/matier-ross/article/Montel-Williams-looks-at-Oakland-s-pot-business-3177337.php; https://www.sfgate.com/politics/article/SAN-FRANCISCO-Newsom-appoints-2-to-city-2622360.php.

94. https://www.sfgate.com/politics/article/SAN-FRANCISCO-Mayor-names-2-to-building-panel-2732503.php; https://www.justice.gov/usao-ndca/pr/former-san-francisco-building-inspection-commission-president-pleads-guilty-multiple; https://sfstandard.com/2023/02/01/san-francisco-city-hall-corruption-scandal-nuru/.

95. https://powersearch.sos.ca.gov/advanced.php.

96. https://sfgov.legistar.com/View.ashx?M=F&ID=1133833&GUID=28B3C475-225F-4108-82F6-2D9DC6466A50.

97. https://missionlocal.org/2024/01/florence-kong-who-bribed-nuru-with-gold-watch-to-be-fined-750k/; https://sfist.com/2024/01/23/florence-kong-former-sf-contractor-linked-to-mohammed-nuru-bribery-ring-gets-one-of-the-largest-ethics-fines-in-city-history/.

98. https://g-a-i.org/fools-gold-reference/.

99. https://sfstandard.com/2023/02/01/san-francisco-city-hall-corruption-scandal-nuru/; https://sfist.com/2023/07/20/chinese-tycoon-admits-to-bribing-mohammed-nuru-gets-sweetheart-plea-deal-from-feds/.

100. https://www.sfgate.com/politics/article/SAN-FRANCISCO-Mayor-handled-own-building-2783601.php.

101. https://www.forbes.com/sites/china/2010/06/21/nows-the-time-to-avoid-dependence-on-china/?sh=4c27913f250f.

102. https://www.theepochtimes.com/chinese-biotech-company-with-military-ties-buys-us-land-to-build-facility-to-breed-monkeys_4773230.html; https://sfmayor.org/article/mayor-lee-announces-crystal-jade-open-san-francisco.

103. https://www.forbes.com/sites/giacomotognini/2021/04/06/meet-the-40-new-billionaires-who-got-rich-fighting-covid-19/?sh=58a870a817e5.

104. https://www.theepochtimes.com/chinese-biotech-company-with-military-ties-buys-us-land-to-build-facility-to-breed-monkeys_4773230.html.

105. https://www.thegatewaypundit.com/2022/09/chinese-biotech-firm-deep-links-chinas-military-covid-19-program-just-bought-land-florida-massive-research-complex/.

106. https://www.wsj.com/market-data/quotes/CN/XSHG/603127/company-people/executive-profile/208109437.

107. https://www.joinnlabs.com/en/news_detail.php?tid=4&id=123.

108. https://www.thegatewaypundit.com/2022/09/chinese-biotech-firm-deep-links-chinas-military-covid-19-program-just-bought-land-florida-massive-research-complex/.

109. https://www.akingump.com/en/experience/industries/education/ag-study-guide/prominent-chinese-academy-of-military-medical-sciences-is-added-to-export-control-blacklist.html.

110. https://www.federalregister.gov/documents/2021/12/17/2021-27406/addition-of-certain-entities-to-the-entity-list-and-revision-of-an-entry-on-the-entity-list.

111. https://www.theepochtimes.com/chinese-biotech-company-with-military-ties-buys-us-land-to-build-facility-to-breed-monkeys_4773230.html; https://www.wuft.org/news/2022/12/19/no-monkey-business-in-levy-county-primate-research-lab-plans-get-nixed/.

112. https://tennesseestar.com/news/desantis-sounds-alarm-over-chinese-purchase-of-florida-land-for-primate-breeding-facility/jtnews/2022/11/06/.

113. https://www.theepochtimes.com/chinese-biotech-company-with-military-ties-buys-us-land-to-build-facility-to-breed-monkeys_4773230.html.

114. https://tennesseestar.com/news/desantis-sounds-alarm-over-chinese-purchase-of-florida-land-for-primate-breeding-facility/jtnews/2022/11/06/.

115. https://www.theguardian.com/us-news/2023/may/09/ron-desantis-bills-ban-chinese-citizens-buying-land-florida.

116. https://www.bizjournals.com/sanfrancisco/print-edition/2012/12/21/chinese-cash-seeks-to-build-next-bio-hub.html; https://opencorporates.com/companies/hk/1820644; https://opencorporates.com/companies/us_ma/001247394; https://opencorporates.com/companies/us_ca/C3579870.

117. https://finance.yahoo.com/news/kidder-mathews-scores-sale-bayer-204233814.html.

118. https://www1.hkexnews.hk/listedco/listconews/sehk/2022/0428/2022042804371.pdf; https://www1.hkexnews.hk/listedco/listconews/sehk/2021/0226/9633736/sehk20101900653.pdf.

119. https://wireless2.fcc.gov/UlsApp/UlsSearch/license.jsp?licKey=3534973.

120. https://wireless2.fcc.gov/UlsApp/UlsSearch/licenseAdminSum.jsp?licKey=3534973.

121. https://www.pbs.org/weta/washingtonweek/web-video/how-nsa-used-special-devices-radio-waves-spy-offline-computers.

122. https://fortune.com/2021/08/18/kweichow-moutai-workplace-drinking-culture-china-baijiu/; https://www.scmp.com/business/china-business/article/3215827/hurun-says-kweichow-moutai-chinas-most-valuable-brand-fifth-straight-year-2022-amid-rising-trust.

123. https://www.theepochtimes.com/china/former-kweichow-moutai-chairman-dies-in-jail-moutai-club-collapses-5497494; https://www.scmp.com/article/735297/booze-smokes-symbols-official-graft.

124. https://www.theatlantic.com/china/archive/2013/11/how-chinas-anti-corruption-campaign-hurts-a-liquor-producing-town/281302/; https://www.scmp.com/news/china/politics/article/3149956/former-chairman-luxury-liquor-firm-kweichow-moutai-sentenced;https://www.businesslive.co.za/bd/companies/retail-and-consumer/2020-07-16-chinas-liquor-giant-moutai-falls-after-corruption-claims/; https://www.theepochtimes.com/china/former-kweichow-moutai-chairman-dies-in-jail-moutai-club-collapses-5497494; https://english.ckgsb.edu.cn/knowledge/article/how-moutai-became-the-worlds-most-valuable-liquor-maker/; https://www.bloomberg.com/news/articles/2020-07-16/china-s-biggest-stock-moutai-sinks-after-state-media-criticism; https://www.chinadaily.com.cn/a/202109/23/WS614c7c34a310cdd39bc6b200.html.

125. https://www.chinadaily.com.cn/business/2010-03/27/content_9652085.htm; https://www.eeo.com.cn/ens/homepage/briefs/2010/01/18/160993.shtml.

126. *Memorandum of Understanding for the Friendly Collaboration between Moutai Group and the City of San Francisco*, October 14, 2017.

127. https://www.prnewswire.com/news-releases/san-francisco-mayor-edwin-lee-visits
-the-production-facilities-of-kweichow-moutai-maker-of-chinas-iconic-liquor
-300537706.html.

128. "Chinese Liquor Maker Shares Surge to New High on Strong Profit Growth," *Xinhua General News Service*, October 26, 2017; https://www.cnn.com/2021/09/24/business
/kweichow-moutai-chairman-jailed/index.html.

129. https://www.calpers.ca.gov/docs/forms-publications/annual-investment-report
-2020.pdf.

130. https://www.calstrs.com/portfolio-holdings-international-equities.

131. https://sfmayor.org/job-creation.

132. https://ajed.assembly.ca.gov/sites/ajed.assembly.ca.gov/files/Select%20Committee
%20Asia%20California%20Trade%20-%20Briefing%20Materials.pdf.

133. https://www.fdiintelligence.com/content/data-trends/bidens-fdi-success-not-an-ex
act-recipe-for-more-jobs-84236.

134. *ChinaSF July 2016–July 2017 Annual Report.*

135. *ChinaSF July 2016–July 2017 Annual Report.*

136. https://trepo.tuni.fi/bitstream/handle/10024/94438/models_for_international
_2013.pdf?sequence+1.

137. https://web.archive.org/web/20160803102121fw_/http://chinasf.homestead.com
/sponsors.html.

138. https://web.archive.org/web/20130618111204/http://sfced.org/china-sf/our-sponsors/.
https://web.archive.org/web/20160803102121fw_/http://chinasf.homestead.com
/sponsors.html.

139. *ChinaSF July 2016–July 2017 Annual Report.*

140. *ChinaSF July 2016–July 2017 Annual Report.*

141. http://www.xinhuanet.com/english/2017-03/31/c_136174805.htm.

142. https://www.computerworld.com/article/1335175/cisco-sues-huawei-over-intellectual
-property.html.

143. https://mashable.com/article/huawei-spy-caught-disguised-as-weihua-employee.

144. https://www.rand.org/content/dam/rand/pubs/monographs/2005/RAND_MG334
.pdf; https://www.latimes.com/projects/la-fg-huawei-timeline/.

145. https://www.nytimes.com/2008/02/21/business/worldbusiness/21iht-3com
.1.10258216.html.

146. https://www.reuters.com/article/us-huawei-3leaf/huawei-backs-away-from-3leaf
-acquisition-idUSTRE71I38920110219/; https://www.latimes.com/projects/la-fg-huawei
-timeline/.

147. https://www.justice.gov/opa/pr/chinese-telecommunications-device-manufacturer
-and-its-us-affiliate-indicted-theft-trade.

148. https://www.cnet.com/news/privacy/huawei-ban-timeline-detained-cfo-makes-deal
-with-us-justice-department/; https://www.cnn.com/2022/11/26/us/us-washington
-huawei-zte-ban-security-risk-intl-hnk/index.html; https://www.reuters.com/article/us
-usa-china-security-universities-insig/u-s-universities-unplug-from-chinas-huawei-
under-pressure-from-trump-idUSKCN1PI0GV.

149. https://www.sfgate.com/business/bottomline/article/ChinaSF-to-open-office-in
-Beijing-3251345.php.

150. https://www.sfgate.com/business/article/Economy-taking-a-break-along-with-investors
-3260958.php.

151. https://youtu.be/qR2PYdsH5z8?si=bWfPk5hlobmrHalf.

152. https://www.reuters.com/article/us-china-unionpay-special-report/special-report-how
-chinas-official-bank-card-is-used-to-smuggle-money-idUSBREA2B00820140312.

153. https://www.ojp.gov/ncjrs/virtual-library/abstracts/triangle-death-inside-story-triads
-chinese-mafia.

154. https://macaudailytimes.com.mo/inquiry-questions-the-star-on-relationship-with
-chau-despite-unsavory-business-associations.html; https://apnews.com/article/sports
-betting-china-business-6c8edb2e86ff291d01cf49d9ed598bec; https://www.asiafinancial
.com/macau-casino-junket-king-alvin-chau-gets-18-years-jail.

155. https://www.cnn.com/2023/01/18/business/macao-alvin-chau-hong-kong-hnk-intl
/index.html.

156. City & County of San Francisco, Statement from Gavin Newsom, 2011.

157. https://www.davidperry.com/newsroom/mayor-lee-announces-new-chinasf-executive
-director.html.

158. https://www.bizjournals.com/sanfrancisco/print-edition/2013/03/15/darlene-chiu
-bryant-hunts-new-deals.html; https://www.globalsf.biz/2023-selectusa-sf-spinoff.

159. https://ajed.assembly.ca.gov/sites/ajed.assembly.ca.gov/files/hearings/Lt.%20
Gov%20Economic%20Growth%20and%20Competitiveness%20Agenda.pdf.

160. https://www.ca.gov/archive/gov39/2013/04/11/news17994/index.html.

161. https://ajed.assembly.ca.gov/sites/ajed.assembly.ca.gov/files/China%20Trade%20
Office%20Report%202014.pdf.

162. https://rct.doj.ca.gov/Verification/Web/Download.aspx?saveas=181214Z10412823
.pdf&document_id=09027b8f80363b2a; https://calmatters.org/politics/elections/2018
/11/gavin-newsom-wins-california-governor-race-dianne-feinstein-us-senate/.

163. https://www.globalsf.biz/latest-news/blog-postchinasf01; https://business.ca.gov/wp
-content/uploads/2019/12/CTIN-Press-Release-2019-f.pdf.

164. https://www.chinatrademarkoffice.com/index.php?c=tdsearch&m=owner&owner=%
E6%BD%98%E6%9D%B0%E5%85%8B%E7%AE%A1%E7%90%86%E9%9B%86%E5
%9B%A2%E5%85%AC%E5%8F%B8&ln=; https://www.registrationchina.com/trade
mark-search/?value=%E6%BD%98%E6%9D%B0%E5%85%8B%E7%AE%A1%E7%90
%86%E9%9B%86%E5%9B%A2%E5%85%AC%E5%8F%B8.

165. https://www.cadewinery.com/; https://plumpjackwinery.com/content/uploads/2019
/08/PJ-Cade-and-Odette-Presentation08.26.19-compressed.pdf; https://financhill.com
/blog/investing/how-did-gavin-newsom-make-his-money.

166. https://web.archive.org/web/20120402112515/https://www.smartshanghai.com
/articles/community/the-agenda-march-12.

167. https://issuu.com/luxurylifestyleawards/docs/lla_asia-small/47; https://www.smart
shanghai.com/venue/14130/t8_bar_and_restaurant_hubindao; https://www.sfgate.com
/travel/article/DESTINATION-Asia-Shanghai-s-chuppies-hang-2664961.php.

168. https://www.shuionland.com/static/docs/club/ShopOffers/SH_Gold_2015_5_14
%E8%8B%B1.pdf.

169. https://www.farmprogress.com/grapes/california-boosts-2010-u-s-wine-exports
-to-record-year; https://www.pressdemocrat.com/article/news/ad-campaign-aimed-to
-educate-booming-nations-middle-class-aboutvalue-qual/; https://winebusinessanalytics
.com/columns/section/26/article/86526/China-Waits-for-the-Sleeping-Tiger; https://
msadvisory.com/wine-market-in-china/#:~:text=The%20wine%20market%20in%20
China,symbol%20of%20status%20and%20sophistication.

170. https://www.usfca.edu/management/news/perfect-pairing.
171. https://www.odetteestate.com/our-story/; https://signumarchitecture.com/wp-content/uploads/2021/06/press-33.pdf.
172. https://plumpjackwinery.com/content/uploads/2018/10/Distributor-List-with-Addresses.pdf.
173. https://www.scmp.com/article/676907/vast-business-empire-grew-entrepreneurs-vision.
174. https://www.chinadaily.com.cn/business/qaceo/2017-03/17/content_28587585.htm.
175. http://www.disclosures.org/wp-content/uploads/2017/08/Newsom_Gavin-2011.pdf.
176. https://www.financeasia.com/article/shui-on-lands-dollar-debt/32290; https://www.scmp.com/presented/business/topics/hkust-biz-school-magazine/article/2093626/cover-story-mapping-out; https://www.scmp.com/presented/business/topics/hkust-biz-school-magazine/article/2093627/one-belt-one-road-connected.
177. https://crsreports.congress.gov/product/pdf/IF/IF11735.
178. https://crsreports.congress.gov/product/pdf/IF/IF11735.
179. https://crsreports.congress.gov/product/pdf/IF/IF11735.
180. https://globalinitiative.net/wp-content/uploads/2021/03/Chinas-New-Silk-Road-Navigating-the-Organized-Crime-Risk-GITOC.pdf.
181. https://www.forbes.com/sites/wadeshepard/2020/01/29/how-chinas-belt-and-road-became-a-global-trail-of-trouble/?sh=ca70b5f443d7.
182. https://www.dailymail.co.uk/news/article-9501919/Chinese-crime-lords-funnelling-drugs-cash-Australia-Belt-Road-scheme.html; https://www.csis.org/analysis/corruption-flows-along-chinas-belt-and-road.
183. https://www.scmp.com/article/75088/shui-site-security-run-gangs.
184. https://globalinitiative.net/wp-content/uploads/2021/03/Chinas-New-Silk-Road-Navigating-the-Organized-Crime-Risk-GITOC.pdf.
185. https://www.scmp.com/presented/business/topics/hkust-biz-school-magazine/article/2093626/cover-story-mapping-out?campaign=2093626&module=perpetual_scroll_0&pgtype=article.
186. https://www.chinadaily.com.cn/a/201803/14/WS5aa8c987a3106e7dcc1419d5.html.
187. States News Service, "Mayor Newsom Launches ChinaSF in Shanghai," *States News Service*, November 12, 2008. https://advance.lexis.com/api/document?collection=news&id=urn:contentItem:4V57-9200-TX4V-207B-00000-00&context=1519360.
188. https://web.archive.org/web/20081116055832/http://www.sfgov.org/site/mayor_index.asp?id=92777; https://www.sfstation.com/china-live-san-francisco-s-grand-opening-and-chinasf-annual-fundraiser-e2308429; https://californianewswire.com/san-francisco-chinas-ndrc-sign-agreement-to-strengthen-ties-in-sustainability/; https://escholarship.org/content/qt77j9z9wk/qt77j9z9wk.pdf; https://sfchamber.com/2016-highlights-sf-chamber/; https://asiasociety.org/files/pdf/101208_Green_Finance_agenda_with_speakers.pdf.

CHAPTER FOUR: THE CALIFORNIA WAY

1. https://www.latimes.com/politics/story/2022-03-08/full-transcript-gov-newsom-state-of-the-state-address.
2. https://www.gov.ca.gov/2022/03/08/governor-newsom-delivers-state-of-the-state-address-3-8-22/.

3. https://calmatters.org/housing/2022/10/california-homeless-crisis-latinos/.
4. https://www.latimes.com/california/story/2021-11-22/storefront-windows-smashed-louis-vuitton-saks-fifth-avenue-beverly-hills-rodeo-drive.
5. https://www.sacbee.com/news/politics-government/election/california-elections/article264329566.html.
6. https://www.reaganlibrary.gov/archives/speech/remarks-opening-american-cowboy-exhibit-library-congress.
7. https://www.sportsbroadcastjournal.com/ronald-reagan-the-great-communicator-advanced-from-the-broadcast-booth-to-the-oval-office/; https://www.hudson.org/domestic-policy/what-ronald-reagan-accomplished-in-his-hollywood-years-a-new-la-times-article-tells-us-the-real-story.
8. https://www.npr.org/2010/07/04/128303672/a-reagan-legacy-amnesty-for-illegal-immigrants.
9. https://calmatters.org/commentary/2018/10/how-california-shifted-from-pro-gop-purple-to-deep-blue/.
10. https://www.latimes.com/archives/la-xpm-2009-nov-17-oe-schnur17-story.html.
11. https://www.latimes.com/archives/la-xpm-1994-11-24-mn-1087-story.html; https://www.latimes.com/politics/la-pol-ca-democrats-supermajority-california-legislature-20181112-story.html.
12. https://www.nytimes.com/2010/03/07/weekinreview/07mckinley.html.
13. https://militarycouncil.ca.gov/s_californiamilitarybases/; https://www.pbssocal.org/shows/blue-sky-metropolis/the-history-and-revival-of-southern-californias-aerospace-industry; https://lamag.com/politics/how-waves-of-latino-immigration-turned-a-purple-state-blue; https://unherd.com/2024/08/the-hollywood-liberals-who-rule-america/.
14. https://www.washingtonpost.com/archive/politics/1996/03/13/effects-of-base-closings-overestimated-studies-say/a96eed05-3223-464e-8b5b-68e6fc969623/; https://unherd.com/newsroom/americas-sanctuary-cities-are-falling-apart/; https://abc7ny.com/archive/8790365/; https://www.cnbc.com/2021/01/23/why-companies-are-fleeing-california.html.
15. https://www.cbsnews.com/sanfrancisco/news/elon-musk-announces-x-spacex-headquarters-to-relocate-to-texas-from-california/#:~:text=Tech%20mogul%20Elon%20Musk%20said%20Tuesday%20afternoon%20that,new%20California%20law%20signed%20by%20Gov.%20Gavin%20Newsom.
16. https://www.fox7austin.com/news/elon-musk-x-headquarters-move-bastrop-texas.
17. https://laist.com/shows/take-two/take-two-for-july-17-2019.
18. https://www.hugheshistoric.com/southern-california-aerospace-industry/.
19. Roger W. Lotchin, San Francisco: From Hamlet to City (New York: Oxford University Press, 1997), 164.
20. https://www.pbs.org/kqed/chinatown/resourceguide/story.html; https://www.sfgate.com/travel/article/Northern-California-historic-Chinatowns-16064369.php.
21. https://www.city-journal.org/article/native-son.
22. https://www.foundsf.org/index.php?title=Beat_Generation_and_San_Francisco%27s_Culture_of_Dissent.
23. https://www.foundsf.org/index.php?title=Beat_Generation_and_San_Francisco%27s_Culture_of_Dissent.
24. https://www.pbs.org/wgbh/americanexperience/features/when-summer-love-took-over-san-francisco/.

25. https://sfist.com/2017/03/02/what_was_the_summer_of_love_an_expl/#google_vignette; https://www.sfgate.com/news/article/Summer-of-Love-40-Years-Later-1967-The-stuff-2593252.php; https://www.gq.com/story/californias-vanishing-hippie-utopias.

26. J. Bell, "Building a Left Coast: The Legacy of the California Popular Front and the Challenge to Cold War Liberalism in the Post-World War II Era," *Journal of American Studies* 46, no. 1 (2012): 51-71, https://doi.org/10.1017/S0021875811001265; https://sfstandard.com/2023/11/27/how-san-francisco-republican-party-died/.

27. https://www.city-journal.org/article/native-son.

28. https://www.city-journal.org/article/native-son.

29. https://www.city-journal.org/article/native-son.

30. https://www.latimes.com/local/obituaries/archives/la-me-edmund-g-pat-brown-19960217-story.html.

31. https://irle.berkeley.edu/wp-content/uploads/2010/08/The-Living-New-Deal.pdf.

32. https://www.sfchronicle.com/opinion/diaz/article/San-Francisco-s-No-1-export-political-13527832.php.

33. https://governors.library.ca.gov/addresses/32-Pbrown01.html.

34. https://www.city-journal.org/article/native-son.

35. https://www.latimes.com/local/politics/la-me-pol-watts-politics-20150806-story.html; https://newsarchive.berkeley.edu/news/media/releases/2004/06/08_reagan.shtml.

36. https://www.sfgate.com/news/article/70s-in-the-Bay-Area-era-of-radical-violence-2654569.php; https://daily.jstor.org/the-summer-of-love-wasnt-all-peace-and-hippies/.

37. https://www.sfgate.com/news/article/70s-in-the-Bay-Area-era-of-radical-violence-2654569.php.

38. https://www.thenation.com/article/archive/remembering-left-wing-terrorism-1970s/.

39. https://newsarchive.berkeley.edu/news/media/releases/2004/06/08_reagan.shtml.

40. https://www.dsausa.org/democratic-left/lessons-from-peoples-park-occupy-and-seattles-capitol-hill-occupied-protest/.

41. https://www.sfchronicle.com/bayarea/article/People-s-Park-at-50-A-recap-of-the-Berkeley-13838786.php.

42. https://www.theguardian.com/books/2019/jul/06/the-battle-for-peoples-park-berkeley-1969-review-vietnam.

43. https://www.fordlibrarymuseum.gov/sites/default/files/pdf_documents/library/document/0011/1683540.pdf.

44. https://www.latimes.com/archives/la-xpm-2008-jan-10-me-flournoy10-story.html.

45. https://jonestown.sdsu.edu/wp-content/uploads/2021/06/Salvation-and-Suicide.pdf.

46. https://jonestown.sdsu.edu/wp-content/uploads/2021/06/Salvation-and-Suicide.pdf.

47. https://jonestown.sdsu.edu/wp-content/uploads/2021/06/Salvation-and-Suicide.pdf.

48. https://www.washingtontimes.com/news/2018/nov/20/jonestown-and-the-jane-fonda-crowd/.

49. Tim Reiterman, *Raven: The Untold Story of the Rev. Jim Jones and His People* (New York: Dutton, 1982).

50. Tim Reiterman, *Raven: The Untold Story of the Rev. Jim Jones and His People* (New York: Dutton, 1982).

51. https://www.salon.com/2012/05/01/jim_jones_sinister_grip_on_san_francisco/.

52. https://jonestown.sdsu.edu/wp-content/uploads/2021/06/Salvation-and-Suicide.pdf.

53. https://www.city-journal.org/article/jim-jones-made-in-san-francisco.

54. https://www.city-journal.org/article/jim-jones-made-in-san-francisco.
55. https://www.city-journal.org/article/drinking-harvey-milks-kool-aid.
56. https://www.city-journal.org/article/drinking-harvey-milks-kool-aid.
57. https://www.fbi.gov/history/famous-cases/jonestown.
58. https://jonestown.sdsu.edu/?page_id=114366.
59. https://www.fbi.gov/history/famous-cases/jonestown.
60. https://www.the-independent.com/arts-entertainment/tv/news/cult-massacre-one
    -day-jonestown-hulu-jim-jones-b2564873.html.
61. https://time.com/longform/jonestown-aftermath/.
62. https://jonestown.sdsu.edu/?page_id=30886.
63. https://www.latimes.com/california/story/2023-02-14/harvey-milk-george-moscone
    -san-francisco-assassination-shaped-dianne-feinstein-career.
64. https://www.nytimes.com/1996/02/20/us/willie-brown-s-performance-is-a-hit.html.
65. https://www.nbcnews.com/id/wbna3672550.
66. https://www.latimes.com/archives/la-xpm-1994-03-02-mn-28983-story.html;
    https://www.sfgate.com/news/article/brown-s-aids-agenda-3123125.php; https://www
    .nytimes.com/1996/02/20/us/willie-brown-s-performance-is-a-hit.html; https://www
    .latimes.com/archives/la-xpm-1985-05-15-mn-8501-story.html.
67. https://www.foundsf.org/index.php?title=Mayor_Willie_Brown.
68. https://www.kqed.org/news/11980202/willie-brown-celebrates-90th-birthday-with
    -california-political-powerhouses.
69. https://www.nbcnews.com/id/wbna3672550.
70. https://www.jstor.org/stable/10.7312/wyss16446.
71. https://www.city-journal.org/article/native-son.
72. https://archive.nytimes.com/www.nytimes.com/gwire/2010/10/08/08greenwire-jerry
    -browns-environmental-record-runs-deep-44334.html?pagewanted=1.
73. WB Rood, "Brown Proposes $2 Billion Revival of Space Program," *Los Angeles Times*,
    September 26, 1979.
74. https://www.latimes.com/archives/blogs/top-of-the-ticket/story/2010-10-25/opinion
    -history-lesson-why-jerry-brown-is-called-moonbeam.
75. https://www.latimes.com/archives/la-xpm-1992-03-31-mn-107-story.html.
76. https://www.latimes.com/archives/la-xpm-2007-feb-19-me-cap19-story.html.
77. https://www.sfgate.com/news/article/FBI-scrutinizes-mayor-s-contractor-pal
    -3077998.php; https://www.sfgate.com/politics/article/the-mayor-s-legacy-willie-brown
    -fbi-s-5-year-2832559.php.
78. https://www.city-journal.org/article/native-son.
79. https://www.governing.com/archive/why-san-franciscos-future-may-be-right-wing
    .html.
80. https://www.latimes.com/archives/la-xpm-2004-feb-01-me-sfchinese1-story.html.
81. https://www.nbcnews.com/id/wbna3672550.
82. https://www.nytimes.com/2011/01/07/us/07bcmayor.html; https://www.sfgate.com
    /news/article/Rose-Pak-SF-political-powerhouse-dies-9230594.php.
83. https://www.sfgate.com/news/article/Newest-S-F-Supervisor-Sworn-In-He-has
    -2853805.php.
84. https://www.sfgate.com/news/article/Newsom-gets-his-political-feet-wet-3134324
    .php.
85. https://time.com/3816952/obama-gay-lesbian-transgender-lgbt-rights/.

86. https://www.msn.com/en-us/news/politics/gavin-newsoms-most-controversial-moments/ar-AA1qgt6I.

87. https://www.msn.com/en-us/news/politics/long-before-gay-marriage-was-popular-kamala-harris-was-at-the-forefront-of-the-equal-rights-battle/ar-AA1qC1Jw.

88. https://www.townandcountrymag.com/society/politics/a34252538/kamala-harris-san-francisco-politics/; https://www.sfweekly.com/archives/looking-back-on-kamala-harris-record-in-california/article_10316c0c-29e1-5ba4-a9c3-aea9effe926c.html.

89. https://www.sfweekly.com/archives/looking-back-on-kamala-harris-record-in-california/article_10316c0c-29e1-5ba4-a9c3-aea9effe926c.html.

90. https://www.sfgate.com/news/article/HERB-CAEN-Twas-the-Day-After-3017150.php.

91. https://web.archive.org/web/20170805043948/http://www.sfweekly.com/news/kamalas-karma/.

92. Peter Schweizer, *Profiles in Corruption: Abuse of Power by America's Progressive Elite* (New York: HarperCollins, 2020), 21.

93. https://www.politico.com/news/magazine/2024/07/31/willie-brown-kamala-harris-campaign-column-00171885.

94. https://www.politico.com/news/magazine/2024/07/31/willie-brown-kamala-harris-campaign-column-00171885.

95. https://sfstandard.com/2024/07/25/willie-brown-kamala-harris-will-tap-gavin-newsom-for-cabinet-role/.

96. https://nypost.com/2024/02/17/business/bill-ackman-accuses-kamala-harris-of-conflict-of-interest-on-herbalife/.

97. https://nypost.com/2024/02/17/business/bill-ackman-accuses-kamala-harris-of-conflict-of-interest-on-herbalife/.

98. https://www.prnewswire.com/news-releases/consumer-watchdog-opposes-california-sen-huesos-bill-that-would-limit-criticism-of-shady-business-practices-shadow-sponsored-by-herbalife-300289474.html.

99. https://www.realclearpolitics.com/articles/2019/08/14/harris_silence_on_diverted_funds_rankles_housing_advocates_141005.html.

100. https://www.pbs.org/newshour/nation/second-brother-testifies-jussie-smollett-paid-for-staged-attack.

101. https://www.breitbart.com/politics/2024/07/26/former-senior-chicago-cop-warns-voters-about-kamala-harris-after-she-backed-jussie-smollett/.

102. https://x.com/KamalaHarris/status/1090361495119187969.

103. https://www.breitbart.com/politics/2024/07/26/former-senior-chicago-cop-warns-voters-about-kamala-harris-after-she-backed-jussie-smollett/; https://www.pbs.org/newshour/nation/actor-jussie-smollett-sentenced-to-150-days-in-jail-for-lying-about-staged-hate-attack.

104. https://freebeacon.com/author/stiles/media/never-forget-its-been-5-years-since-the-mainstream-media-fell-for-jussie-smolletts-hate-crime-hoax/.

105. https://www.nbcnews.com/feature/nbc-out/harris-booker-call-attack-black-gay-actor-attempted-modern-day-n964326.

106. https://www.whitehouse.gov/briefing-room/speeches-remarks/2022/03/29/remarks-by-vice-president-harris-at-signing-of-h-r-55-the-emmett-till-antilynching-act/.

107. https://web.archive.org/web/20240823062529/https://www.nytimes.com/2024/08/23/us/politics/kamala-harris-speech-transcript.html; https://nypost.com/2020/09/03/kamala-harris-rampant-prosecutorial-abuses/.

108. https://www.themarshallproject.org/2024/07/27/kamala-harris-prosecutor
-california-police-election-crime.
109. https://news.grabien.com/story/kamala-brags-about-her-work-to-ensure-every
-transgender-inmate-in-the.
110. https://www.advocate.com/news/2007/06/22/san-francisco-outs-gay-rape; https://
web.archive.org/web/20071215010252/http://www.mensurvivingrape.org/.
111. https://www.hrc.org/news/hrc-president-kamala-harris-exceptional-choice-as-vice
-president.
112. https://nypost.com/2020/09/03/kamala-harris-rampant-prosecutorial-abuses/.
113. https://www.sacbee.com/news/politics-government/capitol-alert/article7965822.html.
114. https://www.latimes.com/archives/la-xpm-2004-jul-01-me-sanfran1-story.html.
115. https://www.sfgate.com/news/article/fewer-homeless-people-on-streets-of-san
-francisco-2730156.php; https://www.insidehousing.co.uk/insight/on-the-streets-of-san
-fran-33326; https://www.politifact.com/factchecks/2018/oct/08/john-cox/fact-checking
-gavin-newsoms-record-solving-homeles/.
116. https://x.com/govern4ca/status/1737538817413062958.
117. https://x.com/govern4ca/status/1737538817413062958.
118. https://www.realclearpolitics.com/articles/2023/10/28/ca_funding_lgbtq_group
_fighting_parental_notification.html.
119. https://freebeacon.com/california/california-group-rebranded-anti-trump-coalition
-hours-after-election-suggest-incoming-windfall-progressive-orgs/; https://www.dailynews
.com/2024/08/30/city-of-la-secures-21-8-million-to-assist-newly-arrived-migrant
-families/.
120. https://therepproject.org/about/.
121. https://www.gov.ca.gov/2019/01/18/governor-newsom-announces-office-of-the-first
-partner/.
122. https://openthebooks.substack.com/p/california-gov-gavin-newsom-reaped.
123. http://oks.substack.com/p/california-gov-gavin-newsom-reaped.
124. https://www.foxnews.com/politics/gavin-newsoms-wifes-films-shown-schools
-contain-explicit-images-push-gender-ideology-boost-his-politics.
125. https://californiaglobe.com/fl/open-the-books-exposes-the-legalized-pay-to-play
-scheme-by-newsom-inc/.
126. https://www.foxnews.com/politics/gavin-newsoms-wifes-films-shown-schools
-contain-explicit-images-push-gender-ideology-boost-his-politics.
127. https://nypost.com/2022/02/16/san-francisco-recalls-gabriela-lopez-faauuga-moliga
-alison-collins-off-citys-school-board/.
128. https://www.nbcnews.com/politics/elections/parents-guilty-murder-raised-radicals
-chesa-boudin-san-francisco-s-n1101071.
129. https://www.foxnews.com/politics/new-san-francisco-da-ayers-chavez;
https://harvardlawreview.org/print/vol-136/san-francisco-district-attorney-chesa-boudin
-recalled/.
130. https://thehill.com/homenews/campaign/3588171-ousted-san-francisco-district
-attorney-wont-run-again-after-recall/.
131. https://www.politico.com/news/2022/07/07/london-breed-replaces-chesa-boudin
-with-brooke-jenkins-00044563.
132. https://www.axios.com/local/san-francisco/2022/08/12/district-attorney-brooke
-jenkins-controversy.

133. https://www.cbsnews.com/sanfrancisco/news/san-francisco-city-workers-charged -corruption-scheme-bribery/.

134. https://www.sf.gov/sites/default/files/2024-11/2024A%20COPs%20MCIP%20-%20 Final%20Official%20Statement.pdf.

135. https://missionlocal.org/2020/01/mohammed-nuru-director-of-san-francisco-public -works-arrested-by-fbi/; https://www.cbsnews.com/sanfrancisco/news/san-fran cisco-mayor-lee-city-leaders-accused-of-corruption-in-court-filing-by-shrimp-boy -lawyers/.

136. Interview between Doug Eckenrod and Susan Crabtree Oct. 17, 2024.

137. https://www.cdcr.ca.gov/covid19/population-status-tracking/; https://ourworldindata .org/mortality-risk-covid.

138. https://californiaglobe.com/fl/californias-latest-crime-events-prove-why-prop-36-to -reform-prop-47-is-essential/; https://www.dailynews.com/2024/01/03/where-los-angeles -county-district-attorney-candidates-stand-on-proposition-47/.

139. https://patch.com/california/murrieta/riverside-county-sheriff-da-attack-california -justice-system.

140. https://calmatters.org/justice/2023/07/california-prisoner-rehabilitation-centers/.

141. https://web.archive.org/web/20230615184000/https:/www.cbsnews.com /sacramento/news/cdcr-inmate-recidivism-report-questions-unanswered/.

142. https://www.cdcr.ca.gov/insidecdcr/2023/04/07/the-california-model-will -transform-corrections/.

143. https://calmatters.org/newsletters/whatmatters/2023/07/california-parole -investigation/.

CHAPTER FIVE: STATE OF DECEPTION

1. https://californiaglobe.com/fr/reedley-lab-owner-arrested/.

2. https://californiaglobe.com/articles/reedley-chinese-covid-lab-received-tax-credit -of-360000-from-gov-newsoms-go-biz/.

3. https://californiaglobe.com/fr/reedley-lab-owner-arrested/; https://californiaglobe.com /articles/reedley-chinese-covid-lab-received-tax-credit-of-360000-from-gov -newsoms-go-biz/.

4. https://californiaglobe.com/fr/reedley-lab-owner-arrested/.

5. https://californiaglobe.com/articles/was-illegal-chinese-covid-lab-in-reedley-a-ccp -biowarfare-lab/.

6. https://presentdangerchina.org/webinar-chinese-carry-out-a-ccp-biowarfare -lab-in-california/.

7. https://selectcommitteeontheccp.house.gov/sites/evo-subsites/selectcommitteeontheccp .house.gov/files/evo-media-document/scc-reedley-report-11.15.pdf; https://gvwire.com /2023/08/10/arias-joins-bredefeld-in-criticizing-fresno-county-over-reedley-lab/; https://www.fresnobee.com/news/local/article278353704.html.

8. https://selectcommitteeontheccp.house.gov/sites/evo-subsites/selectcommitteeon theccp.house.gov/files/evo-media-document/scc-reedley-report-11.15.pdf.

9. https://selectcommitteeontheccp.house.gov/sites/evo-subsites/selectcommitteeon theccp.house.gov/files/evo-media-document/scc-reedley-report-11.15.pdf.

10. https://californiaglobe.com/articles/reedley-chinese-covid-lab-received-tax-credit -of-360000-from-gov-newsoms-go-biz/.

11. https://www.occrp.org/en/news/us-fbi-raids-california-business-suspected-of-green-card-fraud.
12. https://www.justice.gov/usao-cdca/pr/attorney-pleads-guilty-federal-charges-stemming-50-million-scheme-defrauded-eb-5-visa.
13. https://www.occrp.org/en/news/us-fbi-raids-california-business-suspected-of-green-card-fraud.
14. https://www.justice.gov/usao-cdca/pr/attorney-pleads-guilty-federal-charges-stemming-50-million-scheme-defrauded-eb-5-visa.
15. https://www.dailymail.co.uk/news/article-4386478/Father-daughter-accused-massive-visa-fraud.html.
16. https://www.cbsnews.com/sacramento/news/feds-raid-california-business-in-green-card-probe-involving-chinese-investors/.
17. https://www.justice.gov/usao-cdca/pr/attorney-pleads-guilty-federal-charges-stemming-50-million-scheme-defrauded-eb-5-visa.
18. https://www.justice.gov/usao-cdca/pr/us-files-9-lawsuits-seeking-forfeiture-properties-worth-over-30-million-allegedly.
19. https://www.nbclosangeles.com/news/national-international/attorney-guilty-in-multimillion-dollar-fraud-scheme-sentenced-to-one-day-behind-bars/2511151/.
20. https://wikileaks.org/podesta-emails/emailid/55053.
21. https://wikileaks.org/podesta-emails/emailid/49826.
22. https://docquery.fec.gov/pdf/096/201607059020116096/201607059020116096.pdf#navpanes=0; https://docquery.fec.gov/pdf/128/201607059020231128/201607059020231128.pdf#navpanes=0; https://docquery.fec.gov/pdf/009/201509039001599009/201509039001599009.pdf#navpanes=0.
23. https://www.propublica.org/article/operation-fox-hunt-how-china-exports-repression-using-a-network-of-spies-hidden-in-plain-sight; https://docquery.fec.gov/pdf/713/201602019005298713/20160201900529871 3.pdf.
24. https://www.gov.ca.gov/wp-content/uploads/2022/09/SB-1084-VETO-message.pdf?emrc=03208d.
25. https://www.gov.ca.gov/wp-content/uploads/2022/09/SB-1084-VETO-message.pdf?emrc=03208d; https://californiaglobe.com/fr/newsom-vetoes-bill-to-prohibit-foreign-governments-from-buying-ca-agricultural-land/.
26. https://www.politico.com/news/2023/10/07/newsom-california-climate-disclosure-00120474.
27. https://dailycaller.com/2023/10/09/gavin-newsom-signs-law-forcing-investment-firms-to-publish-diversity-data-for-companies-they-back/.
28. https://www.congress.gov/bill/95th-congress/house-bill/13132.
29. https://www.uscc.gov/sites/default/files/2022-05/Chinas_Interests_in_U.S._Agriculture.pdf.
30. https://m.washingtontimes.com/news/2021/aug/3/lawmakers-say-chinese-investment-us-farmland-poses/.
31. https://thesungazette.com/article/news/2023/07/29/sen-hurtado-raises-concerns-on-recent-ag-land-purchase/.
32. https://thesungazette.com/article/news/2023/07/29/sen-hurtado-raises-concerns-on-recent-ag-land-purchase/.
33. https://web.archive.org/web/20111004045554/http://www.yatai.com/english/about-profile.htm; https://www.napawineproject.com/quixote-winery/; https://in.market

screener.com/quote/stock/JILIN-YATAI-GROUP-CO-LTD-6497497/news/Jilin
-Yatai-Co-Ltd-agreed-to-acquire-Quixote-Wine-Co-Ltd-from-Changchun-Zhengmao
-Jiajia-Logisti-35000825/.

34. https://drewaltizer.com/event/14828-plumpjack-quixote-winery-luncheon/.

35. https://sfist.com/2019/11/18/accused-chinese-spy-in-bay-area-linked-to-possible
-scheme-involving-hotel-purchases-and-chinese-investors/.

36. http://blogs.wsj.com/chinarealtime/2015/01/28/chinese-real-estate-firm-looks
-west-to-california/.

37. https://www.foxnews.com/opinion/for-china-buy-american-means-something-else;
https://selectcommitteeontheccp.house.gov/media/press-releases/select-committee
-unveils-ccp-influence-memo-united-front-101.

38. https://www.bizjournals.com/sanfrancisco/print-edition/2016/03/25/first
-and-mission-land-sale-transbay-tmg-oceanwide.html; https://news.theregistrysf.com
/chinas-oceanwide-holdings-looks-to-transform-first-and-mission-site-in-san
-francisco/.

39. https://www.siliconvalley.com/2024/01/17/san-jose-real-estate-buy-land-china
-ranch-build-home-house-develop/.

40. https://www.fsa.usda.gov/programs-and-services/economic-and-policy-analysis
/afida/agricultural-foreign-investment-disclosure-act-afida/index.

41. Peter Schweizer, *Blood Money: Why the Powerful Turn a Blind Eye While China Kills Americans* (New York: Harper, 2023), 49.

42. Peter Schweizer, *Blood Money: Why the Powerful Turn a Blind Eye While China Kills Americans* (New York: Harper, 2023), 49.

43. Peter Schweizer, *Blood Money: Why the Powerful Turn a Blind Eye While China Kills Americans* (New York: Harper, 2023), 49; https://www.sfgate.com/opinion/article
/FEAR-FACTOR-DIVERTS-TORCH-RELAY-3219717.php; http://www.fogcityjournal
.com/wordpress/269/overheard-in-fog-city-2/.

44. https://banks.house.gov/news/documentsingle.aspx?DocumentID=1625#.

45. https://banks.house.gov/news/documentsingle.aspx?DocumentID=1625#.

46. https://californiaglobe.com/fr/calpers-fails-to-answer-rep-jim-banks-questions
-regarding-cios-ties-to-china/.

47. https://californiaglobe.com/fl/calpers-is-heavily-invested-in-chinese-companies/.

48. https://californiaglobe.com/fr/calpers-fails-to-answer-rep-jim-banks-questions
-regarding-cios-ties-to-china/.

49. https://californiaglobe.com/fl/calpers-is-heavily-invested-in-chinese-companies/.

50. https://californiaglobe.com/fl/calpers-is-heavily-invested-in-chinese-companies/.

51. https://www.globalsecurity.org/military/library/report/2020/elements-of-china
-challenge_dos_20201117.pdf; http://web.archive.org/web/20171004004343/http://
society.people.com.cn/n1/2017/1002/c1008-29571359.html; https://perma.cc/J56R
-YJYW; https://www.hup.harvard.edu/catalog.php?isbn=9780674271913; https://www
.wsj.com/articles/beijing-reins-in-chinas-central-bank-11638981078.

52. https://www.californiacitynews.org/2020/08/resignation-calpers-cio-followed
-ethics-complaint.html.

53. https://www.fppc.ca.gov/content/dam/fppc/documents/Stipulations/2024/november
/8-Ben-Meng-Stip.pdf.

54. https://x.com/billessayli/status/1783594900124250203.

55. https://firstamendmentcoalition.org/2019/09/secret-docket-revealed-fac-wins-cal
-supreme-court-rulings-unsealing-clemency-files/.

56. https://www.atthelectern.com/under-the-radar-how-gov-newsom-uses-clemency
-to-engineer-parole-for-recidivist-felons-and-murderers/; https://californiaglobe.com
/fl/under-the-radar-how-gov-newsom-uses-clemency-to-engineer-parole-for-recidivist
-felons-and-murderers/; https://web.archive.org/web/20210610020646/https://www
.sandiegouniontribune.com/news/california/story/2021-06-09/california-supreme
-court-says-killer-can-be-granted-clemency; https://appellatecases.courtinfo.ca.gov
/search/case/dockets.cfm?dist=0&doc_id=2490576&doc_no=S278455&request_token
=NiIwLSEmLkw4WyBJSCM9UElIUFg0UDxTJCBeVz9SICAgCg%253D%253D.

57. https://sfgov.org/sunshine/frequently-asked-questions; https://codelibrary.amlegal.com
/codes/san_francisco/latest/sf_admin/0-0-0-19477#67.2.

58. https://web.archive.org/web/20120315205927/http://www.sfsuperiorcourt.org
/Modules/ShowDocument.aspx?documentid=2860.

59. https://web.archive.org/web/20120315210445/http://www.sfethics.org/ethics
/2011/09/ethics-commission-response-to-the-2010-2011-civil-grand-jury-report
.html; https://web.archive.org/web/20120315205927/http://www.sfsuperiorcourt.org
/Modules/ShowDocument.aspx?documentid=2860.

60. https://www.sfgate.com/politics/article/S-F-panel-Kamala-Harris-violated-sunshine
-law-3247865.php.

61. https://www.forbes.com/sites/adamandrzejewski/2021/09/30/vp-kamala-harris
-is-the-least-transparent-elected-official-in-the-nation/?sh=338106c2286b.

62. https://www.dailymail.co.uk/news/article-13822019/kamala-harris-staff-bully-vice
-president-replaced.html.

63. https://www.politico.com/story/2015/05/brandon-kiel-kamala-harris-aide
-arrested-117683; https://www.theguardian.com/us-news/2015/may/10/bizarre-tale
-kamala-harris-aide-fake-masonic-police-force.

64. https://www.theguardian.com/us-news/2015/may/10/bizarre-tale-kamala-harris
-aide-fake-masonic-police-force.

65. https://www.theguardian.com/us-news/2015/may/10/bizarre-tale-kamala-harris
-aide-fake-masonic-police-force.

66. https://abc7.com/free-masons-masonic-fraternal-police-department-california-of-justice
-fake/701005/.

67. https://www.npr.org/sections/thetwo-way/2015/05/06/404764522/3-arrested
-in-california-for-operating-3-000-year-old-masonic-police-department.

68. https://www.latimes.com/local/crime/la-me-fraternal-police-20160419-story.html.

69. https://www.latimes.com/local/crime/la-me-fraternal-police-20160419-story.html.

70. https://www.sfgate.com/bayarea/article/Judge-rips-Harris-office-for-hiding
-problems-3263797.php.

71. https://www.sfgate.com/bayarea/article/Judge-rips-Harris-office-for-hiding
-problems-3263797.php.

72. Peter Schweizer, *Profiles in Corruption: Abuse of Power by America's Progressive Elite* (New York: HarperCollins, 2020), 24.

73. Peter Schweizer, *Profiles in Corruption: Abuse of Power by America's Progressive Elite* (New York: HarperCollins, 2020), 26. https://spectator.org/why-didnt-kamala-harris-prosecute
-abusive-priests/.

74. https://theintercept.com/2019/06/09/kamala-harris-san-francisco-catholic-church-child-abuse/.

75. https://www.breitbart.com/politics/2020/09/23/kamala-harris-wanted-to-be-a-prosecutor-to-protect-victims-of-sexual-abuse-failed-to-protect-victims-of-priests/.

76. https://www.sfweekly.com/archives/a-secrecy-fetish/article_3040ccdb-d0c9-5d6f-b716-74353af424b7.html.

77. https://calmatters.org/commentary/2019/03/public-records/.

78. https://calmatters.org/education/2022/06/california-schools-stimulus-funds-oversight/; https://www.abc10.com/article/news/local/california/nursing-home-fresno-health/103-6ced0ac0-79cc-487e-837a-1a6b7e9f1358; https://www.abc10.com/article/news/local/california/nursing-home-fresno-health/103-6ced0ac0-79cc-487e-837a-1a6b7e9f1358; https://calmatters.org/politics/2023/04/public-information-california-press/; https://www.modernhealthcare.com/medicaid/california-inks-sweetheart-deal-kaiser-permanente-jeopardizing-medicaid-reforms; https://www.techdirt.com/2023/11/27/california-activists-say-state-isnt-being-transparent-about-how-billions-in-broadband-subsidies-are-being-spent/.

79. https://www.truthinaccounting.org/news/detail/financial-transparency-score-2024.

80. https://www.record-bee.com/2017/05/10/what-does-the-california-state-bar-have-to-hide/.

81. https://www.courthousenews.com/calif-state-bar-blastedfor-lack-of-transparency/.

82. https://webcache.googleusercontent.com/search?q=cache:3LMgcxavAfcJ:https://news.bloomberglaw.com/us-law-week/girardi-probe-reveals-an-internally-corrupt-california-state-bar&hl=en&gl=us&client=firefox-b-1-d.

83. https://www.foxnews.com/politics/democrat-donor-tied-biden-indicted-allegedly-embezzling-millions-suffering-clients.

84. https://www.latimes.com/california/story/2022-11-03/california-state-bar-40-years-complaints-tom-girardi.

85. https://ktla.com/news/local-news/disgraced-former-l-a-lawyer-tom-girardi-indicted-on-client-theft/.

86. https://www.justice.gov/usao-cdca/pr/disbarred-personal-injury-lawyer-tom-girardi-found-guilty-defrauding-clients-out-tens.

87. https://www.justice.gov/usao-cdca/pr/disbarred-personal-injury-lawyer-tom-girardi-found-guilty-defrauding-clients-out-tens.

88. https://webcache.googleusercontent.com/search?q=cache:VD9lD5RBhgUJ:https://news.bloomberglaw.com/legal-ethics/california-bar-looks-ahead-as-girardi-affair-showed-corrupt-ways&hl=en&gl=us&client=firefox-b-1-d.

89. https://www.foxnews.com/politics/gavin-newsom-ties-tom-girardi-lawsuit.

90. https://www.realclearpolitics.com/articles/2020/01/23/suing_california_to_produce_a_state_checkbook_142216.html.

91. https://www.forbes.com/sites/adamandrzejewski/2021/08/31/how-californias-lack-of-transparency-could-flip-the-us-senate/.

92. https://www.ocregister.com/2023/04/23/gavin-newsom-versus-the-california-press/.

93. https://web.archive.org/web/20230423140556/https://www.ocregister.com/2023/04/23/gavin-newsom-versus-the-california-press/.

94. https://fsapartners.ed.gov/knowledge-center/topics/section-117-foreign-gift-and-contract-reporting/section-117-foreign-gift-and-contract-data.

95. https://fsapartners.ed.gov/sites/default/files/2023-04/ReportonInstitutionalCompliancewithSection117oftheHigherEducationActof1965October2020.pdf.

96. https://www.courthousenews.com/feds-abruptly-drop-visa-fraud-charges-against
-chinese-military-scientists/.

97. https://www.latimes.com/california/story/2021-09-01/california-college-financial
-aid-scam-fake-students.

98. https://eccunion.com/news/2023/12/06/human-trafficking-fake-students-suspected
-in-financial-aid-and-enrollment-scams/; https://www.insidehighered.com/quicktakes
/2021/09/02/financial-aid-scam-roils-calif-community-colleges.

99. https://www.latimes.com/california/story/2021-12-17/fake-student-bots-enrolled-in
-community-colleges-one-professor-has-become-a-bot-sleuthing-continues-to-fight
-them; https://www.latimes.com/california/story/2021-09-01/california-college-financial
-aid-scam-fake-students.

100. https://calmatters.org/education/higher-education/2024/04/financial-aid-fraud/.

101. http://web.archive.org/web/20240829102357/https://www.nytimes.com/2024/08/29
/us/california-corruption-huizar.html; https://cdn.ca9.uscourts.gov/datastore/opinions
/2024/09/11/23-972.pdf.

102. http://web.archive.org/web/20240829102357/https://www.nytimes.com/2024/08/29
/us/california-corruption-huizar.html.

103. https://www.justice.gov/usao-cdca/pr/former-los-angeles-politician-jose-huizar
-sentenced-13-years-federal-prison; https://cdn.ca9.uscourts.gov/datastore/opinions
/2024/09/11/23-972.pdf.

104. https://cdn.ca9.uscourts.gov/datastore/opinions/2024/09/11/23-972.pdf.

105. https://www.courthousenews.com/chinese-developer-saw-la-city-councilman-as
-investment-aide-testifies/; https://www.justice.gov/usao-cdca/pr/former-los-angeles
-politician-jose-huizar-sentenced-13-years-federal-prison.

106. https://cdn.ca9.uscourts.gov/datastore/opinions/2024/09/11/23-972.pdf; https://www
.courthousenews.com/chinese-developer-saw-la-city-councilman-as-investment-aide
-testifies/.

107. https://www.justice.gov/usao-cdca/pr/former-los-angeles-city-politician-jose-huizar
-pleads-guilty-racketeering-conspiracy.

108. https://www.justice.gov/usao-cdca/pr/former-los-angeles-city-politician-jose-huizar
-pleads-guilty-racketeering-conspiracy.

109. https://www.justice.gov/usao-cdca/pr/former-los-angeles-politician-jose-huizar
-sentenced-13-years-federal-prison.

110. https://www.nytimes.com/2024/08/29/us/california-corruption-huizar.html.

111. https://www.nytimes.com/2024/08/29/us/california-corruption-huizar.html.

112. https://www.nytimes.com/2024/08/29/us/california-corruption-huizar.html.

113. https://americanarchive.org/catalog/cpb-aacip-45b8d8a9ecd.

CHAPTER SIX: BLEEDING THE BEAST

1. https://www.latimes.com/archives/la-xpm-1996-10-25-fi-57558-story.html; https://www
.cigaraficionado.com/article/grand-havana-room-california-2013.

2. https://ew.com/article/1995/07/28/peak-grand-havana-rooms-opening/; https://www
.seeing-stars.com/Play/GrandHavanaRoom.shtml.

3. https://www.politico.com/states/california/story/2019/03/25/schwarzenegger-plea
-to-beverly-hills-spare-exclusive-cigar-club-from-tobacco-rules-933191.

4. https://lamag.com/news/fbi-agents-corruption-trial-dirty-money-mobsters-and -schwarzenegger-appear-in-filing.

5. https://lamag.com/news/kevin-de-leon-received-hot-money-donations-from-known -mobster.

6. https://lamag.com/news/kevin-de-leon-received-hot-money-donations-from-known -mobster.

7. https://www.latimes.com/california/story/2022-12-13/edgar-sargsyan-los-angeles -con-man-bankruptcy.

8. https://www.yahoo.com/news/l-con-man-posed-attorney-002853793.html.

9. https://lamag.com/crimeinla/bleeding-the-beast-crooked-cops-an-armenian-mob -boss-a-500m-scam-and-an-unlikely-love-story.

10. https://www.wired.com/story/lion-polygamist-and-biofuel-scam/.

11. https://www.latimes.com/california/story/2022-12-13/edgar-sargsyan-los-angeles -con-man-bankruptcy.

12. https://lamag.com/news/exclusive-fallout-1-billion-biofuel-scam-could-decimate -polygamist-sect.

13. https://lamag.com/crimeinla/bleeding-the-beast-crooked-cops-an-armenian-mob -boss-a-500m-scam-and-an-unlikely-love-story.

14. https://www.sltrib.com/news/2020/01/27/polygamy-bribes-luxury/.

15. https://lamag.com/crimeinla/bleeding-the-beast-crooked-cops-an-armenian-mob -boss-a-500m-scam-and-an-unlikely-love-story.

16. https://www.justice.gov/opa/pr/jury-finds-los-angeles-businessman-guilty-1-billion -biodiesel-tax-fraud-scheme.

17. https://www.sltrib.com/news/2020/01/27/polygamy-bribes-luxury/.

18. https://www.wired.com/story/lion-polygamist-and-biofuel-scam/.

19. Inexplicably, the attorney he allegedly paid to commit the fraud—Henrik Mosesi—is still free to practice law in the state of California: https://apps.calbar.ca.gov/attorney /Licensee/Detail/189672.

20. https://lamag.com/crimeinla/bleeding-the-beast-crooked-cops-an-armenian-mob -boss-a-500m-scam-and-an-unlikely-love-story.

21. William D'Urso, "Exclusive: Gavin Newsom Plans to Donate Armenian Mobster's Cam- paign Contribution to Charity," *Los Angeles Magazine*, October 25, 2023, https://lamag .com/news/exclusive-gavin-newsom-plans-to-donate-armenian-mobsters-campaign -donation.

22. https://www.latimes.com/california/story/2022-12-13/edgar-sargsyan-los-angeles -con-man-bankruptcy.

23. https://lamag.com/news/fbi-agent-accused-of-moonlighting-for-armenian-mobsters -fate-now-in-jurys-hands.

24. https://www.latimes.com/california/story/2020-04-28/the-lawyer-who-corrupted -the-fbi-agent.

25. https://lamag.com/crimeinla/conman-edgar-sargysan-fake-beverly-hills-law-firm -christmas-at-home.

26. https://www.justice.gov/opa/pr/los-angeles-businessman-utah-fuel-plant-operators -and-employees-sentenced-prison-billion.

27. https://www.wired.com/story/lion-polygamist-and-biofuel-scam/.

28. https://www.justice.gov/opa/pr/los-angeles-businessman-utah-fuel-plant-operators -and-employees-sentenced-prison-billion.

29. https://www.latimes.com/california/story/2022-12-13/edgar-sargsyan-los-angeles -con-man-bankruptcy.

30. https://lamag.com/news/kevin-de-leon-received-hot-money-donations-from-known -mobster.

31. https://lamag.com/crimeinla/beverly-hills-lawyer-edgar-sargysan-sentenced; https://www.justice.gov/usao-cdca/pr/former-fbi-special-agent-sentenced-6-years -prison-accepting-bribes-paid-attorney.

32. https://powersearch.sos.ca.gov/advanced.php.

33. https://www.breakingbelizenews.com/2022/12/06/john-saldivar-saga-u-s-prosecutors -reveal-during-trial-that-he-facilitated-mob-boss-lev-dermen-and-jacob-kingston/.

34. https://bz.usembassy.gov/designation-of-former-belizean-minister-john-saldivar-for -involvement-in-significant-corruption/.

35. https://schiff.house.gov/30th-district.

36. https://archive.org/details/the-weekly-standard-2000-10-09/page/n11/mode/2up.

37. https://www.latimes.com/archives/la-xpm-2000-nov-08-mn-48886-story.html.

38. https://www.armenian-genocide.org/News.57/current_category.183/offset.50/press _detail.html.

39. https://digitalcommons.law.buffalo.edu/cgi/viewcontent.cgi?article=1028&context=bhrlr.

40. https://www.foreign.senate.gov/press/dem/release/senate-passes-menendez-resolution -recognizing-the-armenian-genocide; https://www.whitehouse.gov/briefing-room/statements -releases/2021/04/24/statement-by-president-joe-biden-on-armenian-remembrance-day/.

41. Troy Anderson, "L.A.'s New Mob Threat; Ethnic Gangs Organizing into Global Problems," *The Daily News of Los Angeles*, March 18, 2001.

42. K.L. Billingsley, "Russian crime families reap 'golden West' in California," *The Washington Times*, December 1, 1996. https://advance.lexis.com/api/document?collection=news &id=urn:contentItem:3RPR-HD90-009B-M4K2-00000-00&context=1519360.

43. Troy Anderson, "L.A.'s New Mob Threat; Ethnic Gangs Organizing into Global Problems," *The Daily News of Los Angeles*, March 18, 2001.

44. Lisa Van Proyen, "Glendale Meets to Work on Conflict Resolution," *The Daily News of Los Angeles*. September 24, 2000. https://advance.lexis.com/api/document?collection=news &id=urn:contentItem:41SJ-J0H0-00D6-M3D6-00000-00&context=1519360.

45. RONE TEMPEST, " California and the West; Medi-Cal Scandal Alarms Armenians; Culture: Leaders stress that those caught are a tiny minority, and that they may have learned such behavior as a survival skill in the former Soviet Union, *Los Angeles Times*, December 8, 1999.

46. Virginia Ellis and Joe Mozingo, "Medi-Cal Fraud Probe Could Reach $1 Billion; Crime: Schemes to File Fake Claims for Medical Supplies May Turn Out to Be One of Largest Scams Against a State. Numerous Guilty Pleas Entered; Many Cases Pending as Probe Continues," *Los Angeles Times*, November 29, 1999. https://www.latimes.com /archives/la-xpm-1999-nov-29-mn-38660-story.html.

47. Virginia Ellis and Joe Mozingo, "Medi-Cal Fraud Probe Could Reach $1 Billion; Crime: Schemes to File Fake Claims for Medical Supplies May Turn Out to Be One of Largest Scams Against a State. Numerous Guilty Pleas Entered; Many Cases Pending as Probe Continues," *Los Angeles Times*, November 29, 1999. https://www.latimes.com /archives/la-xpm-1999-nov-29-mn-38660-story.html.

48. Lisa Friedman, "Stiffer Gang Penalties; Congress to Vote on Mob-Style Statute," *The Daily News of Los Angeles*, May 11, 2005.

49. https://www.huffpost.com/entry/democratic-congressional_b_766162.

50. https://www.nbcnews.com/id/wbna39657964.

51. https://archives.fbi.gov/archives/newyork/press-releases/2010/nyfo101310.htm.

52. https://www.huffpost.com/entry/democratic-congressional_b_766162.

53. https://californiahealthline.org/morning-breakout/house-bill-would-limit-document-requests-in-medicare-fraud-cases/.

54. https://www.govtrack.us/congress/bills/112/hr6575.

55. https://harvardextension.wordpress.com/wp-content/uploads/2010/07/the-armenian-mirror-spectator-july-24-2010.pdf; https://schiff.house.gov/404?news/press-releases/schiff-calls-on-appeals-court-to-rehear-case-regarding-insurance-claims-of-armenian-genocide-victims%27%27.

56. Lisa Friedman, "Court Rejects Lawsuit by Armenian Heirs," *The Daily News of Los Angeles*, August 21, 2009.

57. https://www.latimes.com/california/story/2022-03-23/fraud-los-angeles-cheated-armenian-genocide-victims.

58. https://www.latimes.com/california/story/2022-03-23/fraud-los-angeles-cheated-armenian-genocide-victims.

59. https://www.latimes.com/california/story/2022-04-02/lawmakers-call-for-investigation-of-armenian-genocide-settlement-fraud.

60. https://www.latimes.com/california/story/2022-04-02/lawmakers-call-for-investigation-of-armenian-genocide-settlement-fraud.

61. https://members.calbar.ca.gov/courtDocs/11-O-11759.pdf.

62. https://sandrarose.com/2019/03/mark-geragos-is-michael-avenattis-alleged-co-conspirator-in-nike-extortion-case/; https://www.gainesville.com/story/news/2002/12/07/ryder-trial-ends-with-probation/31621426007/; https://apnews.com/article/jussie-smollett-entertainment-celebrity-los-angeles-michael-jackson-878f1be5fa533dc4009db3fbbd7c17b9; https://www.theguardian.com/us-news/article/2024/aug/21/hunter-biden-lawyer-tax-case-prosecutors.

63. https://www.washingtonpost.com/wp-srv/politics/special/clinton/stories/mcdougal041399.htm.

64. https://casetext.com/case/united-states-v-dermen-5.

65. https://web.archive.org/web/20170621055855/https://www.chambers-associate.com/the-big-interview/mark-geragos-celebrity-lawyer.

66. https://www.latimes.com/california/story/2022-04-02/lawmakers-call-for-investigation-of-armenian-genocide-settlement-fraud.

67. https://www.armeniafund.org/causes/; https://www.himnadram.org/es/1560699079; https://tert.nla.am/archive/NLA%20TERT/Mirror-Spectator/201012.pdf; https://www.himnadram.org/files/2020/12/5265806.pdf.

68. https://www.armeniafundusa.org/news/20120827-gala-press-release.html; https://tert.nla.am/archive/NLA%20TERT/Mirror-Spectator/201012.pdf.

69. https://tert.nla.am/archive/NLA%20TERT/Mirror-Spectator/201012.pdf.

70. https://nationalinterest.org/blog/buzz/what-going-armenia-fund-201339.

71. https://nationalinterest.org/blog/buzz/what-going-armenia-fund-201339.

72. https://hetq.am/en/article/165417.

73. https://www.cbsnews.com/losangeles/news/u-s-is-seizing-los-angeles-mansion-from-family-of-armenian-politician-accused-of-bribery/.

74. https://nationalinterest.org/blog/buzz/what-going-armenia-fund-201339.

75. https://www.armeniafundusa.org/news/20061130-telethon-2006.html.
76. https://www.justice.gov/opa/pr/businessman-charged-fraud-scheme-conceal-38m-irs.
77. https://www.latimes.com/california/story/2022-04-05/california-state-bar-will-investigate-armenian-genocide-victim-payments.
78. https://www.latimes.com/california/story/2022-03-23/fraud-los-angeles-cheated-armenian-genocide-victims.
79. https://apps.calbar.ca.gov/attorney/Licensee/Detail/60631.
80. https://www.justice.gov/usao-cdca/pr/federal-authorities-arrest-9-defendants-charged-relation-scheme-laundered-over-30.
81. https://www.facebook.com/story.php?story_fbid=1476004092495568&id=511855492243771&_rdr.
82. https://www.youtube.com/watch?v=ygkwOAbmIIY; https://ancawr.org/press-release/anca-wr-gala-coverage-2018/; https://www.facebook.com/220458894662821/posts/pfbid0KNN7QSxHSNnBZ5vM6qvVwsAFWg6AYTriNSTF32PnCeSXnNNwqgubnTfwdCbw6Ut9l/?mibextid=cr9u03.
83. https://hyetert.org/2014/12/14/shine-your-light-theme-of-sold-out-diocesan-christmas-ball/.
84. https://clerk.assembly.ca.gov/sites/clerk.assembly.ca.gov/files/adj050318.pdf; https://glendalecitygovernmentwatch.org/2022/08/14/and-then-there-were-three/.
85. https://web.archive.org/web/20181229032158/https://www.latimes.com/socal/glendale-news-press/opinion/tn-gnp-me-mailbag-20181227-story.html.
86. https://g-a-i.org/wp-content/uploads/2021/02/GAI-Cannabis-Final.pdf; https://files.ceqanet.opr.ca.gov/286084-1/attachment/x7iqEWRGwHyf-wjpc72bmR3NYcSdmRvPSdZqZRLmjFBUORxfGDZ9Ty3e4ERMCqe52IFjGv_VWS6c28eN0.
87. https://www.bbc.com/news/election-us-2016-37455372.
88. https://www.consumerfinance.gov/about-us/newsroom/cfpb-orders-citi-to-pay-25-9-million-for-intentional-illegal-discrimination-against-armenian-americans/.
89. https://www.cnn.com/2023/11/08/economy/citibank-armenian-americans-discrimination-accusation/index.html.
90. https://lamag.com/news/fbi-agents-corruption-trial-becomes-thorny-reunion-as-lawyer-testifies.
91. https://www.sfgate.com/cannabis/article/california-illegal-cannabis-grow-17856215.php; https://www.foxla.com/news/california-drug-bust-dozens-ties-sinaloa-cartel-arrested-charged; https://www.nbcnews.com/news/us-news/entire-hells-angels-chapter-arrested-california-police-say-rcna158968.
92. https://www.thedailybeast.com/these-shady-uae-donors-gave-millions-to-clinton-and-trump-while-the-feds-dozed.
93. https://apnews.com/article/4b20d70e110c49329f19865ae8cfa8c7.
94. https://www.chicagotribune.com/nation-world/ct-political-donor-allied-wallet-khawaja-20180802-story.html.
95. https://nypost.com/2018/08/02/shady-payment-processor-gave-millions-to-hillary-and-trump/.
96. https://www.uscirf.gov/news-room/releases-statements/andy-khawaja-appointed-uscirf.
97. https://www.theepochtimes.com/edition/our-nation-51_3173588/3177392.
98. https://www.facebook.com/ancagrassroots/photos/a.172324551858/10156506980596859/?type=3&locale=en_GB&_rdr.

99. https://www.facebook.com/ancagrassroots/photos/a.172324551858/101565069805 96859/?type=3&locale=en_GB.

100. https://www.mayfieldsenior.org/news-detail?pk=782446.

101. https://www.ftc.gov/news-events/news/press-releases/2019/05/operators-payment -processing-firm-settle-charges-assisting-fraudulent-schemes-took-more-110-million.

102. https://www.theepochtimes.com/schumer-names-new-dem-donor-to-replace-his -indicted-appointee-on-u-s-commission-on-international-religious-freedom _3181508.html.

103. https://www.wbtw.com/news/national/mueller-probe-witness-now-faces-child-sex -trafficking-charge/; https://www.nytimes.com/2019/12/04/us/politics/george-nader -ahmad-khawaja.html; https://www.justice.gov/opa/pr/california-ceo-and-seven-others -charged-multi-million-dollar-conduit-campaign-contribution.

104. https://www.justice.gov/opa/pr/businessman-sentenced-35m-foreign-conduit -contribution-scheme.

105. https://www.justice.gov/opa/pr/california-ceo-and-seven-others-charged-multi -million-dollar-conduit-campaign-contribution.

106. https://www.justice.gov/opa/pr/california-attorney-pleads-guilty-multimillion-dollar -conduit-campaign-contribution.

107. https://docquery.fec.gov/cgi-bin/fecimg/?201805249113352523.

108. https://www.justice.gov/opa/pr/california-lawyer-pleads-guilty-fraudulent-credit -card-payment-processing-scheme-and.

109. https://anca.org/press-release/hawaii-recognizes-nagorno-karabakh-republics -independence/; https://www.avvo.com/attorneys/90067-ca-rudy-dekermenjian-201387 .html; https://www.swlaw.edu/sites/default/files/2017-04/SWT112.pdf.

110. https://www.eonline.com/news/398830/lindsay-lohan-s-post-rehab-plans-endorsements -helping-kids-and-overseas-travel.

111. https://www.justice.gov/opa/pr/california-attorney-pleads-guilty-multimillion-dollar -conduit-campaign-contribution.

112. https://edition.cnn.com/2023/11/02/politics/adam-schiff-primary-residence-maryland -california/index.html; https://247wallst.com/city/potomac-md-is-one-of-the-richest -cities-in-the-country/.

113. https://www.thegatewaypundit.com/2024/04/breaking-exclusive-adam-schiff-deep -schiff-evidence-shows/.

CHAPTER SEVEN: UP IN SMOKE

1. https://www.ksby.com/news/fire-watch/2018/11/19/camp-fire-burning-in-butte -county-reaches-66-containment.

2. https://www.nbcnews.com/news/us-news/pg-e-pleads-guilty-84-counts-manslaughter -devastating-camp-fire-n1231256; https://www.usatoday.com/story/news/nation/2020 /06/16/camp-fire-pg-e-pleads-guilty-84-counts-manslaughter-2018-blaze /3199591001/.

3. https://www.kqed.org/news/11792217/1987-report-suggested-pge-study-c-hooks -but-utility-cant-say-whether-tests-occurred.

4. https://www.ocregister.com/2011/08/30/litany-of-failures-led-to-deadly-gas-explo sion/.

5. https://www.nytimes.com/2019/02/23/us/pge-california-politics.html.

6. https://www.sfgate.com/bayarea/article/PG-E-diverted-safety-money-for-profit-bonuses-2500175.php.

7. https://www.kqed.org/news/11737336/judge-pge-paid-out-stock-dividends-instead-of-trimming-trees.

8. https://www.kqed.org/news/11737336/judge-pge-paid-out-stock-dividends-instead-of-trimming-trees.

9. https://www.kqed.org/news/11737336/judge-pge-paid-out-stock-dividends-instead-of-trimming-trees.

10. https://www.nytimes.com/2019/02/23/us/pge-california-politics.html.

11. https://www.nytimes.com/2019/02/23/us/pge-california-politics.html.

12. https://www.courthousenews.com/newsom-lashes-out-at-utilities-as-wildfires-grow-and-blackouts-loom/.

13. https://www.courthousenews.com/massive-wildfire-explodes-overnight-in-northern-california/.

14. https://www.sfchronicle.com/opinion/editorials/article/Editorial-Why-California-can-t-cut-the-cord-14572406.php.

15. https://www.kcra.com/article/pgande-customers-sue-over-california-wildfire-law/28453421; https://leginfo.legislature.ca.gov/faces/billTextClient.xhtml?bill_id=201920200AB1054.

16. https://www.abc10.com/article/news/local/abc10-originals/newsom-pge-protection/103-65ca1d41-8efe-45b4-87bc-0cdecc714378.

17. https://www.capradio.org/articles/2018/11/17/trump-visits-camp-wildfire-as-missing-list-tops-1000-people/.

18. https://www.capradio.org/articles/2018/11/17/trump-visits-camp-wildfire-as-missing-list-tops-1000-people/.

19. https://www.capradio.org/articles/2018/11/17/trump-visits-camp-wildfire-as-missing-list-tops-1000-people/.

20. https://www.npr.org/2018/08/02/634831131/californias-gov-brown-wildfires-are-evidence-of-changing-climate-in-real-time.

21. https://calmatters.org/environment/2020/09/california-governor-climate-emergency/.

22. https://calmatters.org/environment/2020/09/california-governor-climate-emergency/.

23. https://deadline.com/2020/10/california-governor-gavin-newsom-plumpjack-winery-napa-threatened-nearby-glass-campbell-fire-1234589613/.

24. https://pelosi.house.gov/news/press-releases/speaker-pelosi-remarks-at-press-event-on-wildfire-prevention-and-climate.

25. https://www.abc10.com/article/news/local/abc10-originals/pge-gavin-newsom-lobbiest/103-2fc7d4f4-a0e0-492d-ac1d-ec674e58a67b.

26. https://www.kcra.com/article/gov-gavin-newsom-french-laundry-apology-covid-tiers-coronavirus-restrictions/34692431.

27. https://www.abc10.com/article/news/local/abc10-originals/pge-gavin-newsom-lobbiest/103-2fc7d4f4-a0e0-492d-ac1d-ec674e58a67b.

28. https://www.latimes.com/california/story/2020-12-31/questions-linger-newsom-french-laundry-lobbyist.

29. https://sjvsun.com/business/report-newsom-spent-6-7mil-to-craft-protections-for-pge-following-wildfire-manslaughter-convictions/.

30. https://www.msn.com/en-us/money/other/pg-e-fire-victims-will-soon-receive-final-compensation-they-won-t-be-made-whole/ar-AA1lMF5R#:~:text=PG%26E%2C%20

as%20part%20of%20its%20plan%20to%20exit,to%20be%20compensated%20
with%20shares%20in%20the%20company.

31. https://finance.yahoo.com/news/limited-home-insurance-options-california
-134244292.html.

32. https://sfstandard.com/2024/01/09/state-farm-allstate-homeowners-auto-insurance
-increase/.

33. https://www.abc10.com/article/news/local/abc10-originals/newsom-under
-fire-answers-pge-fire-victims-fire-power-money/103-a56a6822-7fde-48ae-9000
-107bae3172bb.

34. https://www.bizjournals.com/sanfrancisco/blog/2015/04/puc-pg-e-1-6-billion-fine
-san-bruno.html.

35. https://www.abc10.com/article/money/pacific-gas-and-electric-company-state
-regulators-gavin-newsom/103-9cffa5af-4f60-48b9-9a42-9c9e6db28bf2.

36. https://consumerwatchdog.org/uncategorized/arnolds-cabinet-secretary-should
-be-shipped-out/.

37. https://consumerwatchdog.org/uncategorized/arnolds-cabinet-secretary-should-be
-shipped-out/; https://www.sec.gov/Archives/edgar/data/1234383/00011046590402
5346/a04-9899_1ex99d1.htm.

38. Interview between Susan Crabtree and Alice Stebbins on Nov. 6, 2023.

39. https://www.courthousenews.com/newsom-must-turn-over-secretarys-pge-meeting
-records-california-judge-rules-in-journalists-favor/; https://www.abc10.com/article
/news/local/abc10-originals/fire-power-money/newsom-advisor-plugs-pge-as-partner
-during-shareholder-event/103-ba3fc8c1-2748-41fa-a5ae-291578398bfa;https://www
.courthousenews.com/newsom-must-turn-over-secretarys-pge-meeting-records
-california-judge-rules-in-journalists-favor/; https://www.sfchronicle.com/california
-wildfires/article/pg-e-agrees-150-million-settlement-deadly-zogg-18107743.php.

40. https://www.cnn.com/2019/12/03/us/pge-transmission-lines-camp-fire/index
.html; https://www.cpuc.ca.gov/news-and-updates/all-news/cpuc-approves-150-million
-settlement-with-pge-for-zogg-fire-2023.

41. Interview between Susan Crabtree and Alice Stebbins on Nov. 6, 2023.

42. Interview between Susan Crabtree and Alice Stebbins on Nov. 6, 2023.

43. https://www.siliconvalley.com/2022/04/07/pge-ceo-patricia-poppe-total-exec-pay
-tops-50-million-wildfire/.

44. https://www.abc10.com/article/news/local/abc10-originals/newsom-pge
-protection/103-65ca1d41-8efe-45b4-87bc-0cdecc714378.

45. https://www.abc10.com/article/news/local/abc10-originals/newsom-pge-protection
/103-65ca1d41-8efe-45b4-87bc-0cdecc714378.

46. https://www.youtube.com/watch?v=kYxda8_WX1w.

47. https://www.siliconvalley.com/2024/01/08/pge-power-bill-electric-gas-consumer
-fire-inflation-economy-rate/.

48. https://abc7.com/consumer-watchdog-jerry-brown-kathleen-sempra-energy/22
69713/.

49. https://www.latimes.com/business/la-fi-puc-scandal-20141009-story.html.

50. https://www.sfgate.com/crime/article/Officials-demand-criminal-probe-of-PG-amp
-E-s-5767564.php.

51. https://www.sfgate.com/crime/article/Officials-demand-criminal-probe-of-PG-amp
-E-s-5767564.php.

52. https://www.sfgate.com/crime/article/Officials-demand-criminal-probe-of-PG-amp
-E-s-5767564.php.

53. www.sfgate.com/search/?action=search&channel=crime&inlineLink=1&searchindex
=property&query=%22Carol+Brown%22.

54. https://www.sfgate.com/search/?action=search&channel=crime&inlineLink=1&search
index=property&query=%22National+Transportation+Safety+Board%22.

55. https://consumercal.org/pges-judge-shopping-outrages-state-puc-employees/;
https://www.sfgate.com/crime/article/Officials-demand-criminal-probe-of-PG-amp
-E-s-5767564.php.

56. https://www.realclearpolitics.com/articles/2020/10/05/critics_harriss_inaction
_against_utilities_helped_fuel_wildfires_144359.html.

57. https://thefederalist.com/2020/10/12/consumer-watchdogs-say-kamala-harris
-looked-the-other-way-while-utilities-set-stage-for-wildfires/.

58. https://www.mercurynews.com/2018/02/03/editorial-ag-must-follow-through
-on-peevey-investigation/.

59. https://www.kpbs.org/news/politics/2016/04/29/deadline-key-allegation-ag-harriss
-san-onofre-prob.

60. https://www.realclearpolitics.com/articles/2020/10/05/critics_harriss_inaction
_against_utilities_helped_fuel_wildfires_144359.html.

61. https://www.sandiegoreader.com/news/2016/apr/24/ticker-attorney-general-kamala
-harri-malpractice/.

62. https://www.sandiegoreader.com/news/2016/apr/24/ticker-attorney-general-kamala
-harris-malpractice/.

63. https://thefederalist.com/2020/10/12/consumer-watchdogs-say-kamala-harris
-looked-the-other-way-while-utilities-set-stage-for-wildfires/.

64. https://www.sfchronicle.com/business/article/Exclusive-Sen-Kamala-Harris
-introduces-bill-to-14830087.php.

65. https://www.govtrack.us/congress/bills/116/s2844.

CHAPTER EIGHT: GREEN WARRIORS, BLACKOUTS, AND BROWNOUTS

1. https://www.winespectator.com/articles/caymus-pays-1-million-for-alleged-violations
-of-napa-county-rules-48765.

2. https://www.pressdemocrat.com/article/opinion/measure-j-sonoma-county-farming/.

3. https://www.agri-pulse.com/articles/21129-cafo-ban-would-cost-sonoma-county
-more-than-400-million-and-1-400-jobs.

4. https://www.dailymail.co.uk/news/article-13351497/world-famous-wineries-revolt
-abusive-bureaucrats-napa-valley.html.

5. https://www.yahoo.com/lifestyle/mystery-among-vines-why-fbi-100045421.html.

6. https://napavalleyregister.com/news/local/ryan-klobas-stolen-records-federal-subpoena
-napa-police-farm-bureau/article_ca98c7c2-0274-11ef-989d-6f39b8b388c8.html.

7. https://www.aol.com/news/mystery-among-vines-why-fbi-100045352.html; https://
internewscast.com/news/us/investigation-into-fbi-inquiry-and-suspicious-death
-unveils-intense-napa-valley-feud-with-eco-mob-extremists-threatening-to-set
-fire-to-famous-wineries/.

8. https://news.uchicago.edu/story/northern-spotted-owls-conservation-timber-jobs
-endangered-species-act.

9. https://www.abc10.com/article/news/local/the-story/northern-spotted-owl-oregon
   -timber-habitat-endangered-species-act/283-33c8a857-668c-4058-abfb-b536a584968a;
   https://news.uchicago.edu/story/northern-spotted-owls-conservation-timber-jobs
   -endangered-species-act.

10. https://pelosi.house.gov/news/press-releases/speaker-pelosi-remarks-at-press
    -event-on-wildfire-prevention-and-climate.

11. https://www.cnn.com/2024/07/03/science/killing-barred-owls-to-save-spotted
    -owls/index.html.

12. https://www.gov.ca.gov/2024/04/22/with-historic-targets-california-will-use
    -millions-of-acres-of-land-to-fight-the-climate-crisis/;https://x.com/CBSEveningNews
    /status/1562936175777955840.

13. https://www.latimes.com/environment/story/2024-05-31/solar-project-to-destroy
    -thousands-of-joshua-trees.

14. https://www.ecowatch.com/solar-project-mojave-desert-joshua-trees-tortoises.html.

15. https://www.blm.gov/sites/blm.gov/files/documents/Nevada_SNDO_Desert_Tortoise
    _Fact_Sheet_0.pdf; https://www.fws.gov/species/desert-tortoise-gopherus-agassizii;
    https://www.usgs.gov/centers/werc/science/desert-tortoise-ecology-health-habitat
    -and-conservation-biology.

16. https://thebreakthrough.org/journal/no-14-summer-2021/green-jim-crow.

17. https://datazone.birdlife.org/the-largest-wind-farm-in-the-world-impacts-birds-of-prey-in
    -california-usa#:~:text=Construction%20of%20the%20world's%20largest,monitoring
    %20programs%20are%20being%20implemented; https://www.dailysignal.com/2023
    /12/28/memo-to-ap-wind-farm-contractors-admit-turbines-harm-whales-dolphins/.

18. https://x.com/CAgovernor/status/1572363201895071746.

19. https://www.newsnationnow.com/climate/record-rain-california-water/.

20. https://water.ca.gov/News/News-Releases/2024/May-24/Benefits-of-the-Delta
    -Conveyance-Project-Far-Exceed-Costs.

21. https://subscriber.politicopro.com/article/2024/05/newsom-unveils-new-cost-estimate
    -for-delta-tunnel-00158380.

22. https://calmatters.org/environment/2024/05/delta-tunnel-new-price-tag/#:~:-
    text=Had%20the%20tunnel%20been%20in,million%20people%20for%20a%20
    year.

23. https://www.capradio.org/articles/2023/10/02/the-bay-delta-ecosystem-is-collapsing
    -california-just-unveiled-rival-rescue-plans/; https://www.thecalifornian.com/story
    /news/local/california/2022/06/22/california-water-officials-review-gov-newsom
    -controversial-sacramento-san-joaquin-delta-tunnel/7700342001/#:~:text=
    California%E2%80%99s%20water%20regulators%20say%20the%20Delta%20
    is%20.

24. https://www.mwdh2o.com/press-releases/metropolitan-issues-statement-on
    -release-of-new-cost-estimate-for-delta-conveyance-project/.

25. https://www.ucdavis.edu/climate/news/decarbonizing-california-transportation
    -by-2045.

26. https://www.sfchronicle.com/bayarea/article/ca-high-speed-rail-100-billion
    -18979091.php?utm_content=cta&sid=65dc09d062e0ab8abc056ad5&ss=A&st
    _rid=03fb6bcb-4376-4932-b65c-548ca236f7ed&utm_source=newsletter&utm_
    medium=email&utm_term=headlines&utm_campaign=sfc_morningfix.

27. https://www.capradio.org/articles/2020/08/17/watch-live-gov-gavin-newsom
-update-on-covid-19-for-august-17/.

28. Interview conducted by Susan Crabtree with Edward Ring May 30, 2024.

29. https://www.kqed.org/news/11970332/rising-utility-costs-compound-californias
-housing-crisis.

30. https://www.kqed.org/news/11970332/rising-utility-costs-compound-californias
-housing-crisis.

31. https://www.kqed.org/news/11970332/rising-utility-costs-compound-californias
-housing-crisis.

32. https://www.kqed.org/news/11970332/rising-utility-costs-compound-californias
-housing-crisis.

33. https://www.publicadvocates.cpuc.ca.gov/press-room/reports-and-analyses
/rooftop-solar-incentive-to-cost-nonsolar-customers-in-2024.

34. https://www.utilitydive.com/news/california-regulators-see-signs-of-a-new-energy
-crisis-can-they-prevent-i/523414/; https://consumerwatchdog.org/uncategorized/no
-relief-rates-power-costs-fall/; https://environmentalprogress.org/big-news/2016/10
/27/in-reversal-pge-now-admits-diablo-canyon-closure-proposal-would-increase
-electricity-rates.

35. Interview between Matt Freedman and Susan Crabtree, 2024.

36. https://www.nbcnews.com/news/us-news/pg-e-pleads-guilty-84-counts-manslaughter
-devastating-camp-fire-n1231256.

37. Interview between Doug Eckenrod and Susan Crabtree Oct. 17, 2024.

38. https://www.kpbs.org/news/environment/2023/11/30/new-california-rules-are
-crushing-the-solar-industry.

39. https://calmatters.org/environment/2022/12/california-solar-rules-overhauled/.

40. https://www.independent.com/2023/01/26/federal-regulators-deny-pges
-request-to-resume-review-of-diablo-canyon/.

41. https://newsroom.edison.com/releases/the-grid-must-grow-quickly-to-achieve
-californias-net-zero-goal-by-2045.

42. https://www.gov.ca.gov/wp-content/uploads/2019/09/9.20.19-Climate-EO-N-19-19.pdf.

43. http://www.auditor.ca.gov/reports/I2021-1/index.html#section3.

44. https://reason.org/policy-study/25th-annual-highway-report/total-disbursements
-per-mile/.

45. https://www.americanmanufacturing.org/press-release/congress-must-act-after-new
-evidence-links-crrc-and-byd-to-chinese-government-and-military/.

46. https://news.yahoo.com/newsoms-secretive-1-billion-mask-190626226.html.

47. https://www.foxbusiness.com/politics/gavin-newsom-hammered-promoting-160000
-chinese-ev-during-china-trip.

48. https://www.foxbusiness.com/politics/gavin-newsom-hammered-promoting-160000
-chinese-ev-during-china-trip.

49. https://www.foxbusiness.com/politics/gavin-newsom-hammered-promoting-160000
-chinese-ev-during-china-trip.

50. https://www.nytimes.com/2020/11/04/technology/california-uber-lyft-prop-22
.html; https://x.com/susancrabtree/status/1771237503015780519.

51. https://reason.org/policy-study/27th-annual-highway-report/california/.

52. https://ballotpedia.org/California_Road_Repair_and_Accountability_Act_of_2017.

53. https://taxfoundation.org/data/all/state/state-gas-tax-rates-2024.
54. https://taxfoundation.org/data/all/state/state-gas-tax-rates-2023/.
55. https://finance.yahoo.com/news/why-gas-prices-in-california-have-gone-ballistic-160544399.html?fr=sycsrp_catchall.
56. https://finance.yahoo.com/news/why-gas-prices-in-california-have-gone-ballistic-160544399.html?fr=sycsrp_catchall.
57. https://dailycaller.com/2024/04/22/biden-admin-california-green-trains/.
58. https://dailycaller.com/2024/04/22/biden-admin-california-green-trains/.
59. https://www.publicadvocates.cpuc.ca.gov/press-room/reports-and-analyses/distribution-grid-electrification-model-findings.
60. https://www.gov.ca.gov/2023/03/28/governor-newsom-signs-gas-price-gouging-law-california-took-on-big-oil-and-won/; https://www.sacbee.com/opinion/article294446334.html.
61. https://www.politico.com/news/2024/10/16/phillips-66-california-refinery-closure-00184058.
62. https://www.eia.gov/todayinenergy/detail.php?id=63944.
63. https://www.nytimes.com/2023/09/23/business/dealbook/california-fossil-fuels-cigarettes.html.
64. https://www.climateone.org/audio/fighting-fossil-fuels-courts-and-ballot.
65. https://abc7news.com/post/californias-air-resources-board-vote-new-fuel-standards-could-increase-gas-prices-65-cents-gallon/15528843/.
66. https://www.kcra.com/article/california-newsom-gas-price-spikes-bill/62474662.
67. https://www.politico.com/news/2024/10/10/california-reject-musk-spacex-00183371.
68. https://www.politico.com/news/2024/10/10/california-reject-musk-spacex-00183371.
69. https://www.usatoday.com/story/money/2024/11/26/tesla-new-california-tax-credits/76601063007/.

CHAPTER NINE: PROFITEERING PANDEMIC

1. https://www.thomaskeller.com/yountville-california/french-laundry/about-wine-program.
2. https://www.nytimes.com/2021/09/14/us/elections/french-laundry-newsom.html.
3. https://www.nytimes.com/2020/11/25/opinion/gavin-newsom-french-laundry-california.html.
4. https://www.sfchronicle.com/bayarea/williesworld/article/Willie-Brown-Newsom-only-hurt-himself-by-15743668.php.
5. https://www.cbsnews.com/news/gavin-newsom-california-face-mask-restaurant/.
6. https://x.com/CAgovernor/status/1312437371460173825?s=20.
7. https://x.com/CAgovernor/status/1312437371460173825?s=20.
8. https://www.cbs8.com/article/news/local/deputies-ticket-22-people-found-violating-stay-at-home-order-in-encinitas/509-05cdc368-ecbb-417c-bf13-da0d52707c43.
9. https://www.deseret.com/faith/2022/8/18/23310356/california-church-violated-covid-19-safety-rules-no-longer-pay-fine/.
10. https://www.deseret.com/faith/2022/8/18/23310356/california-church-violated-covid-19-safety-rules-no-longer-pay-fine/.
11. https://www.nytimes.com/2021/06/09/us/schools-covid.html.

12. https://www.fppc.ca.gov/enforcement/EnfDivCaseResults/stipulated-agreements/2013-sdo/september-sdo/california-strategies-llc,-jason-kinney,-rusty-areias,-and-winston-hickox.html.
13. https://capitolweekly.net/capitol-weeklys-top-100-ten-years-and-counting/.
14. https://www.sacbee.com/news/politics-government/capitol-alert/article247958040.htm; https://www.sacbee.com/opinion/editorials/article247744605.html.
15. https://www.politico.com/newsletters/california-playbook/2020/07/16/rose-parade-cancelled-sf-corruption-probe-widens-newsom-and-davis-lessons-learned-kanye-in-or-out-navarro-slams-fauci-geffen-gives-big-to-project-lincoln-lada-jackie-lacey-vulnerable-489813.
16. https://x.com/KevinKileyCA/status/1294317211914403840.
17. https://www.modbee.com/opinion/article245108720.html.
18. https://www.beckershospitalreview.com/post-acute/5-states-facing-highest-covid-19-nursing-home-deaths.html#:~:text=Here%20are%20the%20five%20states%20with%20the%20highest,York%20-%209%2C038%205%205.%20Ohio%20-%208%2C541.
19. https://www.sacbee.com/news/coronavirus/article249317120.html.
20. https://www.sacbee.com/news/coronavirus/article249317120.html.
21. https://calmatters.org/newsletters/whatmatters/2021/10/newsom-admin-ripped-for-nursing-home-policies/.
22. https://calmatters.org/health/2021/10/nursing-homes-oversight-california-hearing/#:~:text=%E2%80%9CWhere%20is%20the%20proactive%2C%20patient,And%20yet%20here%20we%20are.
23. https://californiahealthline.org/news/article/california-nursing-home-medicaid-funding-performance-during-pandemic/.
24. https://calmatters.org/newsletters/whatmatters/2021/10/newsom-admin-ripped-for-nursing-home-policies/.
25. https://calmatters.org/projects/california-oversight-nursing-homes/.
26. https://www.documentcloud.org/documents/21074143-screen-shot-2021-10-01-at-120607-pm.
27. https://calmatters.org/health/2021/12/rechnitz-nursing-home-fines/.
28. https://calmatters.org/health/coronavirus/2021/10/rechnitz-nursing-home-lawsuit-covid-licensing/.
29. https://law.justia.com/cases/california/court-of-appeal/2024/c098736.html.
30. https://abc7.com/edd-califrornia-unemployment-mom-and-son-homeless-benefits-program/7216092/.
31. https://calmatters.org/economy/2023/05/california-edd-unemployment-appeals/.
32. https://calmatters.org/economy/2023/11/unemployment-benefits-suicide-california-edd/.
33. https://calmatters.org/economy/2023/05/california-edd-unemployment-appeals/.
34. https://calmatters.org/economy/2023/11/california-unemployment-covid/.
35. https://abc7news.com/edd-robocall-autodial-california-unemployment-benefits-backlog/10797950/.
36. https://calmatters.org/economy/2023/05/california-edd-unemployment-appeals/.
37. https://calmatters.org/economy/2023/05/california-edd-unemployment-appeals/.
38. https://abc7news.com/plumpjack-management-group-llc-gov-newsom-winery-sba-releases-detailed-ppp-data-what-business-does-gavin-own/8618229/.

39. https://www.cbsnews.com/sacramento/news/california-paid-400-million-in
-unemployment-benefits-to-inmates/.
40. https://abc7news.com/california-unemployment-tax-refund-seized-edd-fraud
-scam/12002030/.
41. https://calmatters.org/economy/2023/11/california-unemployment-covid/.
42. https://apnews.com/general-news-6b95c7ba4b89b3aabd4d4cc648efbc0c.
43. https://apnews.com/article/biden-julie-su-renominates-nomination-e2e0a2729f0f
77887fad263b855470fb.
44. https://www.nytimes.com/2020/11/04/technology/california-uber-lyft-prop-22
.html.
45. https://www.usnews.com/news/us/articles/2024-01-09/new-labor-rules-aim-to
-offer-gig-workers-more-security-though-some-employers-wont-likely-be-happy.
46. https://www.sacbee.com/news/politics-government/capitol-alert/article240106868
.html.
47. https://www.sfchronicle.com/politics/article/Tom-Steyer-four-ex-California-governors
-to-15209004.php.
48. https://www.gov.ca.gov/2020/11/20/carecoverytaskforcereport/.
49. https://www.politico.com/states/california/story/2020/11/20/newsom-ends-california
-economic-task-force-despite-widespread-pandemic-closures-1337448.
50. https://www.realclearpolitics.com/articles/2021/06/04/newsom_mines_hollywood
_cash_after_covid_carve-out_145876.html#!.
51. https://www.foxnews.com/politics/newsom-shirks-blame-closing-churches-keeping
-hollywood-open-during-covid-we-didnt-know.
52. https://www.foxnews.com/politics/newsom-shirks-blame-closing-churches-keeping
-hollywood-open-during-covid-we-didnt-know.
53. https://www.ocregister.com/2023/03/15/gov-gavin-newsoms-shady-ties-to-failed
-silicon-valley-bank/.
54. https://dfpi.ca.gov/history/.
55. https://www.ocregister.com/2023/03/15/gov-gavin-newsoms-shady-ties-to-failed
-silicon-valley-bank/.
56. https://www.ocregister.com/2023/03/15/gov-gavin-newsoms-shady-ties-to-failed
-silicon-valley-bank/.
57. https://www.nytimes.com/2023/03/12/climate/silicon-valley-bank-climate.html.
58. https://theintercept.com/2023/03/14/cheering-silicon-valley-bank-bailout-gavin
-newsom-doesnt-mention-hes-a-client/.
59. https://theintercept.com/2023/03/14/cheering-silicon-valley-bank-bailout-gavin
-newsom-doesnt-mention-hes-a-client/.
60. https://www.gov.ca.gov/2023/03/11/governor-newsom-issues-statement-on-silicon
-valley-bank/.
61. https://www.whitehouse.gov/briefing-room/statements-releases/2023/03/12
/statement-from-president-joe-biden-on-actions-to-strengthen-confidence-in-the
-banking-system/.
62. https://theintercept.com/2023/03/14/cheering-silicon-valley-bank-bailout-gavin
-newsom-doesnt-mention-hes-a-client/.
63. https://twitter.com/LHSummers/status/1635007265563639808?s=20.
64. https://www.bloomberg.com/news/articles/2023-06-23/fdic-insured-billions-in
-deposits-for-sequoia-other-top-svb-customers?embedded-checkout=true.

65. https://poverty.ucdavis.edu/article/pandemic-learning-loss-california-who-are-most -impacted-after-covid-19-forced-virtual.

66. https://poverty.ucdavis.edu/article/pandemic-learning-loss-california-who-are-most -impacted-after-covid-19-forced-virtual.

67. https://www.gov.ca.gov/2022/10/23/california-outperforms-most-states-in-minimizing -learning-loss-in-national-student-assessment-with-record-investments-to-improve- education/.

68. https://www.usnews.com/news/best-states/rankings/education.

69. https://injepijournal.biomedcentral.com/articles/10.1186/s40621-023-00429-6.

70. https://www.realclearpolitics.com/articles/2021/11/25/teacher_unions_parents _gird_for_2022_battles_146792.html.

71. https://www.realclearpolitics.com/articles/2021/05/18/ca_school_board_dispute _a_test_case_for_teacher_union_clout_145775.html.

72. Susan Crabtree Interview with Ginni Merrifield, executive director of the Parents Association of North County. May 13, 2021.

73. Susan Crabtree Interview with Ginni Merrifield, executive director of the Parents Association of North County. May 13, 2021.

74. https://fox5sandiego.com/news/coronavirus/judge-sides-with-north-county -parents-in-school-reopening-lawsuit/.

75. Susan Crabtree Interview with Ginni Merrifield, executive director of the Parents Association of North County. May 13, 2021.

76. Susan Crabtree Interview with Ginni Merrifield, executive director of the Parents Association of North County. May 13, 2021.

CONCLUSION

1. https://www.newsweek.com/donald-trump-celebrities-leaving-usa-2024-election -1982897.

2. https://variety.com/2024/politics/news/cardi-b-deleted-hurricane-video-election -results-1236202140/.

3. https://www.fox5ny.com/news/nyc-immigration-rally-mass-deportation-fears.

4. https://abc7.com/post/immigrant-rights-faith-labor-groups-speak-la-rally-amid -threat-mass-deportations/15524524/.

5. https://www.yahoo.com/news/california-counties-flipped-blue-red-212216729.html ?fr=yhssrp_catchall; https://www.latimes.com/politics/story/2024-election-live-results -california-congress-assembly-senate-props.

6. https://www.latimes.com/politics/story/2024-election-live-results-district-attorney -la-county-gascon-hochman.

7. https://www.youtube.com/watch?v=OgWJuDqQpRo; https://www.foxbusiness.com /video/6329348595112.

8. https://www.sfchronicle.com/politics/article/gavin-newsom-trump-resistance -19892836.php.

9. https://www.latimes.com/california/story/2024-11-07/newsom-calls-special-session -california-laws-funding-lawsuits-trump; https://www.msn.com/en-us/news/politics /trump-presents-political-opportunity-for-california-governor-newsom-ag-bonta /vi-AA1tIqIx.

10. https://www.latimes.com/california/story/2024-08-09/california-governor-2026
-candidates-newsom-atkins-kounalakis-thurmond-villaraigosa-yee.

11. https://www.kqed.org/news/11865953/newsom-names-east-bay-assemblyman-rob
-bonta-as-californias-new-attorney-general; https://www.kqed.org/news/11865953
/newsom-names-east-bay-assemblyman-rob-bonta-as-californias-new-attorney
-general; https://oag.ca.gov/history/32harris.

12. https://calmatters.org/politics/capitol/2024/10/special-session-gas-prices-newsom/.

13. https://oag.ca.gov/news/press-releases/attorney-general-bonta-announces-lawsuit
-against-oil-and-gas-companies#:~:text=OAKLAND%20%E2%80%94%20Joined%20
by%20California%20Governor%20Newsom%2C%20California,and%20creating%20
statewide%20climate%20change-related%20harms%20in%20California; https://www
.gov.ca.gov/2023/03/28/governor-newsom-signs-gas-price-gouging-law-california
-took-on-big-oil-and-won/; https://www.sacbee.com/news/politics-government/capitol
-alert/article279657054.html.

14. https://www.yahoo.com/news/newsom-calls-special-session-fund-170035935
.html?fr=yhssrp_catchall.

15. https://www.gov.ca.gov/2024/11/07/special-session-ca-values/.

16. https://calmatters.org/justice/2024/11/california-vs-trump-lawsuits/.

17. https://www.pressdemocrat.com/article/news/california-beat-trump-in-court-his
-first-term-its-preparing-new-cases-for/.

18. https://calmatters.org/justice/2024/11/california-vs-trump-lawsuits/.

19. https://x.com/RonDeSantis/status/1730408947268428249.

20. https://www.politico.com/news/2024/09/13/donald-trump-california-press
-conference-kamala-harris-00179155.

21. Joel Kotkin, *The Coming of Neo-Feudalism: A Warning to the Global Middle Class* (New
York: Encounter Books, 2020).

22. https://www.wired.com/story/how-silicon-valley-fuels-an-informal-caste-system/.

23. https://calbudgetcenter.org/resources/californias-poverty-rate-soars-to-alarmingly
-high-levels-in-2023/#:~:text=California's%20poverty%20rate%20increased%20
to,rate%20of%20the%2050%20states.

24. https://www.ppic.org/publication/poverty-in-california/.

25. https://www.gov.ca.gov/2024/07/18/10-ways-ca-leads-the-nation/.

26. https://www.gov.ca.gov/2024/07/18/10-ways-ca-leads-the-nation/.

27. https://www.latimes.com/california/story/2024-03-21/high-speed-rail.

28. https://www.nytimes.com/2022/10/09/us/california-high-speed-rail-politics.html.

29. https://ssti.org/blog/useful-stats-income-inequality-across-states#:~:text=Gini%20
index%20values%20by%20state&text=New%20York%20(Gini%20index%20
%3D%200.5208,value%2C%20behind%20only%20New%20York.

30. https://abcnews.go.com/Health/california-1st-state-offer-health-insurance-undocu
mented-immigrants/story?id=105986377.

31. https://www.cbsnews.com/news/15-house-democrats-call-on-biden-for-border
-executive-action/.

32. https://www.forbes.com/sites/eriksherman/2024/08/31/why-kamala-harriss-25k
-house-down-payment-plan-isnt-a-disaster/.

33. https://www.governing.com/resilience/a-blow-against-californias-ev-tyranny.

34. https://oag.ca.gov/news/press-releases/attorney-general-bonta-announces-lawsuit
-against-oil-and-gas-companies#:~:text=OAKLAND%20%E2%80%94%20Joined%20

by%20California%20Governor%20Newsom%2C%20California,and%20creating%20
statewide%20climate%20change-related%20harms%20in%20California; https://www
.gov.ca.gov/2023/03/28/governor-newsom-signs-gas-price-gouging-law-california
-took-on-big-oil-and-won/; https://www.sacbee.com/news/politics-government/capitol
-alert/article279657054.html.

35. https://www.npr.org/2013/10/13/233449505/15-years-later-where-did-all-the
-cigarette-money-go.

36. https://www.vcstar.com/story/news/local/california/2024/10/11/california-panel
-considers-rules-that-could-increase-gas-prices/75627840007/#:~:text=Analysts%20
say%20motorists%20may%20see%20gas%20prices%20jump,could%20boost%20
prices%20by%2047%20cents%20a%20gallon.

37. https://www.msn.com/en-us/news/us/california-governor-signs-oil-cap-bill-amid
-ongoing-concerns-over-its-impacts-on-arizona-gas-prices/ar-AA1sgEQO.

38. https://www.npr.org/2018/08/28/642795284/california-becomes-first-state-to-end
-cash-bail#:~:text=Under%20the%20California%20law%20those%20arrested%20
and%20charged,algorithm%20created%20by%20the%20courts%20in%20each%20
jurisdiction.

39. https://www.hoover.org/research/california-loses-nearly-10000-fast-food-jobs
-after-20-minimum-wage-signed-last-fall.

40. https://www.reviewjournal.com/opinion/editorials/editorial-california-restaurant
-closings-show-true-minimum-wage-is-0-an-hour-3169513/.

41. https://www.10news.com/news/local-news/13-rubios-stores-closed-in-san-diego
-due-to-rising-cost-of-doing-business-in-california-spokesperson-says.

ABOUT THE AUTHORS

SUSAN CRABTREE is senior White House and national political correspondent for RealClearPolitics.

JEDD McFATTER is the director of research at Peter Schweizer's Government Accountability Institute.